Exploring the intersection of the "domestic" and the "international" in environmental politics, this book presents seven original case-studies which show how the internationalization of environmental protection efforts is altering policy-making processes, policy outcomes, and the effectiveness of policy implementation. The authors argue that while new norms and institutions for the global environment are emerging which are changing policy-making processes at the national and regional levels, sub-state politics continues to influence strongly the nature of national responses to international environmental problems. The volume examines climate change politics in China, Japan and Germany; ozone layer protection in the United States, United Kingdom, Japan, and Germany; East–West environmental cooperation and the former Soviet Union; Zimbabwe and the Convention on International Trade in Endangered Species; biodiversity politics in the United States and United Kingdom; and environmental protection within the European Union.

S0-BRB-430

CAMBRIDGE STUDIES IN INTERNATIONAL RELATIONS: 54

The internationalization of environmental protection

Cambridge Studies in International Relations is a joint initiative of
Cambridge University Press and the British International Studies
Association (BISA). The series will include a wide range of material,
from undergraduate textbooks and surveys to research-based
monographs and collaborative volumes. The aim of the series is to
publish the best new scholarship in International Studies from
Europe, North America and the rest of the world.

CAMBRIDGE STUDIES IN INTERNATIONAL RELATIONS

The internationalization of environmental protection

Edited by

Miranda A. Schreurs

and

Elizabeth Economy

CAMBRIDGE
UNIVERSITY PRESS

PUBLISHED BY THE PRESS SYNDICATE OF THE UNIVERSITY OF CAMBRIDGE
The Pitt Building, Trumpington Street, Cambridge CB2 1RP, United Kingdom

CAMBRIDGE UNIVERSITY PRESS
The Edinburgh Building, Cambridge CB2 2RU, United Kingdom
40 West 20th Street, New York, NY 10011-4211, USA
10 Stamford Road, Oakleigh, Melbourne 3166, Australia

First published 1997

Printed in the United Kingdom at the University Press, Cambridge

Typeset in 10/12.5pt Palatino   [SE]

A catalogue record for this book is available from the British Library

Library of Congress Cataloguing in Publication data applied for

The internationalization of environmental protection / edited by Miranda
    A. Schreurs and Elizabeth Economy.
        p.   cm. – (Cambridge studies in international relations; 54)
    The result of three workshops held at the Center for Science and
    International Affairs at the Kennedy School of Government, Harvard
    University and at the Brookings Institution.
    ISBN 0 521 58499 X (hardback). – ISBN 0 521 58536 8 (paperback)
    1. Environmental law, International.   I. Schreurs, Miranda A.
    (Alice), 1963–   .   II. Economy, Elizabeth, 1962–   . III. Series.
    K3585.6.I56   1997
341.7'62–dc21   96-40354   CIP

ISBN 0 521 58499 X hardback
ISBN 0 521 58536 8 paperback

Contents

Contents

Contributors

Robert Darst is Assistant Professor of Political Science at the University of Oregon, Eugene. He is currently writing a book about conflict and cooperation in East–West environmental politics. He holds a PhD from the University of California at Berkeley and was a recipient of an SSRC-MacArthur Foundation Fellowship on Peace and Security in a Changing World.

Elizabeth Economy is Fellow for China at the Council on Foreign Relations. She holds a PhD from the University of Michigan and was the recipient of an SSRC-MacArthur Foundation Fellowship for research in China and Russia. She has written on both Chinese domestic and foreign policy and taught Chinese foreign policy and international environmental politics at the University of Washington.

Joanne Kauffman, PhD, is research associate and lecturer in Political Science at the Massachusetts Institute of Technology and MIT Associate Coordinator of the Alliance for Global Sustainability. Her fields of research are in comparative politics, and science, technology, and public policy.

Angela Liberatore is scientific officer in the Environment Research Programme of the Directorate General for Science, Technology and Development of the European Commission. She holds a PhD in political and social science. Her fields of research are in environmental policy-making and institutions in Europe and in the interface between science and policy.

Phyllis Mofson is currently working at the Florida Department of Community Affairs where she specializes on land-use policy. She holds a PhD from the University of Maryland at College Park. From 1989 to 1993 she worked as an analyst for international environmental issues in the Office of the Geographer, United States Department of State.

Kal Raustiala holds a PhD in political science from the University of California, San Diego, and is a J.D. candidate at Harvard Law School. A former member of the politics faculty at Brandeis University, and editor of the *Journal of Environment and Development*, he has published in numerous journals. He is also co-editor, with David Victor and Eugene Skolnikoff, of a forthcoming edited volume on the implementation and effectiveness of international environmental commitments.

Miranda Schreurs is Assistant Professor of Government and Politics at the University of Maryland at College Park. She holds a PhD from the University of Michigan and is a former recipient of a Fulbright Fellowship and SSRC-MacArthur Foundation Fellowship on Peace and Security in a Changing World. Her research focuses on environmental policy change in Japan and Germany.

Preface

The idea for this volume emerged out of a discussion we had in a friend's livingroom in Ann Arbor, Michigan in 1992. We had both recently come back from doing research on global environmental policy-making in Asia and shared many substantive and theoretical concerns. Although we had worked in countries with very different political and economic situations, we shared an interest in how the issue of global climate change reached the policy agendas in China and Japan. It was clear that in both countries the internationalization of the environment was influencing normative values and institutional structures. Yet at the same time, domestic politics continued to play an important role in determining how these two states reacted to international negotiations. We both agreed that there was a need for a more systematic appraisal of how international and domestic politics were being linked through the internationalization of environmental politics.

We knew several other scholars with an interest in environmental politics and the linkages between the domestic and international levels and applied to the SSRC-MacArthur Foundation Program on International Peace and Security for support to hold a workshop on this theme. Without this initial support, it is doubtful that this late evening discussion would have led to this book.

The first workshop was titled "Cooperation, Conflict, and the Global Environment." A diverse group of scholars, we met for a weekend to discuss our research and to brainstorm interesting research themes. Our interests covered areas such as the United Nations Conference on Environment and Development (UNCED), the implementation of international environmental agreements, joint implementation schemes, East–West environmental cooperation, and the impacts of migration on the environment. Out of this workshop came the idea to produce a volume that would explore how the internationalization of environmental politics was altering policy-making processes, and what this in turn might mean for environmental protection.

A year later, again with the support of the SSRC-MacArthur Foundation Program on International Peace and Security, we held a second workshop which focused on the major theme that had emerged from the first one – the importance of international and domestic dimensions of global environmental protection. Prior to the second workshop, the group was provided with a set of questions and theoretical guidelines to aid participants in writing revised or new chapters. All those writing on particular regions were selected in part because they had spent substantial periods conducting field research in their areas of expertise. They were also a group that was interested in finding a means to integrate the theoretical insights produced by a growing body of literature in international relations with the theoretical and empirical insights gained from more traditional comparative approaches to the study of politics and policy-making.

The empirical research of the group clearly demonstrated that new linkages were emerging among actors at the international, regional, and national levels and these were influencing environmental policy-making processes, policy outcomes, and the effectiveness of policy implementation. These linkages were important to the formation of new international environmental norms and institutions in the countries we examined as well as internationally. At the same time, however, differences in domestic political institutions and cultures continued to influence policy outcomes.

At the end of the second workshop, we were still not quite ready to sign off on the volume. Many of the chapters were still in draft form and needed revisions that would take into account the theoretical and substantive discussions that occurred during the meeting. We also wanted feedback from external experts who might provide us with an objective critique of the chapters and the volume as a whole. We received funding from the International Studies Association to hold a third and final workshop.

The first two workshops had been held at the Center for Science and International Affairs at the Kennedy School of Government, Harvard University. This final workshop was held at The Brookings Institution; experts in the Washington DC area as well as a few from outside the immediate area were brought in to critique individual chapters and the volume as a whole. This group included Ken Conca, Daniel Deudney,

Maurice Feshbach, Virginia Haufler, Carl Lankowski, Steven Edwards, Robert Percival, Dennis Pirages, Ming Wan, and Paul Wapner. This group of scholars and practitioners offered valuable comments on the substance and theoretical arguments of individual chapters and offered suggestions on how we might improve the volume. Every chapter in this volume has benefited as a result of the time and effort these individuals put into reading and critiquing our work. We are extremely grateful to this group for taking time out of busy lives not only to read and comment on individual chapters but also to spend a full day discussing the volume.

It is a pleasure to sign off on this project knowing that it has produced new friendships and generated rich scholarly exchange. It is also a pleasure to thank the many people who have contributed in various ways to this project. Special thanks go to Karen Stemm, Stacy VandeVeer, Esook Yoon, and Wendy Lynch for the many hours they spent helping with preparation of the manuscript at various stages. We also extend our appreciation to John C. Campbell, William C. Clark, Harold K. Jacobson, Kenneth Lieberthal, and Michel Oksenberg for their mentorship and support in this endeavor. The project would never have gotten so far without the intellectual input and energy provided by a number of individuals who are not represented in this volume. Some produced draft chapters that could not be included – not for lack of quality or potential – but for personal or professional reasons that prevented further work on them. Others came to workshops to offer opinions, guidance, and critique. Yet others spent time reading versions of chapters and making substantive critical analyses. This group includes Alexander Carius, Nancy Dickson, Steven Heydemann, Thomas Homer-Dixon, Karen Jacobsen, Robert Keohane, Vicki Norberg-Bohm, Ronald Mitchell, Ted Parson, Chris Reus-Smit, Michael Ross, Mark Tullis, David Victor, and Hao Yufan. To all of these people, we thank you for your time, your encouragement, and your intellectual contributions. Finally, we wish to acknowledge the support for workshops provided by the International Studies Association and the SSRC-MacArthur Foundation Program on International Peace and Security.

Elizabeth Economy
Miranda A. Schreurs

1   Domestic and international linkages in environmental politics

Elizabeth Economy and Miranda A. Schreurs

Introduction

In Lynton Caldwell's extensive historical account of the development of international agreements for environmental protection, he points to the 1972 United Nations Conference on the Human Environment (the Stockholm Conference) as the turning point in the development of a new paradigm in environmental thinking. As Caldwell writes,

> The Stockholm Conference was a watershed in international relations. It legitimized environmental policy as a universal concern among nations, and so created a place for environmental issues on many national agendas where they had been previously unrecognized … [T]he growth of international environmental cooperation during the 1970s and thereafter is an aspect of a larger social transition. It is an expression of a changing view of mankind's relationship to the earth.[1]

Pollution of the atmosphere, species loss, nuclear power safety, and ocean and sea pollution are some of the problems that are transforming the nature of international politics. As these issues become more and more pressing, the boundaries of states are increasingly blurred. The inefficient use of coal or the inability to treat a communicable disease in one state not only ravages that state's environment and populace but also has direct and frequently dramatic ramifications for other states. Individual states are ill-equipped to respond alone to the myriad challenges posed by transboundary environmental, social, and health problems. As the rapid growth in the number of international environmental agreements since the 1970s attests, the resolution of these types of problems requires extensive cooperation and coordination among states in the formulation and implementation of policies. The United Nations Environment Program (UNEP) has a register that lists close to 200 multilateral environmental agreements or amendments to existing agreements, most of which have been established since the Stockholm Conference. Edith Brown-Weiss has estimated that there were over 900 bilateral and multilateral environmental agreements by the early 1990s.[2]

This represents a major change from the past. Until a few decades ago, environmental policy formation and implementation were primarily local or national matters. In the pre- and immediate post-World War II periods, there were some bilateral environmental agreements to deal with localized transboundary pollution problems and even some international environmental agreements for the preservation of migratory species or the control of nuclear testing. Still, these were exceptional cases. In most instances, environmental policy outcomes were determined primarily by actors within a single state.

In contrast, contemporary environmental politics is a truly global affair. By the time of the United Nations Conference on the Environment and Development (UNCED) in 1992, the international community as a whole evidenced a broader understanding of the complexity and international scope of many environmental problems. This internationalization of environmental politics is transforming the relationship among actors within and among states. Today, international organizations, multinational corporations, international environmental groups, international expert groups (sometimes known as "epistemic communities"), multilateral banks, and other governmental and non-governmental organizations play a central role in influencing environmental policy outcomes. Agenda setting, policy formulation, and implementation are becoming increasingly internationalized.

This volume is concerned with how the internationalization of environmental politics has affected domestic political institutions and policy-making processes. A second and related focus is on the influence of domestic policy priorities on international environmental negotiations. The chapters in this volume are based on extensive interviews and empirical data collection. They explore and contrast how the internationalization of environmental policy-making influences and has been influenced by structures and processes at the domestic or supranational level. The chapters analyze international environmental policy formation in the People's Republic of China, Japan, Germany, the former Soviet Union and its successor states, the United Kingdom, the United States, and Zimbabwe. Because of the special nature of environmental policy-making within Europe, there is also a chapter on the European Union. Our environmental cases include global climate change, biodiversity, stratospheric ozone depletion, trade in endangered species, and acid rain. The chapters examine changes over time in the reaction of states and the European Union to international environmental problems. Importantly, they all find that environmental policy-making processes have been altered by participation in international environmental negotiations. At the same time, they all point to the power that individual states possess to influence the direction or effectiveness of international environmental protection initiatives and call for a more nuanced understanding of international environmental policy formation than many accounts provide.

Each of the authors of this study was asked to explore how, why, and when international linkages matter in shaping domestic policy-making and influencing policy outcomes on transnational or global environmental issues. Our findings suggest that the emergence of new international environmental problems and new coalitions of actors has indeed influenced policy formation and implementation processes at the domestic level. The internationalization of environmental politics has injected new ideas about environmental problems and policy solutions and financial and technical resources into domestic political debates. In some cases, it has altered existing power balances among coalitions operating in the sub-state and international arenas. In other cases, it has provided individual states and sub-state actors with new avenues through which to influence environmental policy debates at the international level. Importantly, however, the international community is not always effective at reaching down into the state to alter domestic politics. If the international community lacks the tools – either financial or educational – to recruit support from the key economic and industrial actors, cooperation is unlikely.

For a volume concerned with the internationalization of environmental politics, our approach is admittedly state-centric. This is intentional. Although the contributors to this volume recognize the growing importance of non-state actors in the international system, we are concerned less with the organization, goals or activities of these new actors than we are with their impact on the state. The contributors to this volume share a belief that not enough empirical work has focused on the question of how international actors and the internationalization of environmental science and politics, more generally, has affected the role of the state in environmental policy formation. The state remains a powerful actor in international politics and continues to play a central role in the establishment and enforcement of domestic environmental laws and international environmental agreements.[3] It is therefore important to understand how the state is influenced by the emergence of new kinds of international environmental problems and the socio-political changes that have accompanied them. It is also important to understand how states are using the internationalization of environmental politics to forward their own policy priorities.

This volume joins a growing body of literature that seeks to bridge the study of international relations and comparative politics.[4] The comparative environmental politics literature points to the importance of domestic political institutions, cultural factors, scientific traditions, interest group politics, and social movements in agenda setting and implementation.[5] In contrast, international relations scholars have focused their attention on international environmental policy formation and its implementation.[6] This literature considers the importance of power relations among states and inter-state bargaining;[7] the ideas held by communities of experts;[8] and treaty design in explaining successes and failures in international environmental cooperation efforts.[9] In addition, there is growing interest in the influence of non-state actors, including international organizations, multilateral corporations, and international non-governmental organizations in policy formation.[10]

Through empirical case studies, this volume draws on and critiques the theoretical insights provided by these schools. Like earlier comparative work it focuses on how domestic political institutions and cultures affect the agenda-setting process and policy implementation at the domestic level. In addition, it draws on international relations theory by focusing on how inter-state negotiations, epistemic communities, and international institutions have introduced new ideas about environmental problems and policy solutions and financial and technical resources into national policy debates. In so doing, this volume joins others in the field of environmental politics that aim to understand the role of domestic politics in international relations.[11]

The volume is also strongly influenced by other bodies of literature. Many of the chapters in the volume follow arguments originating in the state institutionalist literature. This work argues that *domestic* political, social, and economic institutions matter in international relations. Institutions are important because they can structure the relationships among actors in society, influence their preferences, and channel how ideas are brought into domestic decision-making processes.[12] Domestic political institutions can mitigate the effectiveness of international efforts to alter domestic policy priorities and regulations. Institutions tend to be persistent, but occasionally they do change. This may be the

result of exogenous factors (as in the case of the major political trans-
formations in the former Soviet Union); institutional change at the
domestic level may also occur, however, because of international efforts
to bring about such change.

Our work is similar to studies in the field of political economy that
have examined how domestic institutions influence national responses
to international crises or international developments. This literature too
recognizes the importance of domestic institutions in shaping power
relations and influencing the priorities of actors, but in the tradition of
the "second image reversed" also points to the importance of the position of domestic actors within the international political economy. Actor
preferences and behavior can be influenced by their international position.[13] As Robert Keohane and Helen Milner have argued, internationalization also affects the policy preferences of economic and political
actors domestically, and this in turn influences national policy formation and even the shape of domestic institutions.[14]

The internationalization of environmental politics

Before continuing, it is helpful to consider what we mean by the internationalization of environmental politics. At its most basic level, the internationalization of environmental politics is a response to the emergence
of new types of environmental issues. In recent decades, a new class of
environmental problems that are transnational, regional, or even global
in scale have emerged. In some cases, this simply reflects a new understanding of the regional or global impacts of local activities. It is now
understood, for example, that coal-fired power plants in Beijing contribute not only to local air pollution but also to acid rain in Japan as well as
global climate change. There is also growing acceptance of the idea that
species loss in one region of the world is a matter of global concern
because of the still unknown consequences of large-scale losses in biodiversity. Many old environmental problems are now viewed in new
ways.

In other cases, environmental problems have become more international because the internationalization of the economy has intensified
pressures on local ecological systems. Trade in elephant ivory in Asia,
Europe, and North America has contributed to the decimation of elephant populations in Africa. The demand for hardwood in the North
has been an important factor in deforestation in tropical states.
Environmental degradation in eastern Germany is, in part, related to

the transport of waste to this region from the former Federal Republic of Germany. In these cases, environmental issues are internationalized because multiple states have played a role in environmental degradation in a given region of the world.

Finally, new kinds of environmental issues that are global in scale have also been discovered. It is now known that the use of chlorofluorocarbons (CFCs) as a common propellant in spray cans, as a cleaning solvent, and as a refrigerant caused damage to the protective ozone layer in the earth's upper atmosphere. There is also a growing scientific consensus that the burning of fossil fuels is contributing to changes in average global temperatures, or what is commonly known as "global warming." These issues are now widely accepted as issues that require international cooperation if they are to be solved.

The internationalization of environmental policy formation, however, is not just a matter of states responding to the emergence of new kinds of problems or new ways of viewing old ones. The internationalization of environmental politics also reflects the efforts by international actors and institutions to reach down into the state to set domestic policy agendas and influence policy formation and implementation processes.

International actors may attempt to influence scientific or expert discourse within states. There are a growing number of international linkages among environmental non-governmental organizations (NGOs), scientists, and policy experts. Peter Haas argues that transnational expert groups, or what he calls, "epistemic communities," have emerged around specific policy concerns, such as Mediterranean Sea pollution or stratospheric ozone depletion. These expert communities may link scientists, bureaucrats, journalists, and representatives of NGOs who share a common concern and expertise about an issue. Epistemic communities can play a very important role in introducing scientific concerns about an environmental issue into domestic policy debates.[15]

Linkages among states and between actors at the domestic and international level are established through participation in international organizations, the creation of networks among environmental organizations, the activities of multinational corporations, scientific conferences, international political gatherings, the media and telecommunications. International organizations and institutions like the United Nations, the Organization for Economic Cooperation and Development (OECD), or the World Bank bring actors together to address specific environmental issues and to share knowledge, technical expertise, and financial resources. The European Union is another important actor linking actors within states.

The rise in the number of international organizations and interest groups – only some of which emerged in response to international environmental issues – has facilitated the transfer of ideas about policy problems and solutions across national borders. Scientists participating in international conferences have brought new ideas to domestic audiences about how human activities impact on ecological systems. International environmental organizations have formed links with nationally based groups to help spread information about environmental problems and to apply pressures for policy change across national borders. The media has acted as a rapid transmitter of news about environmental disasters. International meetings, such as UNCED, have helped to bring environmental issues to the attention of policy-makers around the world. Through these linkages, the internationalization of environmental policy formation is making states richer in shared knowledge and more aware of the need for cooperation in environmental protection efforts.

Important resources can be transferred from the international to the domestic level through these linkages. These may include, for example, knowledge about the causes and consequences of environmental degradation and technical know-how in the form of computer models, monitoring technology, or energy efficiency strategies. The linkages can promote the exchange of data on such issues as greenhouse gas emissions, the nature of Baltic Sea pollutants, or treaty infractions by a state that is party to an international environmental accord. The internationalization of environmental politics has led to the transfer of funds for environmental protection to developing states, and it has also become a means by which more abstract ideas or values concerning the environment, such as sustainability, North–South equity issues, or concerns of inter-generational responsibility have gained recognition in different national settings.

The extent to which linkages form between actors within a state and actors operating internationally are strongly influenced by the domestic political system. Thus, some of the states we examine have only weak linkages to the international system while others have extensive linkages that have existed for long periods. The end of the Cold War has opened the way at the international level for greater contact among actors in the East and West. Yet, the effectiveness of these linkages is strongly mitigated by domestic politics.

Implications for environmental policy: evidence from the case studies

The case studies in this book illustrate that indeed the internationalization of environmental politics and the emergence of new linkages between the domestic and international levels have encouraged new ways of thinking about environmental problems and policy responses. Multinational corporations helped define the policy debate in the United States and the United Kingdom in the case of the Montreal Protocol. The Convention on International Trade in Endangered Species (CITES) put elephant protection on Zimbabwe's political agenda despite considerable initial domestic apathy and opposition. Events leading up to UNCED elevated levels of concern about air pollution and global climate change in the People's Republic of China. European concerns about transboundary air pollution helped put acid rain onto the former Soviet Union's list of environmental policy problems.

The chapters contend, however, that the effectiveness of linkages in promoting cooperation among states in addressing large-scale environmental problems is strongly mitigated by domestic political and economic structures and institutions. Analyses at the state level highlight the important role played by the different interests of sub-state actors in shaping how a state responds to international pressures for cooperation in environmental protection. The ways in which events at the international level are perceived and defined by relevant policy actors as means for pushing their respective policy priorities greatly influence national responses to international environmental problems. Where the goals of the international community can be effectively linked to the goals of powerful sub-state actors, early cooperation is often the result. Where the goals of the international community are not seen as an effective means for pushing sub-state policy priorities, cooperation is often limited. For politicians involved in international negotiations, it is often necessary to push for a shift in the international debate before participation in an international environmental agreement becomes politically palatable back home. For domestic advocates of environmental protection it is often not until international linkages are successful in legitimizing their demands that political change becomes possible.

In some cases, domestic interest in environmental protection encourages the formation of a cooperative stance. In Germany, for example, the political process permitted and supported the emergence of a strong Green Party. Once this party gained electoral representation and green issues became more important to Germany's established political parties, Germany became a "primary force" in pushing the European Community on the introduction of a Large Combustion Plant Directive and later in the cases of stratospheric ozone depletion and global climate change.

At the same time, the linking of domestic policy concerns with global environmental problems may lead to improvements in domestic environmental protection while not necessarily producing a more co-operative stance on the international environmental issue. In chapter 2, Elizabeth Economy finds that the establishment in China of a leading group to study and develop policy alternatives on global climate change offered the opportunity for the more powerful planning, industrial, and foreign affairs agencies to wrest control of the policy process from the environmental and scientific ministries. Not surprisingly, the outcome of the domestic negotiations resulted in policy prescriptions that reflected these conservative interests.

Similarly, new ideas about environmental protection are often ini-tially rejected by powerful coalitions who feel threatened by the implications of policy change or new environmental paradigms. The phasing out of CFCs and other ozone depleting substances was initially rejected by powerful industrialists in the United States, United Kingdom, and elsewhere who felt economically threatened by environ-mental protection initiatives. In most cases, the critical domestic actors opposing regulation are the relevant economic interests. Industrial interests typically represent the most powerful actors in the state because they can provide jobs and contribute to a nation's GNP. Their leaders are often well-situated politically as well. Unless they see incen-tives in cooperation, industrial actors often possess the power to stymie even the most obvious of cooperative endeavors. In Russia, for example, in the wake of Chernobyl, the nuclear power industry resisted involve-ment by the West because it was afraid that its control over the industry would be undermined.

The power of economic incentive is great. As Joanne Kauffman notes in chapter 4, DuPont became a proactive participant in encouraging the establishment of the Montreal Protocol when it determined that a level regulatory playing field – which could be established only by an inter-national agreement – would "create new markets for more expensive substitutes that only large well-financed corporations could develop." Kal Raustiala (chapter 3) finds in the case of the United States that once the major pharmaceutical and biotechnology firms were persuaded that the biodiversity treaty would not be "dangerous" to their profitability, they threw their support behind the treaty and enabled the Clinton administration to be environmentally proactive without "appearing to sign away American interests in jobs."

The threat of sanction or economic loss has also proved a powerful force in engendering cooperation. According to Angela Liberatore (chapter 8), the introduction of environmental regulation within the European Community was due mainly to economic factors. The European Community wanted to avoid distortion of competition within its member states and to maintain access to foreign markets which might use environmental legislation as a barrier to entry. In China, industry saw no advantages in joining an international accord on global climate change. In the case of stratospheric ozone depletion, however, various industries feared that their market for consumer goods in Asia would be sharply constricted if they did not sign the Montreal Protocol. This same economic rationale emerged in the case of Japan; the Ministry of International Trade and Industry (MITI) finally gave in to the pressure to sign the Montreal Protocol once trade sanctions were considered by the United States.

International linkages can influence these cost-benefit analyses by changing resource balances among actors, altering actors' interests or perceptions, or providing means for pushing other policy priorities. Often this is done through the transfer of funds, technology, and know-how. As Miranda Schreurs remarks in chapter 6, when Japan's politicians, bureaucrats, and economic leaders began to see in global warming a way to promote technological innovation, their attitudes towards participation in an international environmental agreement changed. In chapter 7, Phyllis Mofson finds that when Zimbabwe's political leaders determined that non-participation in CITES could be more costly than participation because non-participation could invite economic sanctions, protection of the African elephant was put on the domestic political agenda. In the United States a change in administration altered the balance between actors in favor of and opposed to the Biodiversity Convention and produced a climate more favorable to the policy change being sought by international actors.

Even wealthier states often balk at environmental cooperation unless adequate financial incentive or risk is demonstrated. Here, too, multilateral institutions are critical players. When financial or technical support is transferred to the typically weak environmental agencies, this process has the potential to alter the context within which environmental policy-making occurs at the domestic level. As Liberatore points out, the European Union became increasingly important in the making of environmental policy in the European states by redistributing funding and offering technical assistance. In China, the World Bank and Asian Development Bank empowered environmental protection advocates during the global climate change negotiations. Although in this case, the effects were limited in terms of policy outcome on the issue of global climate change, the potential longer-term ramifications for the National Environmental Protection Agency's ability to influence policy were substantial.

The internationalization of environmental politics has also altered more fundamental elements of states through the creation of new institutions and the support of traditionally weak societal groups. In states where voices calling for environmental protection are weak, it is often not until linkages force changes in institutional structures or successfully encourage new ways of viewing environmental problems that domestic policy change is possible. Economy's chapter illustrates how the international negotiations leading up to the climate change convention engendered a dramatic increase in information flows both between international and domestic actors and among domestic actors themselves. These types of changes have the potential to alter radically the context within which environmental policy-making occurs at the domestic level. Within China we see that international organizations and bilateral aid programs are empowering environmental protection advocates in a state that is still heavily focused on rapid economic development. In Zimbabwe, weak domestic actors have used international linkages to validate their policy preferences and gain in political stature. For example, Campfire, an NGO based on the principle of fostering sustainable use of wildlife, has gained influence through the CITES negotiations; and the European Union is using international environmental negotiations as a means to strengthen its position as an independent actor.

Importantly, different coalitions of actors linking the international and domestic levels are important at different times and in different ways. International epistemic communities and international institutions contribute foremost to setting the agenda for international scientific discussions and domestic research agendas. As the chapter by Raustiala points out, the International Union for the Conservation of Nature (IUCN) and WorldWide Fund for Nature (WWF) were key actors in identifying biodiversity as an issue of international concern, defining the scope of the problem, and presenting it to domestic audiences in the United States and United Kingdom. International epistemic communities may play a particularly important role in those countries where scientific research of an environmental problem is still at a nascent stage. As Economy notes in her case study, at the time of the international negotiations on climate change, the Chinese had only a very limited research effort underway. Representatives of the international scientific community, most notably from the United States, initiated the Chinese research process by contacting energy specialists in China, bringing them to the United States for training, and supporting their efforts to gain international funding to estimate levels of Chinese CO_2 production. Still, in the end they were not very effective in using these tools to alter policy outcome in China. The same was true in Japan in the stratospheric ozone depletion case. The United States initiated a scientific exchange with Japan in an effort to win Japanese support for the Montreal Protocol. In this case, Japan's position changed.

The impact of epistemic communities is sharply limited by the fact that different actors and issues come into play during the scientific and political portions of the negotiations. Even when there is a relatively strong scientific consensus, as in the case of the Montreal Protocol, the key issues that emerge in the actual treaty negotiations do not hinge on the science of the issue as portrayed by the epistemic community but rather on political concerns such as the financial mechanisms to support implementation of the treaties, technology transfer, and intellectual property rights raised by domestic interests. As Kauffman notes, "while science can be used to justify political positions, national preferences for regulation are determined by commercial and political interests." Raustiala too discovered that epistemic communities are most crucial in the initial stages of negotiation when agendas are being established. In terms of achieving international accord on a treaty, however, the political issues remain relatively uninfluenced by scientific considerations. Instead, domestic political and economic institutions determine actors' perceptions and interests. In the biodiversity case, a community of experts was important in getting states to enter into regime negotiations, but the community played little role in actually shaping the debate around critical issues of the convention. Rather, policy choice was driven by domestic political and economic factors. United States pharmaceutical firms fearing the effects of regulations on their activities proved cautious about the ambiguous language of the accord. British firms that faced a different regulatory structure than that in the United

States were more accommodating. Differences in the political institutions of these states influenced where powerful domestic actors in the debate stood in relationship to the international negotiations.

The dramatic political events of the late 1980s force us to remember that domestic institutions are not static but rather dynamic. Changes in institutional structures and political processes can affect how international agendas are established and policy is implemented. In chapter 5, Robert Darst analyzes the impact of the dramatic changes in domestic politics in the former Soviet Union on the effectiveness of international cooperation for environmental protection. The chapter explores three key East–West environmental issues – nuclear power safety, pollution in the Baltic Sea, and transboundary air pollution. Counter to what one would expect, Darst finds that the period of greatest enthusiasm for East–West cooperation occurred in the second half of the 1980s, at a time when East–West economic integration had yet to proceed beyond a scattering of small joint ventures and when the authoritarian Soviet political order was still firmly in place. In contrast, the successor states to the Soviet Union have been willing to cooperate only when their more affluent neighbors are willing to bear the cost, despite the fact that they are both more democratic and more vulnerable to Western pressures than when they were part of the Soviet Union. In examining the reasons behind this paradox, Darst contributes to an understanding of the possibilities that international linkages provide but also the socio-political factors that can limit their effectiveness. In states where environmental interests are weak, international pressures for change may accomplish little unless these pressures trigger changes in the interests of domestic policy actors or where the goals of the international community can be effectively linked to the goals of powerful sub-state actors. Where the goals of the international community do not match sub-state policy priorities, cooperation is often problematic.

The Soviet case also highlights the difficulty in requiring states with poor financial resources to adopt expensive new technologies or other measures to respond to a transnational or global environmental problem. In such cases, the transfer of funds from multilateral institutions such as the World Bank may be the only means by which a state can be persuaded to sign onto an accord. China's willingness to sign the Montreal Protocol on Stratospheric Ozone Depletion hinged directly on the establishment of a multilateral fund to subsidize the development of CFC substitutes in the People's Republic of China. In Zimbabwe, too, the transfer of funds by international organizations was a critical element in persuading government leaders to recalculate the costs and benefits of participation in CITES.

Finally, internationalization of environmental protection efforts gives states a channel to bring their demands and concerns to the international negotiating table. Strong and weak states alike have been able to inject new issues into international negotiations. While the industrialized states typically have initiated international environmental protection negotiations, the developing states have effectively introduced their concerns about socio-economic development into broader environmental policy debates. For domestic political actors, involvement in international negotiations can legitimize policy solutions that have long been sought, such as energy conservation, the building of more nuclear power plants, or bureaucratic reorganization. Occasionally, domestic actors are able to link domestic issues with aspects of the global environmental problem. In Japan, the promotion of nuclear energy was linked to efforts to address global climate change. Participation in international environmental negotiations has provided a means for developing states to push independent policy priorities, including the transfer of technical know-how and wealth from the developed states.

By bringing their demands to international negotiations strong and weak states alike have been able to alter the text of international treaties. Through a variety of linkages, developing states have effectively introduced their concerns about socio-economic development into broader environmental policy debates. By using the international media, environmental activists have publicized environmental abuses. Weak domestic actors have used international linkages to validate their policy preferences and gain in political stature. National elites have used the internationalization of environmental policy-making as a means to obtain funding for domestic projects.

For many states, participation in international environmental negotiations has provided a means to push independent policy priorities – ranging from the transfer of technical know-how and wealth from the developed to the developing states to improving foreign relations. International environmental negotiations reflect the extent to which a dynamic process of issue linkage leads to a constant redefining of goals and priorities and as a result international negotiations often become a "garbage can" of policy problems and solutions.

Mofson documents the power a developing state can wield in influencing the shape of international environmental agreements. In examining the role of Zimbabwe in the CITES, Mofson argues that Zimbabwe entered the regime because it had little choice. To reject the demands of powerful international actors could prove costly to the state. Once in the regime, however, Zimbabwe found ways to gain greater voice for its own interests and to alter the actual shape of the regime. In doing this, Zimbabwe gained support from the international community by appearing to play a leading role in conservation efforts while using its membership in CITES to subtly alter the regime's power structure and its goals.

Critically, the impact of linkages among international and domestic politics must be understood in the context of an individual state's domestic political structures, policy process, and traditional policy priorities. It is this interaction between the international and domestic levels that best illuminates why and how nations come to cooperate or not on transnational and global environmental issues. The question of how domestic policy-making processes influence and are influenced by the internationalization of environmental politics demands further empirical and theoretical work. It is in this dynamic between the domestic and international levels that international environmental agenda setting, policy formation, and implementation must be studied.

Notes

1. Lynton K. Caldwell, *International Environmental Policy* (Durham: Duke University Press, 1990), p. 21. This is among the most comprehensive histories of the development of international environmental agreements and institutions available.
2. Edith Brown-Weiss, "Global Accords, Institutions, and Legal Developments," in *Global Environmental Accords: Implications for Technology, Industry, and International Relations*, transcripts of a symposium held at The Massachusetts Institute of Technology, September 24–25, 1992. For a list of multilateral environmental agreements see the United Nations Environment Program, *Register of International Treaties and Agreements in the Field of the Environment*, UNEP/GC.15/Inf.2, Nairobi, May 1989.
3. See for example Stephen Krasner, "Approaches to the State: Alternative Conceptions and Historical Dynamics," *Comparative Politics* 16:2 (1984), 223–246, and Theda Skocpol, "Bringing the State Back In: Strategies of Analysis in Current Research," in Peter B. Evans, Dietrich Rueschemeyer, and Theda Skocpol (eds.), *Bringing the State Back In* (Cambridge: Cambridge University Press, 1985).
4. A popular approach is the two-level game elaborated in Robert Putnam, "Diplomacy and Domestic Politics: The Logic of Two-Level Games," *International Organization*, 42:3 (1988), 427–460, and Andrew Moravcsik, "Integrating International and Domestic Theories of International Bargaining,"

in Peter Evans, Harold Jacobson, and Robert Putnam (eds.), *Double Edged Diplomacy: International Bargaining and Domestic Politics* (Berkeley: University of California Press, 1993).

5. For a review of the early comparative environmental politics literature of the industrialized states see David Vogel, "The Comparative Study of Environmental Policy: A Review of the Literature," in Meinolf Dierkes, Hans N. Weiler, and Ariane Berthoin Antal (eds.), *Comparative Policy Research: Learning from Experience* (Hants, England: Gower Publishing Co., 1987). On the importance of domestic politics and institutions in environmental policy formation and implementation see Cynthia Enloe, *The Politics of Pollution in a Comparative Perspective: Ecology and Power in Four Nations* (New York: David McKay Company, Inc., 1975); Donald Kelley, Kenneth Stunkel, and Richard Wescott, *The Economic Superpowers and the Environment: the United States, the Soviet Union, and Japan* (W.H. Freeman: San Francisco, 1976); Lennard Lundqvist, *The Hare and the Tortoise: Clean Air Policies in the United States and Sweden* (Ann Arbor: University of Michigan Press, 1980); Joseph L. Badaracco, Jr., *Loading the Dice: A Five-Country Study of Vinyl Chloride Regulation* (Boston: Harvard Business School Press, 1985); Susan J. Pharr and Joseph L. Badaracco, Jr., "Coping with Crisis: Environmental Regulation," in Thomas K. McCraw (ed.), *America versus Japan* (Boston: Harvard Business School Press, 1986); David Vogel, *National Styles of Regulation: Environmental Policy in Great Britain and the United States* (Ithaca: Cornell University Press, 1986); and Herbert Kitschelt, "Political Opportunity Structures and Political Protest," *British Journal of Political Science*, 16 (1986), 58–95. On comparative social movement theory see Andrew Jamison, Ron Eyerman, and Jacqueline Cramer, *The Making of the New Environmental Consciousness: A Comparative Study of the Environmental Movements in Sweden, Denmark and the Netherlands* (Edinburgh: Edinburgh University Press, 1990) and Russell J. Dalton, *The Green Rainbow: Environmental Groups in Western Europe* (New Haven and London: Yale University Press, 1994).

6. Pioneers in this area include Oran Young, *Natural Resources and the State* (Berkeley: University of California Press, 1981); Robert O. Keohane and Joseph S. Nye, *Power and Interdependence: World Politics in Transition* (Boston: Little, Brown, and Co., 1977); and David A. Kay and Harold K. Jacobson (eds.), *Environmental Protection: The International Dimension* (Totowa, NJ: Allenheld, Osmun, and Co., 1983).

7. See for example John E. Carroll (ed.), *International Environmental Diplomacy* (Cambridge: Cambridge University Press, 1988); Oran Young, *International Cooperation: Building Regimes for Natural Resources and the Environment* (Ithaca: Cornell University Press, 1989); and Gareth Porter and Janet Welsh Brown, *Global Environmental Politics: Dilemmas in World Politics* (Boulder: Westview Press, 1991).

8. Peter Haas, *Saving the Mediterranean: The Politics of International Environmental Cooperation* (New York: Columbia University Press, 1990) and Peter Haas

(ed.), "Knowledge, Power, and International Coordination," *International Organization*, 46:1 (Winter), 1992. For a critique of Haas, see Karen T. Litfin, *Ozone Discourses: Science and Politics in Global Environmental Cooperation* (New York: Columbia University Press, 1994).

9. See especially Peter M. Haas, Robert O. Keohane, and Marc A. Levy (eds.), *Institutions for the Earth: Sources of Effective International Environmental Protection* (Cambridge, MA: The MIT Press, 1993) and Ronald B. Mitchell, *Intentional Oil Pollution at Sea: Environmental Policy and Treaty Compliance* (Cambridge, MA: The MIT Press, 1994).

10. On the importance of non-state, non-sovereign actors in the international system, see James Rosenau, *Turbulence in World Politics: A Theory of Change and Continuity* (Princeton: Princeton University Press, 1990) and Ronnie D. Lipschutz and Ken Conca (eds.), *The State and Social Power in Global Environmental Governance* (New York: Columbia University Press, 1993). On environmental NGOs see Thomas Princen and Matthias Finger, *Environmental NGOs in World Politics: Linking the Local and the Global* (New York: Routledge, 1994), and Kevin Stairs and Peter Taylor, "Non-Governmental Organizations and the Legal Protection of the Oceans: A Case Study," in Andrew Hurrell and Benedict Kingsbury (eds.), *The International Politics of the Environment* (Oxford: Oxford University Press, 1992), pp. 110–141. On the role of the United Nations see Peter S. Thacher, "The Role of the United Nations," in Hurrell and Kingsbury (eds.), *The International Politics of the Environment*, pp. 183–211. On the role of the World Bank see Kenneth Piddington, "The Role of the World Bank," in Hurrell and Kingsbury (eds.), *The International Politics of the Environment*, pp. 212–227. A seminal work on international organizations is Ernst B. Haas, *When Knowledge is Power: Three Models of Change in International Organizations*, (Berkeley, Los Angeles, and Oxford: Oxford University Press, 1990).

11. See, for instance, Jacqueline Vaughn Switzer, *Environmental Politics: Domestic and Global Dimensions* (New York: St. Martin's Press, 1994) which focuses on case studies of several international and transboundary environmental problems, and Andrew Hurrell and Benedict Kingsbury, "The International Politics of the Environment: An Introduction," in Hurrell and Kingsbury (eds.), *The International Politics of the Environment*, pp. 1–50. Case studies taking this approach include Ronald Brickman, Sheila Jasanoff, and Thomas Ilgen, *Controlling Chemicals: The Politics of Regulation in Europe and the United States* (Ithaca and London: Cornell University Press, 1985); Angela Liberatore, "The Management of Uncertainty: Response and Learning Processes Following Chernobyl," Ph.D. Dissertation, Department of Political and Social Sciences, European University Institute, 1992; and Sonya Boehmer-Christiansen and Jim Skea, *Acid Politics: Environmental and Energy Policies in Britain and Germany* (London and New York: Belhaven Press, 1991).

12. For discussions of institutions, see John G. Ikenberry, "Conclusion: An Institutional Approach to American Foreign Economic Policy," *International*

Organization 42:2 (1988); and Kathleen Thelen and Sven Steinmo, "Historical Institutionalism in Comparative Politics," in Sven Steinmo, Kathleen Thelen, and Frank Longstreth, *Structuring Politics: Historical Institutionalism in Comparative Analysis* (Cambridge: Cambridge University Press, 1992), pp. 1–32.

13. Peter J. Katzenstein, "International Relations and Domestic Structures: Foreign Economic Policies of Advanced Industrial States," *International Organization* 30:1 (1976), 1–45; Peter J. Katzenstein, "Introduction: Domestic and International Forces and Strategies of Foreign Economic Policy," *International Organization* 31:4 (1977), 587–606; Peter J. Katzenstein, "Conclusion: Domestic Structures and Strategies of Foreign Economic Policy," *International Organization* 31:4 (1977), 879–920; Peter Gourevitch, "The Second-Image Reversed: The International Sources of Domestic Politics," *International Organization* 32:4 (1978), 881–911; and Peter Gourevitch, *Politics in Hard Times: Comparative Responses to International Economic Crises* (Ithaca: Cornell University Press, 1986).

14. Robert O. Keohane and Helen V. Milner, *Internationalization and Domestic Politics* (Cambridge: Cambridge University Press, 1996).

15. See Haas, *Saving the Mediterranean*, and Haas (ed.), "Knowledge, Power, and International Coordination."

2 Chinese policy-making and global climate change: two-front diplomacy and the international community

Elizabeth Economy

The political and economic reforms that have swept China since 1978 have had a marked effect on China's behavior in the international arena, engendering increased linkages with the international community on a range of issues such as trade, technological development, and arms control. During the late 1980s and early 1990s, there was also a remarkable growth in China's interaction with the international community on environmental issues. This interaction has had a profound impact in several respects on China's participation in international environmental accords on issues such as ozone depletion, biodiversity, and climate change. It has substantially broadened the range of policy alternatives that China considers in response to these environmental problems and has provided the People's Republic of China with access to new technologies and funds that are crucial to any response that China might undertake. At the same time, the influence of the international community remains sharply constrained. In international negotiations, China routinely reiterates its commitment to principles that limit its obligation to respond to global environmental concerns: state sovereignty, Third World–First World inequity, and the responsibility of the advanced industrialized states.

This chapter examines the nature of China's participation in the international negotiations to address one of these environmental issues: global climate change. Specifically, it explores the scientific, energy, and political debates within China that surrounded the issue of climate change; how these debates have influenced China's international negotiating stance; and the process by which international actors influenced both the nature of these debates and China's response strategies in preparation for the United Nations Conference on Environment and Development (UNCED) in June 1992.

Global climate change has the potential to wreak serious havoc on the ecological, economic, and political world by seriously disrupting world food production, inundating millions of acres of coastal and lowland areas, destroying countless animal and plant species, significantly increasing the incidence of pestilence, and creating vast numbers of "environmental" refugees. While some natural phenomena (such as periodic changes in the sun's intensity) may contribute to climate change, a variety of anthropogenic factors in both less developed and advanced industrialized countries, especially fossil fuel production/combustion and deforestation, play a significant role.

Over the period 1988 to 1992, the United Nations conducted its first scientific discussions under the auspices of the Intergovernmental Panel on Climate Change (IPCC) and then proceeded to formal political negotiations through the International Negotiating Committee (INC). These scientific discussions and political negotiations were designed to assess the likelihood of climate change, the potential ramifications for the planet, and the range of response measures available.

The Chinese delegates to the climate change convention negotiations emerged as some of the most aggressive and articulate opponents of a binding convention on climate change. Throughout the negotiation process, they remained committed to only a general framework convention that did not include the delineation of specific responsibilities or commitments for the signatories, especially with regard to curtailing emissions of the principal greenhouse gas, carbon dioxide (CO_2). China held that any action that did not concurrently advance economic growth would have to be funded by the international community. Moreover, Chinese officials rallied the developing states behind their position in an attempt – in large part successful – to establish a united front for bargaining with the advanced industrialized countries.

In attempting to understand how the Chinese arrived at this conservative negotiating position, an explanation based on domestic politics is a useful starting point. There was a long process of negotiation among the key bureaucratic actors in the People's Republic of China that resulted in an ultimate victory by the foreign policy and planning agencies, who were determined to prevent any real policy adjustment in terms of economic growth or energy use. In addition, the process of elite access was highly restricted; the more proactive bureaucracies, such as the environmental and scientific agencies, were given no real opportunity to advance their views to the top leadership. Environmental protection consistently had attracted only a low level of interest among senior Chinese officials, who were committed to rapid economic growth.

Such an explanation, however, would ignore the crucial role played by the international community. International actors intersected with the Chinese in two important respects that significantly shaped the Chinese response.

First, the conservative negotiating position was buttressed by the indifference of key players in the international community. Throughout the process of international negotiation, little pressure was brought to bear on China to adjust its position by its closest partners – the United States, Japan, and Southeast Asia. Essentially, no international actor made any concerted effort to persuade the Chinese to adopt CO_2 emission targets or other highly proactive measures.

Second, and perhaps more importantly, the relatively recalcitrant official stance of the Chinese negotiators masked a range of important activities taking place at a second level of policy-making between the more proactive scientific and environmental communities in China and their counterparts in the international community. An epistemic community emerged surrounding the issue of climate change that sparked a virtual explosion in the amount of information transmitted between the Chinese and foreign specialist communities. Chinese officials and specialists in various disciplines such as energy, the environment, oceanography, and meteorology gained access to ideas as well as to a system of technology and funds transfer. These exchanges and collaborative efforts measurably increased the Chinese understanding of climate change and the range of response measures that they considered, and in some cases actually transformed the thinking of Chinese officials. In addition, international aid and development agencies provided the People's Republic of China with technology and funds that advanced China's response well beyond the position it took in international negotiations.

The environmental setting

By the time of UNCED 1992, China was confronting extensive pollution and environmental degradation stemming from both its rapid industrialization drive during the post-1949 period and its emphasis on continued rapid economic growth throughout the reform period. China's overwhelming reliance on coal, its poor implementation of pollution and efficiency technologies, and its non-market pricing system for coal and other fuels (such as natural gas) brought about severe air and water pollution, transport bottlenecks, and health problems. Pollutants, for example, rendered 86 per cent of the river water that flowed through urban areas unsuitable for drinking or fishing. Acid rain affected almost one-third of China's populated territory and had devastating impacts on agriculture in several provinces. By one estimate, the cost of environmental pollution and degradation cost the state 15 per cent of its annual GNP.

China's patterns of energy usage also had important ramifications for its capacity to address the problem of climate change. By the late 1980s, China was the third largest consumer and producer of energy in the world, with over 75 per cent of its energy derived from coal. Between 1950 and 1990, China's CO_2 emissions – due overwhelmingly to its coal use – rose from 1.3 per cent of the world total to 10.5 per cent, in tandem with its industrial development and its reliance on coal. By 2020, experts predict that China will have surpassed the United States as the leading producer of CO_2.[1]

The overwhelming emphasis on rapid economic growth translated into a history of environmental protection prior to UNCED that was fraught with serious abuse of natural resources. Periodic attempts to redress environmental degradation suffered from a lack of funds and poor enforcement of environmental laws.

Prior to 1972, no environmental laws existed: industry used rivers as drainage systems, and air quality declined steadily. In 1972, however, the confluence of three events sparked a new Chinese approach to the environment. The beach at Dalian Bay became black from polluted shells; tainted fish appeared on the Beijing market from the Guanting Reservoir; and the United Nations Conference on Human Environment was held in Stockholm. The Chinese sent a delegation to the Conference, where they were widely considered disruptive and unconstructive participants. However, when the delegation returned to China, its report prompted Premier Zhou Enlai to organize the first national conference on environmental protection, which was held in June 1973. In addition, an elite group of representatives from the ministries of planning, agriculture, communications, water conservancy, public health, and industry were brought together in a formal capacity to review China's environmental situation and practices and consider what steps China should take to address its environmental problems.[2]

The onset of political and economic reforms in 1978 brought with them a second spurt of activity in environmental protection. In 1979, a draft national level environmental protection law was enacted that was formally promulgated in 1989. It not only established basic principles to protect the environment but also promoted the construction of a legal network for environmental protection. Chinese officials issued a spate of new environmental laws, regulations, guidelines, and organizational changes.[3] At the same time, a nascent environmentalism was growing among members of the Chinese political elite. The National People's Congress – the Chinese legislature – had begun to discuss domestic environmental issues, such as construction of the Three Gorges Dam. In addition, the media initiated exposés of environmental wrongdoing; the universities began instruction in environmental education; and international foundations sponsored nominally non-governmental organizations in environmental protection.

Despite these advances, however, implementation of environmental regulations was haphazard and enforcement remained lax. Chinese leaders were reluctant to back up their laws with adequate environmental protection apparatus for fear that economic development would be hampered. They set fines for polluting so low that they failed to act as an incentive for action; and their investment in environmental protection remained well below the level necessary even to stabilize the environmental situation, let alone to improve it.

The environmental protection tradition that China brought to the UNCED process reflected a continuing battle between desires for rapid economic development and concerns over the ecological ramifications of this development. The problem of global climate change was linked inextricably to the issue of the pace of economic development by virtue of the importance of energy to both issues and China's overwhelming reliance on coal. The policy-making process that the Chinese evidenced throughout the international scientific and political negotiations reflected the primacy of economic concerns. In each of the three domestic debates that surrounded the issue of climate change – scientific, energy, and political – traditional concerns of economic development, as well as sovereignty and Third World–First World relations, dominated the discourse. While the international community had only marginal influence over the actual Chinese negotiating stance, it nonetheless influenced the tenor of the debate by helping to widen the range of issues considered and to assist China in undertaking concrete measures to respond to climate change.

The scientific debate

With the exception of paleoclimatological studies, the Chinese had little history of climate change research. They lacked computers and monitoring equipment and operated without useful data. Also, there were funding shortages and poor collaboration between institutes who often viewed themselves more as competitors than collaborators (by selling data and competing for funds).

However, in 1988, in preparation for the UN-sponsored scientific discussions on climate change under the auspices of the IPCC process, the Chinese began to organize a more sophisticated research effort. The State Council's Environmental Protection Commission (EPC) brought together four agencies – the State Science and Technology Commission (SSTC), the National Environmental Protection Agency (NEPA), the State Meteorological Administration (SMA), and the Ministry of Foreign Affairs (MOFA) – to begin preparations for the scientific discussions. The SMA directed studies on the science of climate change; the NEPA prepared a report on the possible effects of climate change; the SSTC initiated programs to develop response measures; and the MOFA coordinated the negotiating strategy.

By 1989, the SSTC and SPC had negotiated with Beijing for a five-year global climate change research program to determine the sources of global warming in the People's Republic of China, to assess the impact of climate change upon it, and to design political and technical strategies to address the problem. The program encompassed 40 projects and involved about 20 ministries and 500 experts.[4]

Funding, however, was scarce, and Chinese experts turned to the international community for assistance. They were eager for data, technological transfer (such as advanced computing Global Circulation Models), and research design ideas. Not surprisingly, agencies such as NEPA and the SMA, which traditionally had been concerned with issues linked to the debate on global climate change (for example, energy conservation or pollution monitoring) were especially driven to access the ideas of the foreign scientific community.

China had tremendous success in attracting outside assistance, and international organizations and bilateral efforts began to overcome some of the funding and technological shortcomings of the Chinese research program. Support from abroad both reinforced and expanded upon ongoing research and technological developments taking place in China. The World Bank, the Asian Development Bank, the UNEP and the UNDP all took an active interest in providing monitoring equipment for greenhouse gas emissions, sharing computer modeling techniques, offering technological assistance to develop response measures, and training Chinese environmental officials. For example, China's

Energy Research Institute, under the auspices of the State Planning Council, became the focal point for international work on energy and climate change, in large part through the sponsorship of the Battelle Institute in the United States. Battelle offered six-month training programs in the United States for individual Chinese researchers, transferred sophisticated energy-efficiency computer modeling programs, and shared methods for estimating levels of Chinese CO_2 emissions that the Chinese eventually used in their calculations for the political negotiations.[5]

The international community also had an important impact on the range of ideas expressed by the specialist community. The work that emerged from the Chinese scientific community throughout the period of the global climate change negotiations indicated that there were serious differences in approach and understanding of the implications of climate change for China. The international community expanded the range of future environmental and economic scenarios developed by the Chinese and even contributed to a radical reorientation of perspective in some officials. One SSTC official, for example, stated that his basic knowledge of climate change was developed almost entirely through contact with scientists and officials from abroad. This interaction transformed his thinking and encouraged him to assert a proactive position on the extent to which China should respond to the threat of global warming.[6]

Those Chinese researchers who relied on traditional Chinese methodologies or paleoclimatology were less likely to recommend strong action to counter the potential of climate change. Zhou Guangzhao, head of the Chinese Academy of Sciences, who based his thinking in historical analogues, for example, concluded that the climate changes of the past 100 years in China could not be explained by the enhancement of the greenhouse effect. He therefore favored measures that would permit China to adapt to climate change rather than to work to prevent it.[7]

Many researchers in the State Meteorological Administration, who had more extensive access to Western climate models, accepted the validity of global climate change. However, they suggested that the impacts of climate change on China remained uncertain. They noted that regional variation in agricultural production would occur such that the northern part of China would improve its agricultural production, the central area would become unstable, and the region south of the middle and lower reaches of the Yangtze would remain approximately the same. They concluded that it was impossible to discern whether

China would "win" or "lose" in the "global warming sweepstakes."[8] They also suggested that further research was necessary before China would take any action.

The most proactive of the Chinese expert community emerged among those who focused on specific aspects of the impact that climate change might have on society and the environment and those who had more contact with Western experts. One prominent oceanographer argued that sea-level rise due to global warming had the potential to wreak havoc on China's coastal areas, leading to stormtide catastrophic events, sea water invasion landward, soil salinization in coastal lowlands and plains, and beach erosion retreat. This specialist advocated radically redirecting China's energy development strategy away from fossil fuels to renewable resources such as wind, ocean, solar, and hydropower.[9]

Another researcher interested in agricultural production argued that the results of even historical modeling suggested an overall drop in total agricultural productivity in China by 5 per cent due to climatic change.[10] Geographers involved in natural disaster research also argued that climate change would "enhance sharply the amplitudes of climate change," thereby engendering a substantial increase in natural disasters such as floods and droughts.[11]

From the range of the scientific ideas and research reflected by this interaction, the NEPA and the SMA each submitted a formal report to a core Chinese decision-making committee for climate change. The emphasis and concerns of each of these reports, however, varied.

The NEPA report directly credited international research and comments by foreign officials at international conferences concerning China and climate change for their assistance in helping Chinese policy-makers to understand the impact of increased CO_2 emissions on sea-level rise and temperature in China.[12] The report stated that global warming would affect every aspect of society – agriculture, forestry, animal husbandry, marine life, and industry. It acknowledged that the effects of climate change would be complicated: a winter warming, for instance, could produce a bountiful wheat harvest and energy savings. At the same time, however, NEPA reiterated its estimate that overall agricultural productivity would suffer a 5 per cent loss and stated that climate change might also lead to an increase in the frequency of forest fires, soil erosion, and pestilence, thus affecting people's health.

The SMA report was slightly less proactive than the NEPA report. It supported the existence of a relationship between CO_2 and an overall warming of the global climate. However, the SMA researchers argued that a natural cooling might take place and that, given regional discrepancies, it was difficult to discern trends. Furthermore, they stated that it was "difficult to deny that the atmosphere and land temperature wouldn't decrease."[13]

In the final analysis, however, the importance of the science was severely constrained during the actual formulation of the Chinese negotiating position. While the Chinese environmental community tried to present the full range of scientific issues and concerns to the Chinese leadership, the importance of economic development and the weakness of the environmental bureaucracy hampered the success of the more proactive elements of the Chinese expert and official community in transmitting their message.

Moreover, as one science official commented, "The policy-making on climate change depends on social issues not science."[14] Thus, economic modernization (which in China necessarily implies a growing demand for energy to fuel the economic growth) and the debate over who within the international community was "responsible" for global climate change (and what role China should play in international efforts to respond) became far more important in internal policy discussion than the scientific debate.

The energy debate

The second debate that arose surrounding the issue of climate change concerned the accessibility and low cost of energy that were critical components of China's phenomenal economic development throughout the 1980s and early 1990s. Economic reforms that loosened control over coal resources and pricing had fueled spectacular regional and local industrial growth. At the same time, this process of decentralization made environmental monitoring and control far more difficult, led to serious increases in the rates of many air and water pollutants, and was responsible for China's standing as the third largest producer of CO_2 emissions. Thus, in order to respond to climate change in a meaningful manner, China had to shift away from its overwhelming reliance on coal and slow the pace of its economic growth.

The advent of discussions on climate change in the international arena both heightened the salience of an ongoing debate that had been brewing in the People's Republic of China concerning the development of alternative fuel resources and brought increased attention to the importance of improving energy efficiency. The linkage of China's coal use to its climate change policy involved four ministries: the State Planning Commission, the Ministry of Energy, the National Environmental Protection Agency, and the Ministry of Agriculture, all of which attempted to exploit the issue of climate change to advance their interests in energy policy.

The Ministry of Energy and the State Planning Commission were in large part allied in their opposition to a significant restructuring of the energy sector and to any wide-scale introduction of costly new efficiency technologies to limit the level of CO_2 emissions. Much of this stemmed from these officials' belief that continued rapid economic growth was imperative. As Minister of Energy Huang Yicheng argued in a discussion of future near-term energy development, "China wants to double its GNP by the year 2000. It therefore will have to be producing 1.4 billion tons of coal and 200 million tons of petroleum."[15]

In contrast, the director of the National Environmental Protection Agency, Qu Geping, was outspoken in his concern over the reliance of China on fossil fuels. He strongly advocated the development of clean energy such as solar, nuclear, and wind as a means of countering the greenhouse effect.[16] In fact, Qu Geping was so interested in the greenhouse problem that even some high-ranking NEPA officials questioned his attention to the issue given the vast problems involved in China's domestic environmental situation.[17]

Most energy experts also supported the rapid development of energy efficient technologies and a gradual shift away from a coal-based economy, primarily for reasons of long-term economic development; few supported the view that such technologies should be pursued solely for the benefit of the environment. A minority of policy analysts took a stronger tack in advancing environmental claims on energy development. They argued that as the primary consumer of coal and one of the world's major sources of CO_2 pollution, China should coordinate worldwide efforts to decrease the greenhouse effect.[18]

The fundamental question with which these officials grappled was how rapid the pace of economic development should be. They agreed that China could not support the establishment of targets for limiting CO_2 emissions. At the same time, they agreed that there were many serious problems with China's almost total reliance on coal for energy. Chinese energy planners faced a range of challenges: dwindling coal supplies, serious pollution, an overburdened transport system, and an inappropriate pricing system. In 1991, Chinese energy experts estimated that public coalmines were costing the Chinese economy well over $1 billion.[19]

The interaction between the international and Chinese energy specialist communities did have an impact on the thinking of many Chinese energy researchers. An SSTC official, for example, stated that his contacts with American experts made him aware of the possibility of advancing economic growth while simultaneously protecting the environment.[20]

However, the influence of new ideas and methodologies in the policy-making process frequently was limited by organizational constraints. According to one prominent energy specialist, Chinese officials – even those within the energy bureaucracy – typically could not understand the computer models generated to explain Chinese projections of energy usage and pricing, ignored complex reports detailing energy efficiency options, and relied on their traditional methodologies concerning the makeup of China's energy structure which avoided serious consideration of alternative energy sources.

In addition, transmission of ideas from the middle to the top levels of the Chinese government was further constrained by the overall context in which the decision-making process on climate change took place. Leadership legitimacy was premised to a significant extent on successful economic development and on an ability to advance the living standards of the populace. The support of Deng Xiaoping and Li Peng for economic development and their relative lack of attention to environmental issues were critical to the limited nature of the responses eventually adopted by the Chinese. As one official involved in the climate change policy-making process commented, "Since Deng says economic growth must increase, CO_2 will also increase."[21] Deng Xiaoping's proclamations during the 1990–1992 period articulated the necessity of increasing the rate of economic growth but made no mention of environmental protection. These statements were considered inviolable by Chinese specialists and officials.

Chinese participation in the specialized energy group during the IPCC discussions reflected this lack of information transmission and the conservative approach of the Chinese leadership. According to a US participant, the Chinese were determined to avoid any requirements that would limit their use of coal. Even though the Chinese delegate served as co-chair of the group, he participated only minimally in the group's discussions. In addition, he was either unwilling or unable to gather information on China's energy resources and CO_2 emissions for the working group. Instead, US energy specialists from the Battelle Institute, in cooperation with some proactive energy researchers from the SPC's Energy Research Institute, produced the necessary data and brought it to the attention of the UN sub-group.[22]

The domestic debates and discussions over the science of climate change and China's energy development clearly reflected both the influence and limits of the international community on China's decision-making. While foreign experts enhanced the capacity of Chinese actors to explore new ideas and utilize new technologies concerning these issues, bureaucratic and institutional constraints often prevented the effective transmission of these ideas to the key decision-makers. Perhaps more importantly, as the Chinese began to formulate their stance for the international political negotiations, it became evident immediately that the science of climate change would be in large part incidental to the political and economic policy-making. Actors in the planning and foreign ministry bureaucracies remained unresponsive to the scientific claims and policy initiatives put foward by the environmental and scientific agencies, except when they coincided with the former's pre-established interests. One SPC official doubted the validity of NEPA's report, stating, "It is in NEPA's interest to produce such a report."[23]

The political debate

In early 1990, as the focus of the international climate change discussions progressed from scientific debate to formal political negotiations, the Chinese State Environmental Protection Commission established the National Climate Change Coordinating Group. This group consisted of the four agencies involved in the initial climate change leading group – SSTC, NEPA, MOFA, and SMA – as well as the Ministry of Energy and the State Planning Commission.

The actual distribution of decision-making power among these agencies, how this power evolved, and the influence of this evolution on the policies adopted reflected the eventual ascension of officials in the planning and foreign affairs bureaucracies to pre-eminent policy-making positions. While NEPA and the SMA were influential during the scientific aspect of the policy-making process, they became marginal players during the political discussions. The SSTC retained nominal supervision over various aspects of the decision making process; however, the traditionally more powerful institutions such as the Ministry of Foreign Affairs and State Planning Commission assumed real control.

In Spring 1990, prior to the Second World Climate Conference in Geneva, the Chinese began to hammer out in domestic forums their negotiating position in the international arena on climate change. The SSTC, SPC, MOFA, and NEPA convened a meeting with representatives from the Ministry of Energy, the Ministry of Forestry, and the Ministry of Agriculture.

Most officials, even those in the Ministry of Foreign Affairs, who most closely guarded China's sovereignty, believed that China ought to make a contribution to the international effort to respond to climate change in large part because it was a member of the international community, but primarily because it would be affected by climate change agriculturally. Importantly, however, this view also included an argument that any action taken to respond to the threat of global warming should not restrict China's economic development. Furthermore, the reality of the future world energy situation had to include a big increase in China's energy use. Advocates of this perspective called for a new international economic order which would "eliminate those factors not favorable to developing China's economy." They argued that the industrialized countries owed a debt to the developing states for destroying the environment.[24]

The SSTC and NEPA voiced a perspective that emphasized a stronger Chinese commitment to the international community to participate in a climate change accord. They evidenced a sentiment that China belonged to the international community and had a responsibility to participate in a positive fashion because China is an important player. At the same time, these agencies were well aware of the potential benefits that China would receive from such participation: an improved image for the People's Republic of China in the international arena; access to technology and management techniques; and stronger environmental management practices. In this vein, one environmental lawyer stated, "Good intentions in environmental protection will gain us backing internationally and promote international understanding."[25] In a speech to the directors of environmental protection departments, Song Jian, head of the SSTC, stated: "The rapid development of the situation in international environmental protection demands that we do a good job in domestic environmental protection. In particular, we must make considerable progress in promoting the consciousness of all the people with regard to environmental protection, improving the structure of energy resources, and participating in legislation on international environmental protection."[26]

Some social scientists articulated more radical approaches in academic and research journals. These more proactive specialists assumed responsibility on the part of both the industrialized and developing states for the current state of environmental degradation. They advocated a new developmental path for China which included education, moderating consumption, readjusting the basic energy structure, and turning away from the path of high consumption of resources and high living expenses.

At the Spring 1990 meeting, the range of views expressed was distilled to a set of principles that represented the more conservative perspective advocated by the SPC and MOFA. These principles included:

1. Environment and development should be integrated but environmental protection should not be achieved at the expense of the economy. Environmental protection can only be successful when development has been attained.
2. From a historical perspective, the developed countries are responsible for global environmental degradation and the current problems with greenhouse gas emissions. We [China] should not talk about responsibility.
3. Developed countries should provide resources for implementation of agreements or declarations signed. This financial resource should not be considered as assistance, but as the responsibility of the developed states. China believes that this assistance should be viewed as compensation.
4. The developed countries should find suitable mechanisms to develop sustainable programs. In order to accommodate national intellectual property rights, the governments of the developed countries should buy the technology from companies and sell it to developing states at less than international market prices.
5. The sovereignty of natural resource rights must be respected. No country can interfere with the decisions of another with regard to the use of its natural resources.[27]

These principles formed the basis for China's stance throughout the international negotiations. In order to attain the objectives set out in these principles, the Chinese initiated a diplomatic offensive on two fronts. The diplomatic officials worked to restrict any official obligation on the part of China, while the scientific and environmental officials continued to pursue assistance from the international community.

The international political negotiations

In January 1991, the Chinese initiated a well-orchestrated effort internationally to establish the People's Republic of China as the pre-eminent voice for the developing world. This was a position it had not sought actively in almost two decades. Li Xue, deputy director of the Environmental Protection Commission, set out publicly the Chinese position as an appropriate model for other developing countries. He further described UNCED as "an important occasion leading to changes in the present state of international relations and one which would revitalize the North–South dialogue."[28]

In order to accomplish this, the Chinese convened their own international conference in 1991 (14–19 June), immediately preceding the second session of the International Negotiating Committee in Geneva. Forty-one countries gathered at the "Conference of Developing Countries on Environment and Development" in Beijing to discuss global environmental and development issues.

The purpose of the Beijing Conference was to develop a united bargaining position in preparation for UNCED one year later. Despite significant opposition from some of the other developing states, the "Beijing Ministerial Declaration on Environment and Development" was signed by all participants. It essentially reiterated and expanded upon the Chinese principles agreed upon a year earlier. The Declaration included calls for the establishment of a "new and equitable international economic order." It also stated that environmental considerations should not be used as an excuse for interference in the internal affairs of the developing countries, nor should they be used to introduce any forms of conditionality in aid or development financing, nor to impose trade barriers affecting the development efforts of the developing countries.[29]

The developing countries assumed virtually no responsibility for environmental degradation or climate change. Their argument went as follows: "Ever since the Industrial Revolution, the developed countries have over-exploited the world's natural resources. In view of their main responsibility for environmental degradation and their great financial and technological capabilities they must take the lead in eliminating the damage to the environment as well as in assisting the developing countries to deal with the problems facing them."[30] In addition, the declaration stated that the developed countries were responsible for past and present excessive emissions of greenhouse gases and therefore would have to be the ones to take immediate action. The developing countries could not be expected to accept any obligations in the near future.[31]

The Chinese were genuinely concerned about maintaining their sovereignty, which included their right to development. These concerns encompassed not only environmental resource questions but also issues such as human rights and trade sanctions. The conference also brought widespread support for the Chinese position and increased China's bargaining position in discussions with the West, helping to ensure that China, as the developing country with the highest level of CO_2 emissions, would not be singled out and subjected to potentially intense pressures to take immediate action. This was especially important since developing nations such as Bangladesh were expected to be among the most severely harmed by global warming. Finally, funds for climate change assistance from the advanced industrialized states to the developing world were limited; the hard line placed China in the spotlight and probably in a strong position in the competition for international aid.

Although the Chinese representatives presented a unified face at the Beijing Ministerial Conference, according to one observer, there were important differences among the views advocated within the delegation and among the approaches which they proposed at the Conference. The MOFA was far more interested in including language specifically critical of the United States. Because of the interpersonal ties that developed between the SMA, NEPA and the Ministry of Energy and the United States scientific and environmental communities, however, these organizations resisted pointed criticism of the United States. In the end, such criticism was omitted from the declaration.

During the course of the negotiations, China also formed a strong alliance with India; this partnership then became a mainstay of the Chinese negotiating strategy. It was akin to the Sino-Indian alliance that was established during the negotiations on ozone depletion. These two states were widely regarded as the most uncompromising participants, although the Chinese were viewed as more willing to sacrifice their stated principles for financial and technical assistance than the Indians. In the words of one US observer, "the Chinese were willing to cut a deal."[32]

China also suggested that "an appropriate level of economic development" should be the prerequisite for adopting concrete control measures to address climate change.[33] China and India together supported the necessity of a new funding mechanism to help developing countries address climate change. The Chinese also opposed any commitment by all signatories to undertake measures to address climate change "without undue delay." According to some NGO observers, the Chinese were difficult to get along with and had a "bad attitude."

By the advent of the fifth and final session of the INC, China was in the midst of preparing its country report for UNCED. Nominally the responsibility of the SSTC, ultimate control of the report was ceded by the SSTC to the SPC, when SPC officials expressed their interest in directing the project. The resulting document, according to one ranking SSTC official, was of a quality "no better than a high school textbook."[34] The final report provided a broad overview of the Chinese environmental situation and plans for energy technologies development. The measures set forth, however, were fairly limited and went no further than – and, in a sense not as far as – the joint program undertaken with international organizations and other states.

Once at the final sessions in New York, China reiterated its primary interests: a separate financial assistance mechanism, with technology transfer and aid provided without conditions. The Chinese further called upon the governments of advanced industrialized states to purchase patents from private companies and then make the technologies available on concessional and preferential terms. The Chinese also continued to work with the Indians to weaken the implementation and reporting commitments of the Convention.[35]

At the same time as the formal political negotiations were taking place, the Chinese were pursuing a second diplomatic front, searching for funds and technologies to assist them in their efforts simultaneously to respond to climate change and advance economic modernization.

In October 1990, immediately prior to the Second World Climate Conference, Qu Geping, Song Jian, and Ma Hong, president of the Development Research Center of the State Council, convened a three-day, high profile international conference on the integration of economic development and environment in China. The conference was the third in a series of high-level international programs initiated in May 1988 to bring together Chinese leaders and international experts to discuss issues pertaining to the program's directive "China and the World in the Nineties."

This was the first major international conference that China had hosted which focused on environmental concerns. The participants from the international community included such people as prominent United Nations representatives, business executives from Sumitomo and Shell companies, and foundation heads from the Rockefeller Foundation and WorldWide Fund for Nature. At the conference, the Chinese stated that they had several goals: to increase the understanding of the international community of China's environmental problems; to further the idea that the environment is an area in which the international community would be willing to donate funds; and to advance technology and funds transfer to China from the advanced industrialized states, UN organizations, foundations, and corporations.[36]

Qu Geping used the conference to bring international pressure to bear on less environmentally inclined Chinese officials in MOFA, SPC, and the Ministry of Energy. Qu stressed that China's pollution problems stemmed from China's inappropriate pricing system of natural resources, maintenance of the traditional view that resources are inexhaustible, and poor management techniques at local levels. In contrast, the representatives from the Ministry of Energy and SPC stressed the economic imperatives of advancing development at the expense of the environment and the primary responsibility of the developed world to address pollution issues (a responsibility based on the fact that they had consumed global resources and degraded their environment in their drive to industrialize).[37]

According to Chinese environmental officials, the involvement of the international community was critical to any measure that they could take. They also stated that international conferences and agreements served to embarrass the less environmentally inclined Chinese officials into taking environmentally sound measures and strengthening the standing of NEPA. In addition, these international gatherings allowed the NEPA scientists to examine new technologies and further the development of exchange programs.[38]

In some respects, it was the support from the World Bank, the UNDP, the Global Environmental Facility, and the Asian Development Bank that provided the key to even the limited success of the proactive forces in advancing the energy efficiency and technology measures necessary for China to begin to reduce the rate of increase of its CO_2 emissions. The projects funded by these organizations included a large number of research and development efforts. By 1990, the Asian Development Bank had loaned almost \$500 million for China's environmental programs and was planning to have lent an equal amount by 1995. This funding was important both for the opportunity to push the limits of the response measures that China was willing to take to address climate change and for the potential to empower certain agencies (such as the

NEPA) and strengthen inter-agency coordination through international supervision.

At international forums outside of China, however, even the scientific and environmental ministries presented the more conservative stance favored by the planning and foreign ministry bureaucracies on the issue of China's responsibility to respond to global climate change. At the Second World Climate Conference, Zou Jingmen, head of the SMA, and Song Jian articulated more forcefully the responsibility of the developed world. They claimed that the industrialized countries bore a "special responsibility" for the problems of global warming. The developing countries, conversely, were faced with the need to eliminate poverty as well as to develop their economies and improve people's livelihoods. Within this agenda, according to Zou Jingmen, the developing countries needed to place the emphasis on economic development and eliminating poverty. Toward this end, they called upon the developed countries to "provide the necessary funds to help developing countries avoid following the disastrous road taken by the developed countries and transfer to them, under non-commercial preferential conditions, modern technology."[39]

Moreover, the impact of foreign ideas and technologies to some extent was limited even within the official scientific community by a strong desire on the part of the Chinese participants not to denigrate traditional Chinese scientific methodologies. This was especially evident in the continued reliance of many scientists on paleoclimatology and historical analogues for estimating greenhouse gases. There also was a belief expressed by several Chinese scientists that foreign interests in limiting CO_2 were useful in so far as they served concerns about energy efficiency and conservation and technology but that global climate change was an issue to be addressed by advanced industrialized countries. As one Chinese scientist stated, "If the United States wants data for climate change research, it will have to pay for it."[40] In this sense, some members of the scientific community viewed global climate change as an issue with bargaining power in much the same manner as the policy-making community.

Conclusion

The response measures adopted by the Chinese to address climate change resulted from a process of domestic political negotiations which permitted wide-ranging debate but eventually succumbed to traditional interests of development at the expense of the environment. In large part, this was due perhaps to the exclusive focus on development by the top Chinese leadership and lack of interest in environmental affairs. Nonetheless, domestic energy and environmental interests were successful in linking their agendas to that of international organizations and foreign policy-makers. While these linkages were not powerful enough to influence the negotiating position of the Chinese, they did, in fact, advance significantly the range of technical measures and strategies adopted to limit CO_2 emissions within the very conservative stance adopted by the Chinese government.

The impact of the epistemic community on global climate change on Chinese thinking and policies was substantial. China had only a very small scientific community specializing in climate-related issues and these researchers actively sought out access to the cutting-edge technologies such as advanced computer Global Circulation Models and monitoring techniques and equipment. New scientific and technical information often led to a new understanding of the possibilities of addressing climate change. Environmental scientists and energy experts also viewed climate change as an opportunity to advance their own domestic agendas by linking it to concerns in the international arena. Thus, energy researchers, presented with opportunities by experts from the West for new technological understanding of how the People's Republic of China could improve energy efficiency or reorient its energy structure and thereby contribute to limiting global CO_2 emissions, were quick to absorb the new knowledge and incorporate it into their understanding of how China could respond to climate change. This new understanding allowed these experts to link their domestic agenda with an international agenda, although it did not commit them to an overall proactive stance on China's response to global climate change.

At the same time, despite scientific evidence that climate change would have an overall negative effect on the Chinese economy, especially in agriculture, the science of climate change was largely incidental to the political and economic decision-making. The negotiation strategies were rooted in traditional Chinese foreign policy concerns of sovereignty and First World–Third World development issues. This was due in part to the relatively high degree of scientific uncertainty, but primarily to bureaucratic politics. The relative weakness of the environmental and scientific bureaucracies and the historical control of the Ministry of Foreign Affairs over international negotiations were responsible to a significant degree for the Chinese negotiating position. The international community played no real role in the domestic decision-making process.

Once at the international negotiations, Chinese interaction with the international community was critical in two respects. First, the People's Republic of China used its position as a relatively wealthy and powerful developing state to mobilize other developing countries to support its position. The developing states' formal commitment to China's stance ensured that there would be no defections by other players which would permit alliances with the more proactive Western European countries and which would bring pressure to bear on the People's Republic of China. In addition, by asserting a leadership position, the People's Republic of China drew attention to itself and assumed a front-rank position among the developing states in accessing assistance from multilateral organizations and other countries. Second, the lack of leadership by Japan and the United States – China's two most important trading partners – on the issue of global climate change meant that virtually no pressure was exercised in an attempt to persuade China to take a more proactive stance.

Thus, the Chinese leadership pursued a strategy which, in its assessment, maximized China's potential to continue its rate of rapid economic growth while assuming a high moral ground. It rejected the consensus of its own scientific community that climate change would have detrimental effects on China's economic potential in the long run and established a broad-based international alliance orchestrated by the foreign affairs bureaucracy that rooted its position in traditional claims of sovereignty and Third World–First World inequity that rejected any commitments to reduce CO_2 emissions. At the same time, China was able to take advantage of the international community's interest in reducing China's greenhouse gas emissions by permitting, and in some cases encouraging, the scientific and technical bureaucracies to expand their contacts with Western specialists and access new sources of technology, knowledge, and funds that would contribute further to China's development.

Notes

1. William U. Chandler, Alexei A. Makarov and Zhou Dadi, "Energy for Soviet Union, Eastern Europe and China," *Scientific American* (September 1990), p. 125.
2. Geping Qu, "A Synopsis on the Course of Development on China's

Environmental Protection, " in Geping Qu, *Environmental Management in China* (Beijing: China Environmental Press, 1991), pp. 213–220.

3. Ibid.

4. PRC National Environmental Protection Agency official, in an interview with author (New York, March 1992).

5. People's Republic of China State Planning Commission Institute for Energy Research official, interview with author (Beijing, June 1992).

6. State Science and Technology Commission official, interview with author (Beijing, May 1992).

7. Guangzhao Zhou, "Global Change Research in China and International Cooperation," unpublished manuscript, provided to author by East–West Center researcher (Honolulu, March 1992, on file with author).

8. Futang Wang, Shili Wang, Yuxiang Li, and Meina Zhong, "Modelling Experiment of Effects of Climate Changes on the Food Production in the Major Agricultural Areas of East Part of China," (1991) unpublished manuscript, on file with author.

9. Zhanxie Liu, "Modern Sea Level Changes of the Eastern China Seas and Their Influences on Coastal Areas," unpublished manuscript, on file with author.

10. Tao Zhan, "Effect of Global Climate Change on Agricultural Systems of China," presented at symposium "Climate Biosphere Interactions: Biogenic Emissions and Environmental Effects of Climate Change," Beijing, July 1991.

11. Lansheng Zhang and Peijun Shi, "Research into Global Change and Its Impact Assessment," unpublished manuscript, on file with author.

12. PRC National Environmental Protection Agency, "An Assessment of the Impact of Climate Change caused by Human Activities on China's Environment," unpublished manuscript, on file with author.

13. National Climate Change Coordinating Small Group SMA Report, 3rd Conference document, "Since 1980, China's Climate Change Basic Characteristics," unpublished manuscript, on file with author.

14. State Planning Commission Institute for Energy Research official, interview with author (Beijing, May 1992).

15. Tianshen Wen, "China's Energy Resources: Present and Future," *China Today* (February 1990).

16. Foreign Broadcast Information System," *China Daily Report* (10 May 1989), pp. 1–2.

17. PRC National Environmental Protection Agency official, interview with author (Beijing, June 1992).

18. PRC State Science and Technology Commission official, interview with author (Beijing, May 1992).

19. PRC State Planning Commission official, interview with author (Beijing, June 1992).

20. Ibid.

21. PRC State Planning Commission Institute for Energy Research official, interview with author (Beijing, May 1992).

22. United States IPCC delegate, interview with author (Washington, DC, September 1993).
23. PRC State Planning Commission official, interview with author (Beijing, June 1992).
24. "Zhongguo Duiyu Quan Qihou Bianhua de Lichang yu Duice" (China's Position and Countermeasures Toward Global Climate Change), *Zhongguo Huanjing Kexue* 11:6 (December 1991), 457–459.
25. "Taolun Wo Guo de Huanjing Waijiao Zhengce" (A Discussion of China's Foreign Environmental Policy), *Zhongguo Huanjing Guanli* 1(1992), 7–9.
26. Foreign Broadcast Information Service, *China Daily Report* (27 December 1990), p. 31.
27. PRC State Science and Technology Commission official, interview with author (Beijing, PRC, May 1992).
28. Foreign Broadcast Information Service, *China Daily Report* (16 January 1991), p. 41.
29. "Beijing Ministerial Declaration on Environment and Development" (Beijing: SSTC, 1991), pp. 1–3.
30. Ibid., p. 3.
31. Ibid., p. 4.
32. United States Environmental Protection Agency delegate to the INC Sessions, interview with author (Washington, DC, September 1993).
33. Ibid.
34. PRC State Science and Technology Commission official, interview with author (Beijing, June 1991).
35. *ECO* 8 (8 May 1992), p. 2.
36. Martin Lees, "China and the World in the Nineties," Conference Summary Report, Beijing, 25 January 1991, pp. 30–31.
37. Ibid., pp. 9–13.
38. Chinese Academy of Sciences retired official, interview with author (Beijing, June 1992).
39. Foreign Broadcast Information Service, *China Daily Report* (2 November 1990), p. 1.
40. Chinese Academy of Sciences retired official, interview with author (Beijing, June 1992).

3 The domestic politics of global biodiversity protection in the United Kingdom and the United States

Kal Raustiala

Q: Unidentified reporter at UNCED:
"I just wanted to ask about ... the real attitude of the US government towards this summit. Down here your delegation has been very constructive ... But meanwhile, in Washington, senior Administration officials are talking with reporters not for attribution and are calling the proceedings here a circus ... Which of the two approaches does represent the real US position toward this conference?"

A: Michael Young, Deputy Undersecretary for Economic Affairs, US Department of State:
"Circus is not pejorative. I mean, we mean it in the kindest possible way ..."[1]

Introduction

One of two major treaties to result from the United Nations Conference on Environment and Development (UNCED) process, the Convention on Biological Diversity (CBD) addresses one of the most important global environmental problems of our time: the alarming increase in the rate of species extinction and ecosystem destruction.[2] In the words of the eminent biologist E. O. Wilson:

> the one process ongoing in the 1990s that will take millions of years to correct is the loss of genetic and species diversity by the destruction of natural habitats. This is the folly our descendants are least likely to forgive us.[3]

Despite active participation throughout the negotiations, the United States was alone among the advanced industrial states in deciding not to sign the CBD. In taking this (in)action the US government incurred considerable adverse publicity and pressure from traditional allies and enemies alike. The United Kingdom, despite some reservations, signed and has ratified the CBD. This chapter examines the policies of the United States and the United Kingdom – nations similar in many important respects – toward the proposed multilateral biodiversity regime, and seeks to show how domestic politics interacted with international concerns and events to produce this divergence in policy response.[4]

Biological diversity (or biodiversity) typically refers to "the variability among living organisms."[5] The recognition during the 1970s and 1980s that development and deforestation were rapidly destroying the earth's genetic diversity stock led to pressure for a global biodiversity convention.[6] The United States was an early and strong proponent of the proposed new regime.[7] The conservation goals of the treaty include the identification and monitoring of biological resources and the promotion of both on-site (*in-situ*)and off-site (*ex-situ*) conservation. But while the conservation commitments that are the centerpiece of the treaty were relatively conflict-free, seemingly ancillary issues of intellectual property rights (hereafter IPR), financial transfers, technology transfers, and biosafety regulation consumed much of the bargaining process. These were (and remain) complex and contested issues and compounded the work of the negotiators immensely. The result was an incomplete and often ambiguous treaty, which dealt with a host of heterogeneous issues in a manner unsatisfactory to many participants and observers. In the view of one participant:

> It is regrettable that a legal instrument as ambitious as the biodiversity Convention should suffer from basic conceptual and drafting deficiencies. The structure of the negotiations, the haphazard way in which crucial issues were considered, and the pressures of time contributed to a legal instrument whose text should cause the utmost distress for international lawyers and policy-makers.[8]

Despite a change of administration, active private-sector involvement, and continuing diplomatic pressure, it took over a year for the United States to reverse its decision and sign the Convention, and at the time of writing the convention has still not been ratified. The United Kingdom, by contrast, ratified the treaty quickly – less than one year after the UNCED Conference in Rio.

The problem of biological diversity loss

In the decades preceding the start of the CBD negotiations, numerous regional and international conservation treaties had been signed, but no comprehensive treaty regime existed that consolidated the protection of all of the increasingly fragile ecosystems and threatened species populations.[9] Although the reasons for the recent intensified attacks on ecosystems are complex, the conversion of large swathes of tropical rainforest to agriculture and livestock pasture, as well as the worldwide boom in coastal development, are major factors.[10] Tropical rainforest and coral reefs – both areas of extreme diversity – were being destroyed at unprecedentedly high rates, and many species were daily becoming extinct that had never been analyzed by modern biologists. New satellite data graphically documented the extent of the habitat conversion underway. As a result, biodiversity loss came to be viewed as a major and irreversible ecological catastrophe in the making.[11] Nonetheless, little was known about the extent or true severity of the problem. As E. O. Wilson notes, we do not even know the order of magnitude of the number of species in existence, nor how or how quickly they are disappearing.[12]

Why does biodiversity matter? Many ecosystems are delicately balanced, and the loss of certain species can result in unanticipated effects for other species and ecosystems. Moreover, as agricultural strains become more specialized, there is a continuing need for diverse genetic stock suitable for cross-breeding. When California's $160 million barley crop was threatened by a virus, the US Department of Agriculture searched through all 6,500 known varieties of barley before it found one (from Ethiopia) capable of conferring resistance.[13] Many undiscovered pharmaceuticals and chemicals are likewise hidden in tropical forests.[14] Thus, there are clear economic incentives for the preservation of biodiversity, both in terms of direct usage and in "option value."[15] The preservation of biodiversity also helps maintain the robustness of crucial natural processes. Finally, there are ethical arguments; humankind should minimize its destruction of other species to the best of its abilities.

All of these factors played a role in stimulating the creation of the CBD. A comprehensive treaty regime to protect biodiversity worldwide was seen as the best way to slow biodiversity loss. The ecology community increasingly sought to publicize the issue, and the general outlines of a comprehensive treaty were drafted in non-governmental forums. The desire to create a new global biodiversity regime dovetailed with the ecological approach to conservation and the increasing international focus on global environmental issues in the 1980s.[16] The proposed biodiversity treaty, therefore, came to be seen as a logical part of the UNCED process.

The international response

The first steps toward an international biodiversity treaty were taken by members and associates of the International Union for the Conservation of Nature (IUCN), in conjunction with the WorldWide Fund for Nature (WWF) and the World Resources Institute (WRI). IUCN is a leading environmental organization and an unusual hybrid of non-governmental and governmental organizations. WWF is one of the oldest and largest nature conservation groups in the world, and the WRI is a sort of international environmental "think-tank" with an excellent professional reputation.

Between 1984 and 1989 successive drafts of articles for inclusion in a future biodiversity treaty were developed by a team at IUCN, with an eye toward influencing the shape of a future (and at that time still speculative) convention.[17] In addition, members of WRI, IUCN, and the United Nations Environment Program (UNEP) jointly developed an extensive proposal, published under the title *Global Biodiversity Strategy*, which explored the problem of biodiversity loss and offered detailed policy prescriptions oriented around a proposed multilateral treaty regime. These experts played a major role in the process of creating the CBD. But as I describe below, the issues with which these experts were primarily concerned were not always the central issues around which the negotiations focused. Rather, a penumbra of regulatory and redistributive factors affecting biodiversity (IPR, technology transfer) dominated the talks.

In June 1987 UNEP formed an ad hoc working group to explore "the desirability and possible form of an umbrella convention to rationalize current activities in this field [biodiversity], and to address other areas which might fall under such a convention."[18] Utilizing the IUCN text and additional suggestions from the Food and Agriculture Organization (FAO), the UNEP group composed a first draft of a Convention on Biodiversity. The UN General Assembly ultimately chose to create a new intergovernmental body – the Intergovernmental Negotiating Committee (INC) – to negotiate the proposed treaty, as was also done for the contemporaneous climate change negotiations. The INC met four times during 1991 and 1992. As the negotiations proceeded, the scope of the convention was broadened to include all aspects of biodiversity and its protection – conservation, sustainable use and development, access to genetic resources, technology transfer, IPR, genetically-modified organisms, biosafety, and finances. The talks were difficult, and considerable differences divided North and South. The final negotiating session, just prior to Rio, was inconclusive and acrimonious (one observer termed them "extremely bad tempered") and many delegations, particularly the United States, were unhappy with the final product.[19] In the limited time available, the United States announced its formal intention not to sign the treaty, while the United Kingdom, despite expressing serious concerns about the financial mechanisms, made clear its intention to sign.

Specific issues

In order to understand national behavior and domestic–international interactions during the process of regime formation, it is critical to review some of the details of the CBD. The central conservation commitments include the identification and monitoring of components of biological diversity; the establishment of a system of protected geographical areas; the adoption of measures for both in-situ and ex-situ conservation; the integration of genetic resource conservation considerations into national decision-making; and the adoption of incentives for the conservation of biological resources. The treaty takes, for the first time, a comprehensive rather than a sectoral approach to the conservation of biodiversity, and formally proclaims the intrinsic value of biological diversity. It also includes a number of issues that were the focus of heated negotiations – the worldwide structure of IPR; concerns over genetically modified organisms ("biosafety"); and financial and technology transfers from the developed world to the developing world.

IPR became a central issue in the biodiversity negotiations because genetic resources (often taken from developing nations) form the basis for many pharmaceutical, agricultural, and biotechnological products. These industries depend upon the protection of IPR for their profitability. As a spokesman for the pharmaceutical giant Merck & Co. noted:

> [f]or no industry is intellectual property protection more fundamental to innovative research than the pharmaceutical industry ... [the CBD] leaves key provisions open to alternative interpretations.[20]

Many developing nations, by contrast, have tended to view the entire IPR structure as unjust, and have sought to restrict or undermine IPR.[21] While the CBD negotiations were taking place, negotiations on the Uruguay Round of the General Agreement on Tariffs and Trade (GATT) were drawing to a close. One of the central issues in the GATT round was over Trade-Related Intellectual Property Rights, or TRIPs, and here the confluence of the biodiversity negotiations and the GATT-TRIPs negotiations proved critical. In the eyes of the US negotiating team, the developing nations were attempting to use the terms of the biodiversity convention to "hollow out" IPR concessions in the important TRIPs agreement, thus heightening US opposition.[22] Developed nations also feared that the treaty might make access to genetic resources too costly, inhibiting the growth of the extremely profitable biotechnology, pharmaceutical, and agricultural industries.

The financial aspects of environmental treaties are always contentious, and biodiversity proved no exception. At the heart of the dispute was the issue over who would control the institutional structure in charge of disbursing funds to developing countries to help defray their treaty implementation costs. The developing states sought to place the financial mechanism under the control of the Conference of Parties, and not under the Global Environment Facility of the World Bank, which was dominated by donor states. In the end, the Global Environment Facility was designated the interim financial mechanism *only* if it was fully restructured, including the installation of a "democratic and transparent system of governance."[23] Language was rejected which would have limited developing country treaty compliance to the extent that they received the financial and technological resources needed; instead contributions were to be determined in accordance with the Conference of Parties' decision regarding the amount of resources needed. This issue was very controversial as it appeared to invest the Conference of Parties (which operates on a one-nation one-vote system) with the power to determine the financial contributions of the rich nations. In response, eighteen industrialized country delegations joined in a declaration which vehemently asserted their right to determine the amount of their contributions.[24] The United Kingdom was particularly concerned about the funding issues; although British Secretary for the Environment Michael Howard signed the UNCED treaty, he continued to denounce the proposed funding mechanism.[25]

Technology transfer was likewise a major issue in the biodiversity treaty, as it has been in nearly every environmental treaty where technology is involved. One Western analyst wryly observed that "the treaty might just as appropriately have been designated the 'Convention on Biotechnology Transfer'."[26] The developed countries attempted to insert language into the treaty which would make the access to genetic resources and technology contingent solely on "mutu-

ally agreed terms." The developing nations, however, resisted this ter-
minology, and the use of the term in the final agreement is not consistent.[27] The statements of some less-developed countries, led by India,
that they would interpret the treaty to grant them the right to use compulsory licensing laws, fueled the fears of those in the West who viewed
the convention as unraveling the delicate gains of the TRIPs negotiations.

The issue of "biosafety" and biotechnology regulation contained elements of both IPR and technology transfer. Biosafety refers to concerns
over dangers arising from biotechnology – specifically what the treaty
terms "living modified organisms" (LMOs), more commonly known as
genetically-modified organisms.[28] At the first session of the working
group of legal and technical experts a UNEP report was submitted on
the linkages between biotechnology and biodiversity.[29] This report
stressed that the chief linkages, though still minor, were positive.
Biotechnology and biosafety received little further attention until the
Malaysian delegation called for the inclusion of biotechnology regulation in the biodiversity talks.[30] Fearing that they would be used as
testing and dumping grounds for LMOs, the developing countries
made the biotechnology issue a central focus of the negotiations. While
the final treaty language – due to US pressure – no longer calls for a
biosafety protocol, biosafety is a continuing concern of the less developed countries, and remains a source of North–South tension. At the
meetings of the Conference of Parties in 1994 and 1995 the parties
agreed to continue to explore the need and modalities for a protocol on
biosafety, and it is likely that the first protocol negotiated under the
convention will be not on forest, ocean, or coral reef protection – or
even on the serious problem of natural alien species – but instead on
biosafety.

The US response to global biodiversity loss

The United States was instrumental in getting the negotiations for an
integrated framework convention started, but as the negotiations progressed (and were increasingly consumed by what the US government
considered ancillary issues), the United States began to back away from
its initial support. In the view of many government officials the treaty
was concentrating on economic issues rather than conservation, and
disturbing important areas of international affairs. The tone of the IPR
language, for example, ran counter to US efforts in the GATT.

Technology transfer proposals deeply concerned many businesses which feared that they would be forced to turn over proprietary technology innovations to developing country governments. Finally, the financial mechanism was of concern to all potential donor nations; the prospect of turning over the power to determine their financial contributions to a Conference of Parties dominated by poor countries was not welcomed.

Domestically, the United States was concerned about the treaty's impact on the federal-state structure of land-use. White House sources were quoted as saying that the treaty language "would make our life ten times worse" because it would strengthen the Endangered Species Act (ESA) and ongoing wetlands conservation efforts that the Bush Administration officials sought to weaken.[31] Unlike the United Kingdom, the United States has numerous indigenous peoples of its own with a complex and often ambiguous legal status vis-à-vis the federal government, and therefore it had great concerns about treaty language relating to indigenous peoples' rights.

As in the United Kingdom, in the United States the societal actors most concerned with the CBD were the biotechnology, pharmaceutical, and agricultural industries (though the latter only much later in the process).[32] US environmental NGOs devoted much more of their energy to the simultaneous climate negotiations.[33] Some in the NGO community attributed this asymmetrical focus to the anticipated weakness of the CBD, fostered by State Department officials "badmouthing" the treaty from the onset of the negotiations.[34]

As the negotiations continued, the United States hoped to postpone their conclusion until after UNCED, thus creating more time to work out the extensive problems.[35] Interest at higher levels of government intensified; the Interior Department delegate, previously a Ph.D. with a natural science background, was replaced by a senior political appointee.[36] Two officials of the Council on Competitiveness (a regulatory watchdog office chaired by Vice-President Quayle) argued in an April 1992 memo to William Kristol, Quayle's Chief of Staff, that in their view the economic harm and legal hassles from signing the treaty would substantially outweigh its environmental benefits:

> The draft convention is a major problem for the US ... the Endangered Species Act and the National Environmental Policy Act would need to be greatly expanded ... it could greatly increase litigation ... [and] proposes to regulate biotechnology in a manner totally unacceptable to the US ... The current draft convention is so extensively flawed that it

is highly unlikely that sufficient corrective action could be accomplished at a single negotiating session, and thus, any final convention that might be completed in May would remain seriously flawed.[37]

The Quayle Council had paid close attention to the negotiations, sending faxes almost daily to the delegation.[38] The final treaty text that emerged out of meetings in Nairobi addressed many, but not all, of their concerns.[39]

While President Bush had campaigned as "the environmental president," when challenged by right-wing Republicans critical of his moderate environmentalism in the primary campaign he increasingly focused on the costs of environmental measures. The continuing recession and lack of credit for his environmental efforts (for example, the Clean Air Act of 1990) encouraged Bush to return to core Republican themes – job creation and small government – and to disavow his intention to support stronger environmental regulations.[40] These pressures influenced deliberations on the CBD. In an official statement explaining the US decision to reject the CBD, the State Department cited objections to the language on IPR, biotechnology development, and funding, and emphasized that the US "does not and cannot sign an agreement that is fundamentally flawed merely for the sake of having that agreement."[41] The United States was immediately and widely castigated for this position.

Key US businesses, however, were supportive of the decision to reject the treaty. As a spokeswoman from one biotechnology firm stated, "[we] agree with the treaty's noble goals for protection, but the treaty oversteps its boundaries by beginning to tamper with [IPR] and international trade issues."[42] The Pharmaceutical Manufacturers Association (Pharma), the Association of Biotechnology Companies (ABC) and the Industrial Biotechnology Association (IBA) all sent letters to the White House in the weeks preceding the Rio conference urging the President not to sign the treaty.[43] Richard Godown, president of the IBA, stated that "[w]e stood up and said it was a lousy deal ... it seems to us highway robbery."[44] Gerald Mossinghoff, president of Pharma, wrote to President Bush that the treaty "would undermine the great progress your Administration has made in encouraging other countries ... to strengthen their patent laws."[45] Firms within these industries often rely upon genetic resources as the basic feedstock for production, and therefore are concerned about any potential barriers to supply. IPR is particularly important to these industries; pharmaceutical companies lose an estimated $6 billion annually from the pirating of patented medicinals.[46]

On 3 June, EPA chief William Reilly made a last-minute effort to convince the Bush Administration to reverse its position. In a classified memo that was subsequently leaked, Reilly noted that the United States's formal announcement not to sign was a major topic of concern at the conference, and he proposed modifications to key sections of the treaty.[47] These modifications had reportedly been worked out with the help of the Brazilian government; the leakage of the memo was a major incident at Rio. The changes, however, were deemed "minor" by the Administration and insufficient to justify a change in position.[48] The leaking of Reilly's memo caused a considerable stir among the delegates at UNCED and among the international press, and served to further isolate the United States, vilify Bush, and embarrass Reilly internationally.

In a press conference following the leak, President Bush stated that while the United States had a long history of environmental protection, the CBD was clearly dangerous for American jobs.[49] The United States increasingly appeared to be a lone renegade in the international environmental community, especially since it had also fought hard for the retraction of language in the climate convention that discussed firm targets and timetables for CO_2 emissions reductions. President Bush argued in his Rio speech that "sometimes leadership requires that we stand alone."[50] Meanwhile reports circulated that behind-the-scenes the United States was attempting, to no avail, to gain allies in its decision through diplomatic pressure and the offer of trade concessions. In any event, the US decision created so much publicity about the treaty that other nations clamored to sign on; in a heavily ironic gesture, in late 1992 the head of UNEP allegedly thanked Curtis Bohlen of the State Department for making the treaty such a success.[51] In declining to sign the CBD, the US government stated that:

> It is deeply regrettable to us that – whether because of the haste with which we have completed our work or the result of substantive disagreement – a number of issues of serious concern in the United States have not been adequately addressed ... the text is seriously flawed in a number of respects. As a matter of substance, we find particularly unsatisfactory the text's treatment of [IPR]; finances, including, importantly, the role of the [Global Environment Facility]; technology transfer, and biotechnology. In addition, we are disappointed with the development of issues related to environmental impact assessments, the legal relationship between this Convention and other international agreements, and the scope of obligations with respect to the marine environment ...[52]

With the election of Bill Clinton in November, many in the American environmental community correctly anticipated a switch in US policy toward biodiversity. Nevertheless, this switch did not occur easily. In a private initiative, a working group of NGOs and pharmaceutical and biotechnology firms – including Merck, Genentech, and WRI – was formed shortly after the election, and met for several months to discuss various aspects of the treaty language. This group carefully evaluated the treaty and eventually drew up an interpretive statement supportive of US accession.[53] Its success in convincing several of the major pharmaceutical and biotechnology firms that the treaty was "safe" (or at least not immediately dangerous to their profitability) and that US accession was critical to protecting their interests was an essential element in the Clinton Administration's decision to accede to the treaty. At the same time a rigorous government review of the treaty was taking place. The core finding of the inter-agency review was that the treaty required no new legislation and could be implemented through existing programs and statutory authority.[54]

In June 1993, with much fanfare, the United States announced that it had reconsidered the terms of the treaty and would become a signatory. Several interpretive statements, with stronger domestic than international legal significance, were issued to address US concerns. In the fall of that year, the Clinton Administration presented the treaty to the Senate for ratification; however, at the time of writing some three years later, the treaty had still not been ratified. Opposition continues on several fronts: the most recent round of interest group pressure against the CBD came from the cattle and livestock associations concerned about the land-use implications of the treaty. The outlook for US ratification is not particularly promising at this time.[55]

The British response to global biodiversity loss

The United Kingdom shared the enthusiasm of the United States for the core conservation goals of the proposed regime, and was also an early supporter of a framework convention. Martin Holdgate, the head of IUCN, was a British citizen well-connected with government. Environment was an increasingly hot issue in British politics; Margaret Thatcher had begun to make speeches on the subject, though the British press considered this new-found environmentalism blatantly political: "The Prime Minister's first public statement of any note on the environment in more than nine years in office has launched a movement in the competition among Britain's political parties to woo the green voter," and, some suggested, to head off other rising Tory leaders like Michael Heseltine.[56] In the 1980s the United Kingdom had earned the sobriquet "Dirty Man of Europe" and now it sought to shake it off.

As in the United States, the related issues (for example, IPR and financial transfers) that were raised in the CBD negotiations received less support. With minimal coordination by the European Community (now Union) on the biodiversity negotiations, the United Kingdom was relatively free to formulate an independent negotiating position.[57] Of primary concern to the British government throughout the course of the negotiations were the issues of financial contributions and the structure of the financial mechanism. While this concern with financial issues was shared by the US government, the United Kingdom did not share the United States's high level of concern over technology transfer, IPR, and biotechnology regulation issues.

At the start of the international negotiations, the British government created an advisory group of private-sector actors which met periodically to review the draft texts. This group was similar in composition to that formed privately in the United States in the wake of the Rio conference. The express intent was to bring together the business, scientific, and environmental protection communities in a consultative process; included in this group were representatives of the WorldWide Fund for Nature, Imperial Chemical Industries, the Congress of British Industry, Cambridge Monitoring Centre, and Kew Gardens.[58] In the view of the UK chief negotiator, this advisory process led to greater levels of understanding among both business and environmental groups, and a higher level of domestic consensus on the relative merits of the emerging treaty regime.[59] However, while these meetings allowed certain NGOs some input and information, the overall level of NGO interest remained low.[60]

Within the British pharmaceutical and, especially, biotechnology industries concern over the treaty language was far less vehement than that of their US counterparts. This difference existed despite the fact that the US Office of Technology Assessment reported in 1991 that:

> United Kingdom intellectual property laws are strict, comprehensive, and rigorously enforced. The government's positions in international forums, such as the World Intellectual Property Organization and the [GATT] talks (Uruguay Round) have been virtually identical to US positions.[61]

Moreover, the report stated that in biotechnology "the [United Kingdom] most closely parallels the [United States], with a strong research base, an emphasis on basic research, and a reluctance on the part of government to articulate a clear ... industrial policy." Its pharmaceutical industry is also world class. While the UK's biotechnology sector is smaller and less developed than that of the United States, it nevertheless includes over 300 firms, some of them world leaders in the field; moreover, the UK economy is one-sixth the size of the US economy. Yet the public statements of British firms immediately prior to UNCED reflected their comparatively high level of comfort with the treaty terms. While the head of the American Industrial Biotechnology Association referred to the treaty as "a lousy deal" favoring the "highway robbery" of biotechnology firms, the executive director of the British BioIndustry Association (BIA) stated that "[H]aving reviewed the convention, we do not share the concerns expressed by the US government."[62] Another BIA official struck a moral note: "[w]e think it's quite right morally to let developing countries have the technology ... We don't feel that it's interfering with our profitability, and it's helping people, so what's wrong with it?"[63] The BIA believed that because the text was so ambiguous it posed little threat to industry.[64] The division of the Department of Trade and Industry responsible for the chemical and biotechnology industries also assured British firms of the non-threatening nature of the treaty language.[65]

As the negotiations progressed the British government did become increasingly concerned about the financial language. In the words of one government negotiator, the United Kingdom felt there was "already far too much money in the Montreal multilateral fund," which provided financing to the developing world as part of the stratospheric ozone treaty, which they considered a relatively finite problem in comparison to global biodiversity.[66] They feared that erecting a similar funding structure would rapidly get out of hand. Driven by these concerns, the United Kingdom, more than any other actor, fought for the placement of the financial mechanism within the Global Environment Facility rather than under the control of the Conference of Parties – an effort that was only partially successful.

Despite serious apprehensions, however, the United Kingdom chose to join the new regime. For the UK chief negotiator, the Convention represented a last effort before her retirement; she thus had a personal incentive to shepherd the agreement through the government and to push hard for British signature. In announcing the United Kingdom's intent to sign, Conservative Environment Minister Michael Howard stated that his government would outline its interpretation of the treaty at signature, and made a point of noting that the United Kingdom did not share the United States's apprehension over the IPR language.[67] Rather, he stated, financing was and remained the United Kingdom's uppermost concern.[68] Upon signing and at ratification (June 1994), the United Kingdom included a careful interpretive statement:

> The Government of the [United Kingdom] … declare their understanding that the decisions to be taken by the Conference of the Parties under paragraph 1 of Article 21 concern "the amount of resources needed" by the financial mechanism, and that nothing in the Article 20 or 21 authorizes the Conference of Parties to take decisions concerning the amount, nature, frequency or size of the contributions of the Parties under the Convention.[69]

In the United Kingdom, ratification occurred fairly quickly – less than one year after Rio. Debate was minimal and wholly unlike the process that has taken place in the United States since 1994: senators have raised issues of the treaty's effects on private rights of action, future amendments of environmental legislation, status vis-à-vis American law, binding dispute resolution, future protocols, denial of reservations, and so on.[70] Three main factors encouraged swift British ratification: the restructuring of the Global Environment Facility; agreement among the EU members that they would seek clearer rules about financial procedures; and the repetition of the interpretive declaration quoted above, which was seen as affording a degree of legal protection vis-à-vis the financial mechanism.[71] In the months following UNCED, Michael Howard continued to exert pressure on the US government to sign the treaty, arguing publicly that "it is absolutely pointless having a global convention of this kind unless the United States is a signatory."[72]

UK and US foreign environmental policy and the biodiversity convention

Neither the United States nor the United Kingdom are particularly biodiverse, nor is their respective reliance on biodiversity markedly different (while agriculture is clearly of greater importance to the United States, agricultural interests and issues played a relatively small role in the negotiation of the CBD). The expected "regime effects" are quite similar for both states. Moreover, both are advanced industrial democracies, ruled at the time by anti-regulatory, free-market conservative governments. The scientific communities in both are tightly linked, and they often take similar stances in international environmental negotiations. For all these reasons, their response to the biodiversity problem might reasonably have been expected to be similar. What then explains the divergent policy choices of the United States and the United Kingdom?

Miles Kahler has suggested that there are two main theoretical approaches which address national preferences for international cooperation: knowledge-based and interest-based approaches.[73] A central knowledge-based approach revolves around transnational communities of experts known as "epistemic communities." These communities of like-minded, policy-oriented scientists have been argued to be central actors in several international regimes.[74] This chapter compares this perspective with an approach which is specifically focused on the domestic politics and economics of biodiversity protection. This latter perspective emphasizes the importance of the supporting coalitions of governments, the economic effects of regime rules on key societal actors, and the ways these anticipated effects shape the domestic politics of international cooperation. This chapter argues that what I term "regulatory politics" played the central role in the decision-making processes of both states. While a biodiversity epistemic community existed, and indeed critically shaped the agenda and the initial debate, it had relatively little influence on national positions and decisions.

Epistemic communities and biodiversity

Epistemic community analyses emphasize the important role played by transnational expert coalitions in fostering and shaping state preferences for international cooperation. The environment as an issue-area is considered particularly prone to the influence of epistemic communities, and much of the work in this tradition is oriented around international environmental affairs. While it is argued that epistemic communities help to shape and create state preferences for cooperation through the knowledge they possess, they also exert influence through the institutionalization of community members into government policy-making bureaucracies. Thus their influence is claimed to be both cognitive and bureaucratic.

Uncertainty is argued to correlate positively with epistemic community influence.[75] Biodiversity is a problem exhibiting relatively high levels of uncertainty.[76] The depth and significance of the problem, as well as its dynamics (for example, does all habitat destruction matter equally) are imperfectly understood. Many scientists – primarily ecologists, botanists, and zoologists – were concerned with the rapid rate of habitat destruction and very eager to see a stronger conservation regime in place. Other experts, concerned with forest preservation, recognized that species conservation was a powerful means of inhibiting deforestation. These concerns provided a scientific foundation for the emergence of a new regime for biodiversity protection.

Defining an epistemic community is always a contestable proposition. A community is not generally self-defined, nor is it organized in the sense that its membership can be readily ascertained. But the members of WRI, IUCN, and WWF involved in biodiversity issues, and in particular in the creation of the *Global Biodiversity Strategy* volume, do fulfill standard criteria: a network of professionals with special expertise and policy-relevant knowledge within a given domain.[77] Their entrepreneurial efforts resulted in influential agenda-setting roles, offering interpretations, analyses of the problem, as well as proposing solutions. Without the attention and perseverance of these global biodiversity experts, a comprehensive conservation regime might not have been proposed, or might only have been proposed much later when the problems of species and ecosystem loss were far more intractable.

The members of the epistemic community involved in biodiversity issues were instrumental in encouraging UNEP to create an ad hoc working group on a biodiversity convention, and as noted earlier, an IUCN team produced the draft text which served as the basis of the subsequent treaty negotiations.[78] Some of the principles, obligations, and language they proposed survived in the final treaty text, albeit in various mutations. In this sense, governments – or at least intergovernmental organizations as the agents of governments – turned to the epistemic community to alleviate both causal and policy uncertainty. As epistemic theory predicts, these experts provided national governments with both a causal understanding of the problem and a set of policy prescriptions. However, even though some of their positive and normative interpretations of the biodiversity problem were adopted by government policy-makers, the environmental experts failed to extend their influence very far into the actual national and international decision-making processes. Although conservation issues provided the impetus for the treaty, they did not, despite the efforts of the epistemic community, fundamentally shape the policy responses of either the United States or the United Kingdom. Indeed, as one negotiator stated, for many important issues "much of the IUCN language was discarded as the negotiations got down to business."[79]

When biodiversity experts did offer interpretations and prescriptions about issues "peripheral" to pure conservation, such as IPR protection, this advice was rarely heeded. For example, while many in the NGO and scientific communities supported greater equity in the genetic resource trade, and sought to have indigenous peoples reap greater benefits from the local genetic material they husbanded, their influence in determining governmental positions on these issues was minimal.[80] The expert community was most influential as a catalyst for action, with the shape and scope of that action determined by other factors. The influence of the epistemic community was reasserted, at least in the United States, in the process leading up to the signing of the treaty by the Clinton Administration. With the support of key industry groups, the President could accomplish his environmental objectives without appearing to sign away American interests or jobs in the process.[81]

In sum, in this case the relevant epistemic community was important as a shaper of international agendas rather than of state interests. The environmental community was able to establish both constraints and opportunities: constraints on acceptable and defensible policy positions, and opportunities for those pursuing certain policy options, or solutions, to gain their preferred policy outcomes.[82] The comprehensive approach of the proposed regime allowed many new issues to be addressed. Most importantly, the epistemic community was a critical catalyst for action in prioritizing the issue of biodiversity loss. Without the actions of biologists, ecologists, and environmental lawyers deeply concerned over the exponential growth rate of extinctions, a treaty on biodiversity would have been highly unlikely. This core community was able to draft a proposed treaty and encourage UNEP to push hard for the onset of the negotiations which ultimately resulted in the creation of the CBD.

"Regulatory politics" and biodiversity conservation

While the impetus for a broad-based convention on biodiversity stemmed from the biodiversity epistemic community, the negotiations were not driven by purely conservationist concerns. This section explores the political economy of the CBD, focusing on economic and political variables operating at the domestic level that help to determine state interests toward international environmental policy.

The key elements of the regulatory politics approach are as follows:

1. The *electoral commitments* of governments shape policy responses because they structure the political costs and benefits of undertaking certain policies. Different governments will have different supporting coalitions, and thus will favor different policies.

2. *Societal actors* are often interested in the shape and scope of international environmental treaties – they have "regime interests" – and they lobby governments accordingly.

3. *Domestic political institutions* can shape the demands of these societal actors, while also shaping the direct concerns of governments themselves. Different institutions will promote or inhibit different policy responses.

This analytic approach views international environmental agreements as regulatory arrangements, and suggests that the politics this form of regulation engenders and the institutional setting in which this occurs best explains foreign policy choice.[83]

The electoral commitments of the governments of the United Kingdom and the United States differed in important ways. President Bush stated that he was not "going to go down there [to UNCED] and forget about people that need jobs in the United States of America."[84] In the United Kingdom, while the Conservative party had traditionally been a foe of regulatory initiatives, beginning with Margaret Thatcher's well-noted speeches on environmental themes in 1989 and 1990, they had moved towards a more green image. Additionally, for domestic reasons the Department of Trade and Industry (DTI) had begun to re-orient its policies toward regulation of firms and away from industry sponsorship.[85] As a result, pro-environment policies faced less dissension within bureaucracy and the Cabinet.[86]

Regulatory systems played a crucial role in determining the different preferences of the United States and United Kingdom *and* of US and UK firms – the societal actors most involved in the CBD process. British firms considered the CBD non-threatening. This view was clearly not shared by American firms, who interpreted the same ambiguity as potentially quite dangerous. This variance in industry preferences is an important part of the biodiversity story.[87] As many analysts have extensively documented, the United States and the United Kingdom have very different styles of environmental regulation, and these differences can significantly vary the practical effect of the treaty obligations at the domestic level.[88] Legal and administrative structures and practices may refract international commitments through the "domestication" and implementation processes, thereby altering their practical significance and content – and thus actor preferences towards them.[89] Brickman et al. observe that "[i]n spite of their shared common-law heritage, Britain and the United States seem to hold radically different views about the role of law in implementing public policy."[90] In the United States, environmental regulation has been marked by adversarial, court-like, rule-making proceedings, court challenges, extensive citizen and public-interest group input and litigation, and Congressional technol-ogy-forcing and action-forcing measures.[91] American environmental legislation often contains "private attorneys-general" clauses, by which citizens or citizens' groups can bring suit against violators or even the government itself.[92] Many of these characteristics stem from the separa-tion of powers enshrined in the US Constitution. Congress, the presi-dent, and the courts reflect distinct constituencies and distinct interests, and compete to control regulatory policy. Coupled with a widespread distrust of industry, the result is a combative, open, and litigious regu-latory style.

In Britain, by contrast, regulation is performed with extensive private industry consultation, greater flexibility, a minimum of court-like pro-ceedings, and comparatively little litigation. Individualized imple-mentation is the British way. The British regulatory style flows from a particular philosophy and institutional design: the executive and the legislature are fused in the body of the Cabinet, and courts are relatively weak bodies.[93] Parliamentary oversight is minimal and judicial review of standards "virtually unknown".[94] Moreover the United Kingdom, as a rule, relies on formal environmental regulation much less frequently than the United States and it is much less controversial:

> [T]he most important technique for controlling the private sector is through heavy reliance on official discretion to make individualized orders. Typically, Parliament identifies a problem and enacts a general enabling statute conferring broad discretion on defined officials ... [a] graphic example is the control of air and water pollution.[95]
> In the USA, the substance of regulations and the procedure by which they are made present issues which generate enormous controversy in political, judicial, and academic circles. In Britain, nearly everyone seems satisfied with (and hardly anyone seems interested in) pro-cedural and substantive aspects of delegated legislation [regula-tions].[96]

The structure and process of regulation in their respective countries influenced the expectations – and therefore the demands – of American and British firms. A US industry official observed, "[w]e had to think in terms of a worst case interpretation of the convention." American firms feared that US courts would find something in the treaty text that could, for example, obligate the forced transfer of technology through compulsory licensing.[97] They worried about court challenges and extensive – and expensive – regulatory processes. As one legal expert noted, the CBD's language "was so fuzzy that it [could have] set a precedent for future disputes in US courts."[98] Conversely, the collegial, flexible, and individuated style of British regulation allowed the British firms to be less concerned.[99] Enduring expectations about regulation, resulting from differing historical practice and institutional setting, shaped the responses of the industries to the anticipated treaty-driven regulation. These variations in turn reflected and amplified more fundamental differences in political philosophy and the relationships between courts, legislatures, and executives.

Ultimately, as one US official observed, the American firms demanded a "clear domestic signal" about implementation before they could accept the treaty.[100] That signal was provided by the interpretative statements made by the Clinton Administration upon signing, which reflected industry concerns over IPR, biosafety, and technology transfer. While of limited international legal significance, these statements can constrain how a US court would "interpret the treaty provisions as applied here in the United States."[101] With this assurance in hand, and the realization that they could exercise more influence inside the regime than outside it, key companies gave their blessing to the treaty accession in 1993, propelling the US decision to sign.

What of other interested parties? Other societal actors potentially interested in the convention, such as environmental NGOs, were surprisingly uninvolved at the domestic level in both countries.[102] Within the United Kingdom, select NGOs were involved through the consultative process, but beyond this interaction pressure was minimal. And one analyst of the negotiations noted that, "remarkably, some US delegates remarked to WRI representatives that they had not been lobbied by any ENGOs at any time in the lead-up to, or at the actual negotiations."[103] Thus within both the United States and United Kingdom individual firms and industrial associations were the dominant voices in the policy process.

The preceding has shown how institutional structures – in this case, regulatory institutions which are reflective of more general constitutional structures – shape the interests of interested parties like biotechnology firms. Interest groups are an important part of the story, but

institutions – by aggregating, refracting, and encouraging and dis-
couraging political interests and behavior – also influence state
responses. In a federal system, for example, international commitments
cannot be made which contravene constitutionally mandated powers.
One of the chief fears of the US government – particularly the Interior
Department – was that the terms of the CBD would encroach upon the
complex structure of US federal and state wildlife law.[104] The jurisdic-
tional issues of whether the states or the federal government control
wildlife and natural resources are complex. In the view of the Bush
Administration, the CBD could demand actions which might force the
extension of "the responsibilities of government beyond our current,
extensive federal management of biological resources."[105] The US chief
negotiator repeated this fear during the negotiations, stating that US
domestic law recognizes the right of states to manage their own wildlife
programs, and that the proposed treaty text would be difficult to adapt
to such a federal system of wildlife management.[106] The United States
fought successfully for language changes which mitigated these problems, but Administration critics remained skeptical. For the United
Kingdom, as a unitary state, local autonomy was not a factor in the decision-making calculus, and concerns over constitutional barriers to
implementation did not inhibit the Major Government from signing the
accord.[107]

Differing institutional structures make particular policy options seem
more or less attractive. The possibility of court-mandated compliance –
a common feature of US administrative law – served to accentuate
cautiousness in undertaking ambiguous international commitments.[108]
The power of the courts in the United States dovetailed with political
concerns over the rights of property owners and the economic costs of
environmental regulation to form a potent domestic source of opposition to the CBD. Administration officials were very concerned about the
legal implications of the treaty language vis-à-vis the Endangered
Species Act and wetlands protection.[109] They feared that the treaty, at a
minimum, would inhibit the rollback of the ESA they sought, and could
even encourage further extension of the act. This concern was central to
the Bush Administration's decision not to sign. The interpretive statements made by the Clinton Administration lessened, but did not eliminate, this ambiguity. The Senate Foreign Relations Committee has
continued to express concerns about the treaty's impact on domestic
courts and legislation.[110]

In general, the US delegation sought language which would not require new domestic legislation to implement.[111] This concern reflected the very real constraints posed by the American separation of powers and by divided government, as well as the particularities of federalism and a powerful judiciary – itself a concomitant of the separation of powers. Any implementing legislation would have to pass through both houses of Congress, and perhaps be subjected to amendments and riders of limited interest to the president. Moreover, implementation, whether occurring through new statutes or under existing laws, would take place in a complex and competitive adminstrative system. For the United Kingdom, ratification and implementation was far more straightforward. The nature of the British parliamentary system, with the executive highly dominant vis-à-vis the legislature, meant that a decision to accept the CBD entailed little uncertainty about the process of putting the CBD into practice. Possible reinterpretations and potential obstacles, legal and political, to implementation were unlikely for the United Kingdom but potentially serious for the United States. Coupled with a strongly anti-regulatory administration wedded to limited governmental intervention and land-use reform, the CBD stood little chance of support in the United States. Only a significant change in the White House and in the views of key industry members – and the realization that the CBD could be implemented solely with existing legislation – allowed the United States to move forward. Nonetheless, the United States has still failed to ratify the CBD, though it remains a player in the ongoing activities of the regime.

Conclusion

The problem of biodiversity loss combined scientific uncertainty about key aspects of the problem with a relatively high degree of consensus regarding the need for rapid action. As epistemic community theory would suggest, a tightly-knit group of conservation experts was able to play an important role as a catalyst for the formation of a regime to coordinate international policy on an environmental issue of critical importance. However, the epistemic community was unable to significantly shape the debate around the most contentious issues of the convention. As soon as an administration came to power in the United States that was more amenable to environmental issues the epistemic community was able to reassert its role in the political debate, rallying the political and industrial support necessary for the Clinton Administration to sign the CBD. The epistemic community, therefore, was most influential in the pre-negotiation and post-negotiation phases, rather than during the negotiations themselves.[112]

The actual policy directions taken by the United States and the United Kingdom are best explained through an analysis of the regulatory politics engendered by the regime commitments and their expected implementation. The CBD posed distinctly different political, institutional, and legal ramifications to the United States and the United Kingdom due to divergent domestic structures. The Major and Bush administrations each had to estimate the costs and benefits of accession to the CBD and especially of the implementation of its commitments in light of their differing institutional constraints and political commitments. Implementing the norms and rules of the CBD would entail different sets of actions, stimulate different actors, and involve different institutions in each nation. Of key importance to the decision-making calculus of the two states were their regulatory styles, the strength and scope of judicial influence, and the constitutional structure of their governments. British firms were reasonably confident in their ability to negotiate and resolve in their favor any difficulties that might emerge in the domestic implementation of the treaty. US industry and government, on the other hand, feared the impact of loosely worded commitments. Given the highly technical and complex arena of US environmental regulation and the difficulties inherent in the federal–state separation of powers, worst-case scenarios were credibly advanced by powerful domestic actors: that the treaty would be a threat to US competitiveness, that it would instigate heated internal political battles, and ultimately that an independent judiciary could force actions that were not politically or economically acceptable to these actors.

In short, the domestic politics of international regulation were crucial for the policy responses of two major industrial democracies. Because international regulatory agreements so frequently involve extensive processes of implementation, and invoke many institutions and many actors, domestic political factors loom large in national decision-making. Regime effects are in many ways a product of the marriage of international commitments and national institutions. While I have argued that concerns over implementation were particularly acute for the United States – as a result of its particular constitutional structure – and that a distinctive set of concerns arose, all states are likely to look to the ultimate, domestic impact of a regime in the negotiating process. The regulatory politics approach outlined here focuses on these crucial politics of regime implementation in regulatory settings – arguably a rapidly growing area of international law.[113]

Finally, policy stage emerges as an important factor in the comparative efficacy of the analytic approaches; in the pre-negotiation stage, epistemic communities can and often do play a major role. In the actual regime formation process, however, the regulatory politics approach outlined here appears much more useful. In the post-negotiation stage, epistemic communities can reassert their influence, though this finding may be particular to the case at hand. Policy stage thus operates as a sort of "meta-variable," indicating which set of variables is most likely to be influential. Future analyses of environmental regime formation and national actions within regime negotiations should benefit from close attention to both theoretical perspectives and to their respective "home stages" within the regime formation process.

Notes

1. US Department of State Dispatch, vol. 3 (July 1992), p. 22 ; from a press briefing by the US delegation to UNCED.
2. The other treaty was the Framework Convention on Climate Change, though formally these were negotiated separately from the "UNCED process" but opened for signature at the summit. A proposed convention on forests was downgraded to a resolution of forest "principles." For a recent assessment of the CBD see Kal Raustiala and David Victor, "Biodiversity Since Rio: The Future of the Convention on Biological Diversity," *Environment* (May 1996), 17–45.
3. E. O. Wilson, quoted in WRI, IUCN, UNEP, in consultation with UNESCO and FAO, *Global Biodiversity Strategy: Guidelines for Action to Save, Study, and Use Earth's Biotic Wealth Sustainably and Equitably* (Washington, DC: World Resources Institute, 1992), p. 19.
4. The United States and the United Kingdom make an interesting comparison. Both are advanced industrial states, with a common language, shared political traditions, free-market oriented governments (the Republican–Tory tie is a close one), close-knit scientific communities, strong environmental NGOs, and flourishing biotechnology and pharmaceutical industries. On comparable cases, see Arend Lijphart, "The Comparable-Cases Strategy in Comparative Research," *Comparative Political Studies* (July 1975) and "Comparative Politics and the Comparative Method," *American Political Science Review* (September 1971).
5. CBD, Article 2. Ecologists typically refer to genetic, species, and ecosystem diversity; for overviews see E. O Wilson and Francis Peter (eds.), *Biodiversity* (National Academy Press: 1988); and for a discussion, see WRI et al., *Global Biodiversity Strategy.*
6. Paul and Anne Ehrlich, *Extinction: The Causes and Consequences of the Disappearance of Species* (New York: Random House, 1981); David Tilman et al., "Habitat Destruction and the Extinction Debt," *Nature* 371(1 September 1994), p. 6

7. Gareth Porter, "The United States and the Biodiversity Convention: The Case for Participation," EESI Papers on Environment and Development, no. 1, 1992, p. 2.

8. Melinda Chandler, "The Convention on Biodiversity: Some Issues for the International Lawyer," *Colorado Journal of International Environmental Law and Policy* 4:2 (1993), 174. Ms. Chandler was a member of the US negotiating team.

9. For an overview of these treaties see Simon Lyster, *International Wildlife Law: An Analysis of International Treaties Concerned with the Conservation of Wild Life* (Cambridge: Grotius, 1985). The economic issues are covered in Timothy Swanson, *The International Regulation of Extinction* (Washington Square, NY: New York University Press, 1994).

10. WRI, et al., *Global Biodiversity Strategy*, pp. 12–18, lists six root causes: an unsustainably high rate of population growth and resources consumption, the failure to properly value environmental goods, inequities in ownership and management of benefits from biological resources, deficiencies in knowledge, and institutional systems that promote unsustainable exploitation.

11. See, for example, National Science Board, *Loss of Biological Diversity: A Global Crisis Requiring International Solutions* (NSB: 1989).

12. Ibid. For an argument that we need not worry, see Wilfred Beckerman, *Small is Stupid* (Duckworth, 1994)

13. Albert Gore, *Earth in the Balance* (New York: St. Martin's Press, 1992), pp. 126–140.

14. For a recent estimate of the value of these pharmaceuticals, see R. O. Mendlesohn and M. Balick, "The Value of Undiscovered Pharmaceuticals in Tropical Forests," *Economic Botany* 49:2 (1995), 223–228; also C. M. Peters, A. H. Gentry, and R. O. Mendlesohn, "Valuation of an Amazonian Rainforest," *Nature* 339 (26 June 1989), 655–656.

15. David Pearce, *Economic Values and the Natural World* (Earthscan, 1993), chapter 2 and *passim*.

16. Frank Benjamin Golley, *A History of the Ecosystem Concept in Ecology: More than the Sum of its Parts* (New Haven: Yale University Press, 1993).

17. IUCN, "Legal Measures for Supporting the Conservation of Biological Diversity: A Background Document for IUCN General Assembly Workshop 3," n.d., p. 4.; and Françoise Burhenne-Guilmin and Susan Casey-Lefkowitz, "The Biodiversity Convention," *Yearbook of International Environmental Law* (Norwell, MA: Kluwer Academic Publishers Group, 1992).

18. Françoise Burhenne-Guilmin and Susan Casey-Lefkowitz, "Introduction," in *The Convention on Biological Diversity: An Explanatory Guide*, IUCN Environmental Law Centre/Draft Text, October 1993, p. 2.

19. Tony Brenton, *Greening of Machiavelli* (Earthscan, 1994), p. 203.

20. "Swift Senate Action on Biodiversity Pact Seen as Best Protection for Business," *BNA International Business and Finance Daily*, April 14, 1994.

21. See, for example Vandana Shiva, "Farmer's Rights and Convention on Biological Diversity," in Vincente Sanchez and Calestous Juma (eds.), *Biodiplomacy* (Nairobi: ACTS Press, 1994).
22. Interviews, US Department of State and US Patent and Trade Office (Commerce Department).
23. Biodiversity Convention, Article 39. Global Environment Facility restructuring occurred in 1994.
24. "Declaration made after the Adoption of Agreed Text of the Biodiversity Convention;" UK Government.
25. "Declaration by the United Kingdom of Great Britain and Northern Ireland at the Time of the Signing of the Convention on Biological Diversity," UK Government, 12 June 1992.
26. Dan Burk et al., "Biodiversity and Biotechnology," *Science* 260 (25 June 1993).
27. See IUCN-The World Conservation Union, "The Convention on Biological Diversity: An Explanatory Guide" draft text, October 1993, pp. 76–83 and *passim*.
28. The phrase "living modified organisms" appears to connote a much larger array of organisms than does "genetically modified organisms". Indeed, any organism which has been modified purposefully by man – such as a dog, or a rice strain – could be considered an LMO.
29. UNEP/Bio.Div./SWGB.1/3 (12 October 1990), Val Giddings and Gabrielle Persley, "Biotechnology and Biodiversity."
30. Interview, US delegation. This may have been an attempt to kill the treaty, which made Malaysia nervous due to its large tracts of (diminishing) moist tropical forest.
31. Unnamed White House source, in *BNA Daily Report for Executives* (Regulation, Economics and Law section), 8 June 1992.
32. Later, once the treaty was being considered for ratification, cattlemen, sheep-farmers, and other livestock interests began to view the treaty with some alarm.
33. A WRI researcher described the NGOs as "non-existent" (interview, March 1995).
34. Interviews, NGO members, Washington DC. I have asked this question of many Washington-based NGO members and they often express bewilderment as to why biodiversity got so little attention.
35. Eleanor Savage, leader of the US delegation, stated in May that the "United States has never felt there was a mandate to complete this convention before the Earth Summit." (quoted in "Chief US Negotiator Unsure Whether Bush Will Be Able to Sign Pact in Rio," *BNA International Environment Daily*, 21 May 1992, p. 1; similar points were made in interviews, US State Department and UK delegates).
36. Interview, US Government, April 1995.
37. Members of the Council also sat on the inter-agency group which was handling the treaty internally. The quote is from a memo from David McIntosh

and John Cohressen to Bill Kristol, 14 April 1992 (courtesy of EDF). The convention's possible impact on domestic legislation and in particular the ESA was of great concern to the Interior Department; in the words of one Administration source, "The biggest thing Interior fought about was endangered species. They don't want any reference to genetic diversity ... we are battling to go even as far as US law allows" (interview, courtesy of Gareth Porter).

38. Interview, US government, April 1995.

39. For discussions of some of the internal politics, see Porter, "The US and the Biodiversity Convention"; and Russ Hoyle, "Deep-sixing Biodiversity," *Biotechnology* (August 1992). This was a feat of negotiating for the US.

40. Patrick Buchanan's challenge, while unsuccessful, forced George Bush to move away from the middle ground and towards the Republican core constituency, which did not favor international agreements perceived as disadvantaging American business.

41. UPI, 30 May 1992, BC cycle.

42. Systemix spokeswoman Kathryn Comba, quoted in Lawrence Aragon, "Diversity collides with biotechnology R&D; intellectual property rights stymie United States backing of biological diversity treaty," *The Business Journal –San Jose* 10: 9 (15 June 1992).

43. Richard Stone, "The Biodiversity Treaty: Pandora's Box or Fair Deal?" *Science* 256 (19 June 1992).

44. Quoted in Andy Coghlan, "Biodiversity Convention a 'lousy deal,' says US; agreement signed at Earth Summit protecting wildlife," *New Scientist*, 4 July 1992.

45. Mossinghof was head of the Patent and Trademark Office during the Reagan Administration. Quoted in Burk et al., "Biodiversity and Biotechnology". Compare with Mossinghoff's later letter to Senator Conrad in which he states: "It is essential for the Senate to ratify this treaty ... we declare our support for the Biodiversity Treaty and ask for yours." (Letter to Senator Kent Conrad, from the presidents of the Biotechnology Industry Organization, Pharma, and the American Seed Trade Association, dated 8 August 1994).

46. Porter, "The US and the Biodiversity Convention," p. 10.

47. Blame tended to fall on the Quayle Council. Assistant Secretary of State for Oceans and International Environmental and Scientific Affairs, E. U. Curtis Bohlen, stated that "it is outrageous that a member of the Administration, a member of the Vice President's Council, would leak a classified document. It was a great disservice to President Bush" (in *BNA Daily Report for Executives* [Regulation, Economics, and Law Section], 8 June 1992). Senator Tim Wirth called the move "disgraceful pandering to the right wing" (ibid.).

48. Senior White House official quoted in Keith Schneider, "The Earth Summit: White House Snubs US Envoy's Plea to Sign Rio Treaty," *New York Times*, 5 June 1992, Section A, p. 1. See also Robert Szaro, "Blending Science and Policy: The Convention on Biological Diversity" (manuscript, 1993), p. 8.

49. Ibid.
50. Brenton, *Greening of Machiavelli*, p. 205; Phillip Shabecoff, "Real Rio: Behind the Scenes at the 92 Earth Summit," *Buzzworm* (Sept.–Oct. 1992), 38–39. Shabecoff was the NYT's environment reporter for many years.
51. Interview, US government, May 1995.
52. Declaration of the United States of America.
53. Interviews, US government, February 1995; WRI, March 1995; Energy and Environment Study Institute, March 1995.
54. This was a goal of the US negotiators from the beginning.
55. While the biotechnology and pharmaceutical firms have come to view accession to the treaty as a superior option, Senator Helms has been a consistent foe of the treaty, and has raised many issues concerning it; see "Letter to Majority Leader Mitchell," dated 5 August 1994, signed by many members of the Committee on Foreign Relations (on file with author). For a recent attack that focuses on the biotechnology aspects of the treaty, see Henry Miller, "Is the Biodiversity Treaty a Bureaucratic Time Bomb?" *Hoover Institution Essays in Public Policy* 56 (1995). Miller advocates abandonment of the treaty. The US appears to be behaving in ways similar to the aftermath of the Law of the Sea negotiations, in which it essentially implements the treaty without ratification occurring.
56. Environmental Data Services Report 165, September 1988, p. 5. The memberships of Greenpeace UK and Friends of the Earth UK increased by 600 percent between 1985 and 1989; Brenton, *Greening of Machiavelli*, p. 126.
57. See Nigel Haigh, "The European Community and International Environmental Policy," *International Environmental Affairs* 3:3 (Summer 1991).
58. Interviews, UK government, June and October, 1994.
59. Ibid.
60. Ibid.
61. OTA, 1991, p. 242.
62. Dick Godown, quoted in Andy Coghlan, "Biodiversity Convention a 'lousy deal' says US," *New Scientist*, 4 July 1992, p. 9.
63. Ibid., p. 10.
64. Interview, Executive Director, BIA, May 1994. The major firms did not dispute this; interviews, DTI, June 1994.
65. Interview, Executive Director, BIA.
66. Interview, UK government, June 1994. See also chapter 4 by Joanne Kauffman in this volume.
67. UPI June 9, 1992, BC cycle. Howard stated that these had been dealt with: "[w]hen we first looked at the text, we identified some points of difficulty ... we have now succeeded in finding solutions to these difficulties."
68. Ibid.
69. Declaration of the United Kingdom of Great Britain and Northern Ireland; UNEP "Convention on Biological Diversity," Na.92-8314.
70. Letter to Mitchell and "Memorandum of Record"; cited in fn 55.
71. Interview, UK government. Despite this, Department of Environment

Minister John Gummer has made statements to the effect that the UK would withdraw if the Conference of Parties attempted to dictate financial resource amounts (ibid.).

72. "UK Environment Secretary Encouraging Clinton to Sign Biodiversity Convention," *BNA National Environment Daily*, 4 March 1993.
73. Miles Kahler, *International Institutions and the Political Economy of Integration* (Washington, DC: The Brookings Institution, 1995), pp. 8–11.
74. For relevant literature see chapter 1, fn 8.
75. Peter Haas, "Introduction," in Peter Haas (ed.), "Knowledge, Power, and International Coordination," *International Organization* 46:1 (1992), p. 3.
76. For an overview of the scientific literature on biodiversity and biodiversity loss see E. O. Wilson (ed.), *Biodiversity*.
77. Haas (ed.), "Knowledge, Power, and International Coordination."
78. This text, which actually began the INC process, contained elements of the IUCN draft but was compiled by UNEP; interview, US delegation.
79. Interview, UK government. The IUCN draft text was rejected early on in part because of its forays into financial issues, such as royalties arising from the use of biomaterials; see Szaro, "Blending Science and Policy." Szaro was Alternate Head of Delegation for the United States.
80. The LDCs did tend to like their proposed language, because it benefited them.
81. See Letter to President Clinton, 15 April 1993, from the directors of Merck, Genentech, WWF, WRI, EESI, and Shaman (on file with author). The draft interpretive statement provided along with the letter was used almost verbatim by the US government.
82. On this issue see John Kingdon, *Agendas, Alternatives, and Public Policies* (Boston: Little, Brown, and Co., 1984).
83. The literature on regulation is enormous; for an introduction to the political economy approach see George Stigler (ed.), *Chicago Studies in Political Economy* (Chicago: University of Chicago Press, 1988); Roger Noll (ed.), *Regulatory Policy and the Social Sciences* (Berkeley: University of California Press, 1985); James Q. Wilson (ed.), *The Politics of Regulation* (New York: Basic Books, 1980); and Roger Noll and Bruce Owen, *The Political Economy of Deregulation* (Washington: American Enterprise Institute, 1983). All contain case studies of regulation (and deregulation) examining the role of self-interested actors in the political process.
84. Phillip Shabecoff, "Shades of Green in the Presidential Campaign," *Issues in Science and Technology* 9 (Fall 1992).
85. Wyn Grant, *Business and Politics in Britain*, 2nd edn (Houndmills, Basingstoke: Macmillan, 1993).
86. For a discussion of these issues see Marc Levy, "The Greening of the United Kingdom," paper presented at the 1991 APSA, Washington, DC.
87. Many observers stress the key role played by members of the Quayle Council in whipping up anti-treaty sentiment. While this cannot be proven, it is most likely accurate. Nonetheless, the argument of this

chapter is unaffected – without a set of beliefs about regulation and its consequences such sentiment would not have been credible. The regulatory expectations I discuss shaped firm preferences, and made plausible interventions by Administration officials.

88. David Vogel, *National Styles of Regulation* (Ithaca: Cornell University Press, 1986); Ronald Brickman, et al., *Chemical Regulation and Cancer: A Cross-National Study of Policy and Politics* (Program on Science, Technology, and Policy, Cornell University, 1982); Sheila Jasanoff, "Cultural Aspects of Risk Assessment in Britain and the US," in B.B. Johnston and V.T. Covello (eds.), *The Social Construction of Risk: Essays on Risk Selection and Perception* (Boston: D. Reidel, 1987), p. 359; Michael Asimow, "Delegated Legislation: The United States and the United Kingdom," *Oxford Journal of Legal Studies*, 3: 2 (1983).

89. On the importance of implementation and domestication see Marc Levy, Oran Young, and Michael Zurn, "The Study of International Regimes," IIASA Reprint, RR-96-7 (June 1996); Steinar Andresen, Jon Birger Skjaerseth, Jorgen Wettestad, "Regime State and Society: Analyzing the Implementation of International Environmental Commitments" (IIASA Working Paper WP-95-43); and Kal Raustiala, "The Domestication of International Commitments" (IIASA Working Paper, 95-115).

90. Brickman, et al., p. 63.

91. See especially Martin Shapiro, *Who Guards the Guardians?: Judicial Control of Administration* (Athens: University of Georgia Press, 1988); Richard Stewart, "The Reformation of American Administrative Law," *Harvard Law Review* 88:7 (1975); Keith Werhan, "The NeoClassical Revival in Administrative Law," *Administrative Law Review*, 44:3 (Summer 1992); and Cass Sunstein, *After the Rights Revolution: Reconceiving the Regulatory State* (Cambridge, MA: Harvard University Press, 1990); Shep Melnick, *Regulation and the Courts: The Case of the Clean Air Act* (Washington, DC: The Brookings Institution, 1983); P. S. Atiyah and R. S. Summers, *Form and Substance in Anglo-American Law: A Comparative Study of Legal Reasoning, Legal Theory and Legal Institutions* (Oxford: Clarendon Press, 1987); and Asimow, "Delegated Legislation."

92. On private attorneys-general or citizen-suit provisions in US legislation see Richard Stewart and Cass Sunstein, "Public Programs and Private Rights," *Harvard Law Review* 1982; Cass Sunstein, "What's Standing After Lujan? Of Citizen Suits, 'injuries,' and Article III," *Michigan Law Review* 1992; and Lettie M. Wenner, "Environmental Policy in the Courts," in Norman Vig and Michael Kraft (eds.), *Environmental Policy in the 1990s* (Washington, DC: Congressional Quarterly Press, 1994).

93. R. M. Punnet, *British Government and Politics*, 5th edn (Prospect Heights, IL: Waveland Press, 1988); Simon James, *British Cabinet Government* (London and New York: Routledge, 1992); Gary Cox, *The Efficient Secret* (Cambridge: Cambridge University Press, 1987).

94. Jasanoff, "Cultural Aspects of Risk Assessment," p. 360. There is some evi-

dence, however, that this is beginning to change. For an analysis of recent changes in British administrative law, see Bernard Schwartz, *Lions Over the Throne: The Judicial Revolution in English Administrative Law* (New York: New York University Press, 1987). Much of the "revolution" is in areas tangentially related at best to environmental regulation – in part because regulation is seen as something distinct from law. And in the key area of mandamus the revolution has barely taken hold; Schwartz, pp. 103–104.

95. Asimow, "Delegated Legislation," p. 271.
96. Ibid., p. 253.
97. Porter, "The US and the Biodiversity Convention," p. 10. The concern with the domestic use of the treaty text by courts continues: see "Letter to Majority Leader Mitchell from the Committee on Foreign Relations" (5 August 1994) for an elaboration. The Administration's response is in "Memorandum of Record from Secretaries Christopher, Babbitt, and Espy" to Mitchell (16 August 1994). The letters highlight several core issues: private rights of action created by the Convention, restraints on the amendment of environmental legislation, such as the ESA, future protocols, etc. (on file with author).
98. Stanford Law School professor John Barton, quoted in Stone, "Pandora's Box".
99. Despite perceptions that UK biotechnology firms are more highly regulated already than are American firms, the evidence is mixed. The "regulatory increment" added by the treaty provisions may be greater in the United States than in the United Kingdom if this perception is true. But a recent study by British industry and government officials found no strong evidence for this view; see Department of Trade and Industry Overseas Science and Technology Expert Mission Scheme, "Report of an Ostems Mission to Investigate the Regulation, Patenting, and Public Perception of Biotechnology in the US" (July 1993). This mission was organized by the UK BioIndustry Association and contained members of the House of Lords, BIA officials, and industry representatives.
100. Interview, US government, Feb. 1995.
101. See "Administration gets high marks on interpretation of biodiversity treaty," *Biotechnology Newswatch*, 6 December 1993, p. 4. The interpretive statements were also seen within the US government as a sort of estoppel action; if other parties did not object to the statements when they were made, this fact would be used in future disputes.
102. IUCN and WRI, as professional/scientific organizations, did little direct lobbying. Moreover, IUCN is not a true NGO, having a strong intergovernmental component.
103. Vanessa McMahon, "Environmental Nongovernmental Organizations at Intergovernmental Negotiations," in Susskind, Moomaw, and Najam (eds.), *Papers on International Environmental Negotiation*, vol. 3, The Program on Negotiation at Harvard Law School, 1993.
104. Chandler, "The Convention on Biodiversity"; Porter, "The US and the Biodiversity Convention"; and interviews, US government.

105. Memo quoted in "White House Memo Warns of Problems with Draft Biodiversity Convention," *BNA Environmental Law Update*, 8 May 1992. International conservation treaties have allowed the federal government to usurp certain powers in the past; see *Missouri v. Holland* (1921). The US had language inserted which limited certain obligations "subject to its [a party's] national legislation"; e.g. Article 8-j. These clauses, and the many qualifiers in the treaty, reflected a purposeful attempt to ensure that no new legislation was required to implement the treaty obligations.

106. *BNA International Environment Daily*, 21 May 1992.

107. While there are salient legal divisions within the United Kingdom, it remains a unitary state; Arend Lijphart, *Democracies: Patterns of Majoritarian and Consensus Government in Twenty-one Countries* (New Haven: Yale University Press, 1984).

108. See Sunstein, *After the Rights Revolution*; Shapiro, *Who Guards the Guardian*; Richard Stewart, "The Reformation of American Administrative Law"; and Robert Paarlberg, *Leadership Abroad Begins at Home: US Foreign Economic Policy After the Cold War* (Washington, DC: The Brookings Institution, 1995), pp. 41–45 and 75–82. Paarlberg notes that "the mere possibility of domestic litigation can discourage US entry into international environmental agreements. Not wishing to be taken to court, the US government tends to avoid formal environmental commitments abroad" (p. 76).

109. Interviews, US Government.

110. *Biotechnology Newswatch*, "Administration gets high marks," p. 4; see "Letter to Majority Leader Mitchell" (5 August 1994) and "Memorandum of Record" from Secretaries Christopher, Babbitt, and Espy (16 August 1994).

111. This quest was successful; see Office of the President, "Letter of Transmittal to the Senate" (indicating that the treaty provisions can be implemented under existing statutory law).

112. Janice Gross Stein, *Getting to the Table: The Process of International Prenegotiation* (Baltimore: Johns Hopkins University Press, 1989). This idea is also discussed in the environmental context in Oran Young, *International Governance: Protecting the Environment in a Stateless Society* (Ithaca: Cornell University Press, 1994), pp. 170–172.

113. See, for example, A. Chayes and A. Chayes, *The New Sovereignty* (Cambridge, MA: Harvard University Press, 1995).

4 Domestic and international linkages in global environmental politics: a case-study of the Montreal Protocol[1]

Joanne M. Kauffman

Introduction

Global environmental agreements require reconciliation of an inherent tension between narrow business interests and broad public benefits. This difficult feat was achieved in the successful negotiation of the Montreal Protocol on Substances that Deplete the Ozone Layer. This global treaty is heralded as the most successful attempt at protection of a global commons – in this case, stratospheric ozone, a thin layer of gas that protects the earth from the sun's harmful ultraviolet rays (UV-B). States initially disagreed on the need for an international agreement and over its form. In this chapter, I explore why states with such different initial responses to this global problem were able to reach agreement to take precautionary action that would phase out an entire industry. Recognition of favorable international market conditions prompted key industry actors to play a proactive role internationally and domestically to shape state preferences for stringent global regulations. The participation of industry helped to ensure the creation of international regulations that would be implemented.

Since the 1970s, when the advanced industrialized countries of the world intensified national efforts to control pollution, national decision-makers increasingly have been confronted with the challenge of reconciling the economic benefits of industrialization with the environmental benefits that derive from placing constraints on economic activity. At the same time, as consciousness of this dilemma increased at the national level, a gradual shift in perception of environmental problems from the local and national to international and global levels also occurred. This shift in perception led to a plethora of "global" negotiations and a concomitant rise of "global environmental politics" in which both the economic and environmental stakes are extremely high.[2] The causes of global environmental problems – pollutants emitted as a result of worldwide industry, energy consumption, transportation, farming, and forestry – are embedded in industrial and agricultural practices that lie at the very core of the highly competitive economies and lifestyles of the industrialized world.[3] These practices are also central to strategies for rapid economic growth in developing countries; any attempt to constrain them will be met with strong resistance. As at the national level, the international resolution of these problems requires a reconciliation of an inherent tension between private and public benefits. Difficult to resolve at the national level, these problems are even more problematic in the international arena where countries strive to gain economic advantage in an increasingly competitive and interdependent world. Nevertheless, it has been done.

The Montreal Protocol signed in September 1987 established a concrete schedule of reduction for chlorofluorocarbons (CFCs) and halons, culminating in a 50 percent reduction in production and consumption by 1998. This schedule was made more stringent in subsequent negotiations which led to worldwide agreement to phase out an entire class of chemicals by the turn of the century. Developing nations were given a ten-year period of grace to meet the agreed phaseout.[4] We would expect the process of international negotiations to result in a watering down of attempts to constrain economic activity. In this case, however, just the opposite occurred – the negotiations resulted in strengthening the protocol. Why this was the case and the conditions under which we might expect such an outcome are the central concerns of this chapter. In this context, it is particularly interesting to consider the role of actors whose activities overlap both domestic and international arenas – in this case, two of the world's leading CFC producers, DuPont in the United States and Imperial Chemical Industries (ICI) in the United Kingdom. While initially opposed to any restriction on markets, both companies changed their positions over time. DuPont actually sought – and ICI soon after accepted and supported – the international regulation of CFCs. While DuPont managers insist that scientific evidence, and not business interests, accounted for the change in the company position, the fact is that the producers could benefit from global regulations.[5] A level regulatory playing field could create new markets for more expensive substitutes that only large well-financed corporations could develop. Examination of the role of these economic actors across the domestic and international negotiating arenas demonstrates the importance of their participation in shaping national negotiating posi-

75

tions, which in turn affect the pace and timing of international agreements.

The remainder of this chapter is divided into three sections: first, an overview of the problem of ozone depletion and the divergent policy positions on the regulation of CFCs that had to be reconciled in order for there to be agreement at the international level; second, a consideration of the extent to which the recognition of market opportunities by the world's two major CFC producers affected the formulation of the US and UK positions; finally, an examination of the theoretical implications of these findings for international relations and in particular for their consequences in the intensifying arena of global environmental politics.

Overview of the problem

From the very beginning of international negotiations on ozone depletion in the 1970s through the Vienna Convention of 1985 and up to the protocol negotiations in 1987, the divergent US and UK positions were rationalized on the basis of different interpretations of scientific data and associated uncertainties. Although these uncertainties had not been dispelled when the Montreal Protocol was signed in 1987, countries with divergent policy positions ultimately surrendered a small degree of sovereignty in the interest of international cooperation to address a common resource problem. The following section addresses this puzzle through an examination of the role of industrial actors in determining state preferences for regulation.

Until the 1970s, CFCs were thought to be among a handful of miracle chemicals – inert, inexpensive, and very useful. In the 1930s DuPont began marketing them as Freon, a fire retardant. Since then, their many applications have included use as fire retardants, coolants (widely used in refrigerators and air conditioning systems), aerosol propellants, solvents for cleaning electronic circuit boards, and foam-blowing agents in the manufacture of styrofoam packaging. Between 1960 and 1974, production and use increased at an annual rate of about 13 percent.[6] In 1974, the peak year for worldwide production and sales of CFCs, two scientists, Sherwood Rowland and Mario Molina, announced their belief that chlorine loading in the stratosphere from the decomposition of CFCs could lead to significant reductions in stratospheric ozone, which protects the earth from harmful UV radiation. Their hypothesis had significant implications for US and UK industries. That year the United States accounted for nearly 50 percent of the world production and consumption of CFCs, while chemical companies in the European Community (EC) accounted for 38 percent of production. At that time, 50 percent of American and 80 percent of UK production was used as aerosol propellants.[7]

Once the popular press publicized the Rowland/Molina hypothesis, US consumer response was swift and significant. Sales of spray can products fell rapidly with the appearance of reports like the *Time* magazine cover story picturing an aerosol spray can over the world with the ominous headline, "Not with a bang but a PSSSSST?"[8] In addition, the theory galvanized US environmental activists to join the scientists in calling for a CFC ban. In 1975, the Natural Resources Defense Council sued the Consumer Product Safety Commission and demanded a ban on CFCs in aerosols. In this climate, Johnson Wax announced its intention to phase out CFC use in all of its products, and other consumer product companies soon followed suit. In the United States, a battle over the accuracy of the Rowland/Molina hypothesis and control of CFC production and use ensued. This battle, the so called "ozone war," was played out in the media, in state and federal government hearings, and in scientific forums.[9] Industry was opposed to any kind of regulation. Eventually however, industry lost this first round, and the Environmental Protection Agency (EPA) banned the use of CFCs in aerosols. Direct effects of the ban were minimal. Even before the EPA ban of non-essential usage of CFCs went into effect in 1978, the American CFC aerosol market had bottomed out. However, economic disruptions in the user industry were minimal due to the availability of low-cost propellant substitutes such as hydrocarbons and nitrous oxide. The EPA also permitted use of CFCs as propellants if no suitable alternative propellant was available.[10]

Reaction in Europe, and in the United Kingdom in particular, to the CFC-ozone depletion link theory was quite different from that in the United States. The economic consequences of an aerosol ban loomed large in the highly concentrated UK market, where the bulk of CFC use was in aerosols. UK press accounts differed markedly in their treatment of the subject from those in the United States, reflecting the attitude of many British scientists that the United States was overreacting. The public response was also less intense in Britain than in the United States where an apocalyptic image of the problem was often portrayed in the popular press.[11]

Despite pressure from the Americans, among OECD countries only Canada, Norway and Sweden imposed comparable bans. European governments, led by Britain and France, remained steadfast in their resistance to an aerosol ban. Germany and the Netherlands proposed an aerosol ban within the EC, but the United Kingdom held firmly to the position that regulation was unnecessary. A UK Department of the Environment pollution paper in 1976 predicted that in any case the use of CFCs in aerosols would decline by at least 30 percent without any form of regulation. Data from the Chemical Manufacturers Association showed that between 1976 and 1979 CFC sales in the EC fell by 22.8 percent thanks to consumer demand and voluntary changes to propellant substitutes by many manufacturers of personal care products and some industrial aerosols.

Although economic disruptions – to manufacturers, their employees and the public – caused by unilateral action on aerosols did not come anywhere near predictions, differences in regulatory response across the Atlantic did cost the United States a significant share of the global market for CFCs, and DuPont alone lost one-third of its CFC business.[12] More troubling to the producer industry was the fact that the Carter Administration had made it clear that it intended to press for even further regulations. Not wanting to lose further market share, DuPont fought domestic regulation with two arguments – the first that scientific evidence did not warrant regulations, and the second that the issue should be dealt with in an international rather than domestic arena. Steps in that direction were already being taken.

In 1977 the United Nations Environment Program (UNEP) sponsored a meeting in Washington, DC that launched an international program aimed at developing a "World Plan of Action on the Ozone Layer." Highly scientific in character, the working groups that evolved out of this meeting provided the foundation for negotiations in Vienna eight years later to establish an international plan of action for ozone layer protection.

The US aerosol ban and worldwide consumer response to the ozone depletion problem resulted in declining CFC production and consumption in the late 1970s. This drop, however, was short-lived. By 1986, worldwide figures returned to their pre-1978 heights.[13] There were a number of reasons for this rise including the declining estimates of ozone depletion by the National Academy of Sciences and UNEP, economic recovery from the worldwide recession of the early 1980s, and new markets for a compound that had not been affected by the aerosol ban, CFC-113, which proved to be an effective solvent in a wide range of industries (especially electronics and military uses). During this time, the CFC market share had nearly reverted to what it had been, with the EC accounting for 43 percent of the reported world total and the United States dropping to 40 percent.[14] In the United Kingdom, production almost doubled between 1974 and 1986 – from about 65,500 tons to 123,700 tons annually.

By 1986, the value of the EC's production of CFC-11 and CFC-12 was over 50 percent higher than that of the United States. Although CFC sales for use as aerosol propellants declined, it still accounted for 60 percent of the UK market.[15] In contrast, CFC-propelled aerosols which still accounted for over half of CFC-11 and -12 sales within the EC, had virtually disappeared in the United States. Moreover, EC exports rose 43 percent from 1976 to 1985. Export activity was particularly pronounced in the growing markets of the developing world. In contrast, the United States consumed almost all the CFCs it produced. A major factor in the recovery of the CFC market in the United States was the rise in applications for CFC-113, especially in the burgeoning electronics industry.[16]

Another effect of the lower depletion estimates was a slackening of interest by DuPont and ICI in developing CFC substitutes. While both had identified CFC alternatives for aerosol, refrigeration, and foam-blowing applications in research carried out in the mid-1970s, the substitute products were deemed too expensive to introduce into the market. DuPont invested virtually nothing in R&D for CFC alternatives in the early 1980s, and ICI discontinued its entire alternatives research program around 1981.[17] With domestic levels of concern dropping in the United States, negotiations shifted largely to the international level. In the United States, a new administration more sympathetic to industrial interests than its predecessor began in 1981 to push the CFC issue into the international arena using the argument that it properly belonged there as an issue that affected all nations. This action was taken at the urging of the Alliance for Responsible CFC Policy, a CFC-producer/user industry lobby that DuPont strategists created after the Carter Administration took unilateral action against aerosol sprays.

Domestic politics and international negotiations

After years of slow-moving preparations, 1985 saw the delegates of leading CFC-producing countries meeting in Vienna to discuss formulation of an international agreement for ozone layer protection. Differences existed among states regarding the need for an agreement and the shape any such agreement should take. The positions of both

79

the EC and US delegations going into the negotiations reflected their existing market situations. US negotiators and their supporters pressed hard for an 80 percent reduction in production or a complete ban in non-essential aerosol use of CFCs, while the Europeans favored a production capacity cap plus a 30 percent cut in non-essential aerosol use – an amount that had already been reached in most European countries through voluntary transitions to alternative technologies such as the vacuum pump.[18] In the end, neither side won in the Vienna negotiations; the meeting concluded with nothing more than an agreement to follow the scientific developments and to meet again in two years to negotiate a protocol if the situation warranted international controls.[19]

The appearance of the Antarctic ozone hole six months after the Vienna Convention was signed was a surprise to scientists, to environmental groups whose attention to the ozone problem in the early 1980s had been diverted to other more immediate domestic environmental problems, and to industry. It jarred industry's complacence with regard to the development of CFC substitutes. Although no evidence at the time supported a causal relationship between CFCs and ozone depletion, chlorine deposits from CFCs remained a primary suspect. Powerful and evocative pictures of ozone depletion simulations appeared in magazines all over the world and prompted a shift in the political ground. Some recognized this shift earlier than others. In Washington, DC, the chief lobbyist for the Alliance for Responsible CFC Policy knew that the politics would change, and that it would be just a matter of time before regulations were erected.[20] From his point of view, this strengthened the need for an international, as opposed to a purely domestic, response. At DuPont headquarters in Wilmington, Delaware, the head of the division that produced CFCs, Joseph Glas, asked company scientists for current estimates of chlorine-loading based on the recovering CFC market.[21]

A Harvard Business School case-study indicates that following the appearance of the Antarctic "ozone hole," DuPont's investment in R&D on CFC substitutes jumped from virtually zero between 1981 and 1985 to $5 million in 1986, and doubled to $10 million in 1987.[22] At the same time, the DuPont Freon Division's marketing strategy changed from one of short-term profit maximization to mitigating potential regulatory impacts on DuPont and its customers in the long term. In fact, because of the aerosol ban and the worldwide recession of the early 1980s, the market for CFC-11 and -12 had been flat for several years. Only CFC-113 was showing significant profits (23.5 percent earnings on production costs compared to less than 1 percent for CFC-11 and -12).[23] As one DuPont official put it, "If we raise the price to the market clearing price, we may drive some of the low-value consumers out of business; then, they won't be around when we introduce substitutes. We might instead want to maximize the number of current customers so we can switch them to other products later."[24]

DuPont knew from its research in the 1970s that coolant substitutes, although costly, were in fact possible. By revealing this publicly in 1986, DuPont broke ranks with the international industry position vis-à-vis CFC controls. That position essentially maintained that CFCs were unique and irreplaceable, and that their elimination would result in a devastating impact on the quality of modern lifestyles as well as on national economies. DuPont said that appropriate economic incentives would bring forth substitutes; for example, worldwide limits on production without limiting demand (as had happened with aerosols in the US) could stimulate rather than depress the CFC market for a company in the vanguard of producing those substitutes. Importantly, an international action would also stave off unilateral control by the EPA which was under increasing pressure from environmental groups and some members of Congress to act on its own to curb CFC emissions. This proposal threatened many foreign industries with the prospect that the huge US market in CFC-containing products – like refrigerators, automobiles, and electronic equipment – would be cut off from exporters who did not comply with the more stringent US regulations. For DuPont and other US CFC producers, the prospect of unilateral US action would certainly mean a loss of market share and loss of a level playing field internationally.

To the chagrin of its European competitors and some of its allies in the Alliance for Responsible CFC Policy, in mid-1986 DuPont announced its support for concerted international action to limit CFCs. Although reluctant at first, the Alliance joined DuPont in its support for the negotiations. Once US industry revealed its support for international controls, both the British and the French representatives to the UNEP negotiations had a strong incentive to hold out as long as possible for minimum production reductions until their companies could develop substitutes.[25] Thus, with the United Kingdom in control of the EC Council Presidency, the Community adhered to its very limited position. Despite stronger environmental policy recommendations from a majority of the EC countries (led by the Netherlands and Germany), this protectionist position prevailed. Under the terms of the Treaty of Rome, the EC Council had to adopt a unanimous position. As such, the industries of England and France effectively determined what that position would be by successfully advancing their interests through their national delegations.[26] This did not change until the eleventh hour in the negotiating process when Belgium took over the presidency of the EC Council, and Germany, under increasing political pressure from its burgeoning Green Party, refused to go along any further with the intransigent position. Other commercial interests besides those of CFC producers (i.e., exporters of CFC-containing products) were also at stake, and some European countries, as well as Japan, feared the trade imbalances that could result from the United States taking unilateral action if the international negotiations failed.[27]

In fact, the 50 percent reduction ultimately agreed upon at Montreal was unlikely to have any impact on European industry, which could quite easily meet the reductions through belated switches to readily available aerosol substitutes. Moreover, by restricting the supply of CFCs through an incremental phaseout plan, a protocol could stimulate the development of higher priced substitutes and a potentially more profitable market for large producers.

Recognizing what was going on in the negotiations to protect commercial interests, UNEP Executive Director Mostafa Tolba later lamented:

> The difficulties in negotiating the Montreal Protocol had nothing whatever to do with whether the environment was damaged or not. It was all who was going to gain an edge over who; whether DuPont would have an advantage over the European companies or not.[28]

Ultimately, the Protocol did not confer an advantage on either side but did reward both of the large producers over smaller companies who were less able to invest in the development of substitutes.

The market was dramatically affected soon after the signing of the Montreal Protocol when the Ozone Trends Panel released its findings in 1988 which provided the "smoking gun" linking CFCs to ozone depletion. Within a week DuPont announced that it would phase out the chemicals entirely. What that announcement did, according to then EPA Administrator Lee Thomas, was to "send a message that substitutes can be made readily available in the near future."[29]

Although the substitutes issue is far more complicated than Thomas characterized it,[30] the DuPont action most certainly sent a message to customers and competitors alike. It enhanced the company's credibility by keeping its 1974 promise to phase out the compounds if scientific evidence demonstrated that CFCs would damage health or the environment. Second, it also signalled DuPont's advanced stage of substitute development and this in turn convinced customers to stay with DuPont until substitutes became available. Finally, it effectively isolated any recalcitrant position of potential competitors.

In August 1988, ICI joined DuPont's pledge to phase out existing CFCs and rapidly develop substitutes. One month later a report by the British Department of the Environment urged a rapid phase-out of "man-made carriers of chlorine and bromine to the atmosphere."[31] This reversal of the department's position of the previous year can be explained only in part by the close and cooperative relationship of industry and government in UK policy-making. In fact, the marketplace for CFCs was changing. As consumer demand for non-CFC technologies grew, political pressure to alter the United Kingdom's pro-producer industry position also increased, and by 1988, the Conservative Government was feeling increasing pressure from its own closest adherents to change its anti-green stance.

From Montreal to London: the growing influence of green politics

Several analysts of the Montreal Protocol negotiations attribute its success to the strong pressure exerted by the United States on the EC countries to accept an agreement or face the trade consequences of US unilateral action.[32] The strength of that pressure was due in no small measure to the role of domestic environmental groups and their allies in the Congress. From the public relations campaign launched in the aftermath of the announcement of the Rowland/Molina hypothesis in 1974, to the 1984 Natural Resources Defense Council lawsuit, which was designed to force the EPA to take action on ozone depletion under the Clean Air Act, to the pressure exerted by environmental NGOs on Congress to introduce legislation calling for unilateral action and trade sanctions against countries that did not take action to protect stratospheric ozone from manmade effects, these events were important in communicating the seriousness of the US commitment in keeping the international negotiations in the forefront of the American agenda.[33] In addition to the pressure this placed on European governments to participate in international negotiations, activities of environmental groups also leveraged support for international controls from US industry. American CFC producers were eager to avoid further unilateral action by the EPA or Congress, which they feared would be tantamount to turning world markets over to European competitors, as had happened in the aerosol market.

Similar pressures from different quarters in Europe were to have a significant impact on the EC position as well. Although formal environmental groups in Europe did not have official standing during the Montreal Protocol negotiations, or access to domestic policy-making channels similar to those available to interest groups in the United States, a "green wave" in European politics created a political climate that generally favored controls. Under pressure from its strengthened Green Parties, in 1986 Germany established a Ministry for the Environment. Whereas the CFC issue had been handled by the Interior Ministry, which focused on advancing the economic goals of the state, competence for coordinating the German negotiating position now went to the newly created environment ministry. Although many of the key people working on the issue were transferred to the new ministry, their constituent base changed from predominantly domestic industrial interests to the growing environmental movement. Hence, the German position took on an increasingly green hue in the EC-level negotiations. Moreover, although the EC regulations implementing the Montreal Protocol initially copied the protocol verbatim, political and commercial pressures had begun to mount to strengthen the provisions almost before the delegates returned from Canada.

One of the most significant elements of the Montreal Protocol is its amendment procedure, which requires the signatory parties to review and assess control measures at least every four years.[34] Following on the heels of the discovery of the ozone hole over Antarctica, the Ozone Trends Panel Report prompted media coverage and public debate at a level to rival that in the United States in the mid-1970s.[35] Only this time, it broke out on both sides of the Atlantic in equal force.

In the United States, as noted above, DuPont pledged it would phase out all CFC and halon production by the end of the century because of their ozone depleting potential.[36] Environmentalists urged immediate renegotiation of the protocol to strengthen its provisions. But negotiators, noting the amendment process already in place, did not call for immediate action.[37] In Europe, environmental and consumer groups began to call for stricter limits by the EC, and called upon industry to voluntarily reduce CFC production and use beyond the level for which the Protocol called. Product boycotts were threatened, and the amount and tone of media coverage began to change. Environmentalists were supported by members of the European Parliament who recommended that the EC members adopt stricter national standards.[38]

Although these pressures and recommendations did not prevail in the immediate aftermath of the Protocol negotiations, they set the stage for what ultimately would be a complete turnaround of the EC position. On 2 March 1989 the Council of Ministers of the EC took the unexpected decision to eliminate CFCs completely by the end of the century. What happened to allow this dramatic change, especially in the United Kingdom and France? The answer is found in shifting commercial and political interests which fostered changes in the interpretation of, and attitudes toward, scientific findings. Several environmental disasters in the United Kingdom gave rise to growing support for environmental NGOs in the late 1980s. Between 1985 and 1990, membership in British environmental groups increased by more than 40 percent. The focus of their attention increasingly turned to the large and traditionally heavy polluting industries, especially chemicals. As Britain's flagship chemical producer, ICI was a highly visible target for the environmental movement's growing demands for industrial change.

The pressure by consumer and environmental groups on British industry to cut CFC production and use voluntarily began to take effect almost immediately after the Montreal Protocol was signed. In May 1988 the British Association of Aerosol Manufacturers recommended that its members label CFC-free products. Similarly, ICI headquarters became more sensitive to damage to its image caused by its perceived anti-environmental posture. In response, the company established a public relations unit for the first time to work with the external community in defining and communicating its position on policy matters.[39]

But the seminal event signalling a fundamental change in the British position was the October 1988 speech by Prime Minister Margaret Thatcher to the Royal Society in which she effectively legitimized the environmental movement's claims. "The environment and the balance of nature," she said, "are one of the great challenges of the late 20th century." Emphasizing the importance of global environmental problems, and in particular the hole in the ozone layer and global warming, the prime minister promised that Britain would begin to play a leadership role in finding solutions. She further noted that spending on the environment was "money well spent because the health of the environment and the health of our economy are totally dependent upon each other".[40] Only one year earlier, she had referred to environmentalists who accused Britain of dragging its feet in the international environmental arena as "subversives" and "the enemy within."[41]

Mrs. Thatcher had trained as a chemist, and some claim that the compelling evidence presented by the Ozone Trends Panel convinced her of the urgent need for Great Britain to deal with this problem.[42] Foremost, however, she was a politician, and there were compelling political reasons for a change in the prime minister's attitude. Public opinion polls in the EC showed a marked change in British public attitudes toward the environment during the 1980s.[43] In 1982, 50 percent of those polled said that protecting the environment was more important than keeping prices down. By 1985, the figure increased to 60 percent, and in 1988 it stood at 74 percent.[44] Moreover, polls taken in the United Kingdom in 1988 indicated that those most concerned about environmental issues were Conservatives – members of Mrs. Thatcher's own party.[45] Public opinion polls between December 1988 and July 1989 indicate that the environment moved from being mentioned as an important issue by 5 percent of the public to 35 percent, placing it ahead of all other public concerns, including the health service and unemployment.[46] What was worse, the public had been relatively satisfied with government efforts to control water and air pollution in the 1960s and 1970s. But, thanks in part to the economic recovery of the 1980s, and the government's generally unsympathetic view toward environmental actions that might have affected that recovery, British environmental quality deteriorated in the 1980s.[47]

In addition, other dramatic incidents sensitized the British public to environmental concerns, including a mysterious massive death of seals in the North Sea. The accident at the Chernobyl nuclear power plant, a chemical spill of toxins in the River Rhine in 1986, and the enduring problem of acid rain had already sensitized Europe in general to the fact that environmental disasters are not contained by borders. In December 1988, *The Washington Post* noted, "A drumbeat of emergencies has intensified the environmental debate this year in Europe, when public concern about pollution has never been higher."[48]

That concern translated into significant growth in environmental organizations, and into votes in the 1989 European Parliament elections. According to press reports, 20,000 Britons per month joined environmental groups in 1988/1989. Paid membership in Friends of the Earth alone that year climbed from 31,000 to 125,000. In the 1989 elections Europe's Green Parties added seventeen seats to the twenty they already held, which made environmentalism one of the biggest "winners" of the election.[49]

The "green wave" that had begun in Germany and spread across the continent had clearly crossed the channel by the end of the 1980s. Nor was France immune to the effects of the green wave. Unlike DuPont and ICI, France's major CFC producer, Elf-Atochem, did not produce products for the consumer market, and therefore felt buffered from direct public attack and consumer demands. But the French government, while protective of the state-owned industry, did feel the international political heat. In 1989, just prior to the March EC Council meeting, France announced support for substantial reductions in CFC production and use.[50]

When the Council met, in what seemed to be a struggle for green one-upmanship, France called for a complete phase out of CFCs by the year 2000 rather than the 85–95 percent that had been proposed earlier by various delegations. As Jachtenfuchs notes, "In this case, the desire to improve the EC's image in the field of environmental protection prevailed over the proposal to allow some uses of CFCs in cases where the possibility of their replacement by other substances was not yet clear."[51] These changes in EC policy opened the way for significant amendments to be made to the Montreal Protocol in London in 1990. Domestic political and commercial interests had at last converged to create the political will necessary at the national level for taking strong regulatory measures.

Ironically, while a burgeoning green movement in Europe strengthened political resolve in the EC for stronger regulation, the political impact of environmentalists in the United States seemed to wane. In London, the USA joined the USSR and Japan in opposing EC member country recommendations for a total phase-out of CFCs by 1997, and hindered the creation of a fund and of technology transfer mechanisms to assist developing countries in meeting the obligations of the protocol.[52] Only after assurances from the Alliance for Responsible CFC Policy that the industry in fact supported the international proposals were key policy-makers in the White House (namely John Sununu and Office of Management and Budget chief Richard Darman) persuaded to take the stronger stance.[53] In meetings of the Parties to the Montreal Protocol in 1992 and 1993, the regulations were strengthened even further, and most of the industrialized countries and some of the developing countries have indicated that they will phase out ozone depleting substances ahead of the agreed time frame.

Nonetheless, problems remain. The international dialogue on ozone depletion shifted from the need for creating international regulations to compensating developing countries for the loss of the use of the inexpensive technologies being phased out under the terms of the Montreal Protocol. In fact, the 1987 Protocol granted the developing countries a ten-year period of grace before being required to implement the Protocol provisions. During this time, their unconstrained production and consumption of CFCs and other ozone depleting substances have increased significantly. This has put added pressure on industrialized countries (which will complete their phaseout of most ozone depleting substances by the turn of the century) to ensure that the developing countries, with burgeoning economies and potential CFC markets, make the transition to substitutes as soon as possible.

The Multilateral Fund for the Montreal Protocol was established in 1990 to provide compensation for the incremental costs to developing countries of phasing out ozone depleting substances. However, while uncommonly successful in attracting the commitment of most nations of the world to a complete CFC phaseout and ensuring a merit-based approach to project selection, implementation of the projects has been bogged down in bureaucratic delays and disputes over technological choice and transfer.[54] Thus, while the Montreal Protocol is widely hailed as the first application of the "precautionary principle" on a global scale, it may not be an effective model for other even more complex global environmental problems.

Conclusion

The story of the Montreal Protocol is ultimately about the complex intersection of science, politics, and markets on both domestic and international levels. Without further scientific evidence (since the WMO/UNEP report) that CFCs were the cause of ozone depletion, a stronger case for international action could not be made. However, although the anti-regulatory positions of France and the UK might have been expected to prevail, they did not. Clearly, other factors were at play to bring about the change that led to the negotiation of an international agreement. Commercial interests and politics had to converge before a compromise for international action could be forged. What the ozone negotiations suggest is that although scientific evidence can be used to justify political positions (in this case, both for and against regulation), national preferences for regulation are determined by commercial and political interests. The more uncertain the science, the more interest group politics will come into play. As scientific uncertainty declined, industry and activist positions converged. For example, in the 1980s, scientific predictions of lower levels of ozone depletion did not prevent international negotiations from moving forward. Likewise, despite the fact that no hard scientific evidence linked CFCs to ozone depletion, the Montreal Protocol was signed in 1987. To this day, scientific uncertainty continues to surround debate on the cause and effect of ozone depletion, the speed with which it is occurring and, most importantly, the anticipated environmental and health effects of ozone depletion. In short, the scientific evidence of ozone depletion was less certain than the anticipated economic effects of regulation.

Negotiators of the Montreal Protocol clearly had to strive to reconcile both domestic and international imperatives, often finding themselves in the position of negotiating simultaneously in both arenas. Of equal importance, however, was the pivotal role of the actors through whom the two levels intersected. In the case of the Montreal Protocol this included the affected industries, environmental organizations, and green movements.

This chapter does not argue with the importance of scientific evidence in identifying complex threats to health and the environment, nor with the fact that a significant degree of scientific consensus is a prerequisite for international action. Rather, the Montreal case demonstrates that these conditions are not sufficient to explain what leads countries to recognize the need for international regulation, to take responsibility, and to cooperate. Bureaucratic elites responsible for formulating negotiating positions are subject to a complex array of pressures in the political process which affect their negotiating position. Some of these include institutional factors[55] and exogenous pressures[56] which have been studied in the context of the Montreal Protocol. In the case of the Montreal Protocol the appearance of the Antarctic ozone hole was a major catalyst for progress by creating political pressures. But as the foregoing analysis has demonstrated, equally important are interest-based politics operating simultaneously at the national and international levels. In the case of the Montreal Protocol, we see how domestic interests – from coalitions of activist scientists to environmental NGOs to industry lobbyists and representatives of specific firms – log-rolled with government decision-makers and negotiators to advance positions that supported their interests and goals.

In the United States these various interests competed with each other for control over the country's negotiating position, each using arguments about international environmental cooperation and the broader public interest to justify the promotion of a self-serving position.[57] However, in the long run their interests were best served and advanced not through lobbying activities, but through participation in the generation and interpretation of scientific knowledge and events at national and international levels. Representatives of industry with scientific and technological credibility on the issue of stratospheric ozone depletion were able to participate in and effectively utilize forums for building knowledge to assist and support decision-making in the international arena. At the same time, this participation provided them with a window on to the international processes of decision-making and an opportunity to use this information to develop company strategy. For this reason, for example, DuPont – a company with representation on the Ozone Trends Panel – was able to understand and interpret the significance of the panel's findings sooner than other corporations which initially had access only to the Executive Summary of the Panel Report. It was DuPont's historical knowledge and current expertise due to its ongoing R&D capabilities which garnered it a place on the Ozone Trends Panel in the first place – not its domestic lobbying activities. The importance of that involvement to the outcome of the Montreal Protocol is underplayed in most analyses of the negotiations but may well be pivotal.

Competing interests did not appear at first to be a factor in the UK's deliberations. Rather, the traditional relationship between government officials and corporate representatives prevailed in the development and articulation of its negotiating position until the unexpected intervention in the mid-1980s of a third variable – public demand. At this time, demands for greater environmental sensitivity in the wake of a series of domestic environmental problems prompted industry and government to seek visible ways to mitigate their anti-environmentalist image. That opportunity was present in the concurrent negotiations on ozone depletion. By shifting the British stance in the international negotiations from opposition to cooperation, the UK negotiators, and by implication the prime minister, could, if not satisfy, at least offer a modest bow to emerging domestic pressures (especially those emanating from the prime minister's own political party) without compromising economic interests. In resisting international regulations, the interests of ICI changed once its competitor, DuPont, signalled that the development of substitutes was possible under new market conditions. The DuPont announcement weakened industry's argument for an antiregulation stance and opened the way for UK negotiators to adopt a conciliatory posture towards regulation without harming industry. In short, it provided the opportunity for a win-win situation. With both the necessary capacity and capital to go into substitution production, both companies stood to gain from the protocol requirements.

The identification of the Antarctic ozone hole in 1985 and the ensuing media images of a hole in the sky brought public opinion into play in ways that affected both business and government sectors. The emergence of strong public opinion in favor of an international response to the threat of ozone depletion was not enough in itself to change negotiating positions, but it played a catalytic role in one very important sense. The threat of a tarnished corporate image and angry consumer boycotts probably helped to stimulate manufacturers to speed up R&D efforts aimed at finding CFC substitutes. Similarly, by riveting public attention on an international problem, the appearance of the Antarctic ozone hole ironically helped Conservative British politicians meet complaints of their own party members about their insensitivity to England's deepening environmental crisis. Although the growing public discontent with the Thatcher government's environmental record played a fairly minor role in altering the UK position in the 1987 negotiations, it was central in the later reversal of that position to one calling for stringent regulations.

What does this analysis of the development of the Montreal Protocol say about international relations theory generally and about global environmental politics in particular? It supports recognition of the links between diplomacy and domestic politics. Furthermore, it suggests that those linkages may be best understood through analysis of the roles of actors operating simultaneously in national and international arenas. During the Montreal Protocol negotiations, industrial interests lobbied both domestic and international negotiators through informal meetings and formal industrial association channels, such as CEFIC at the EC level and Chemical Manufacturers Association at the US and international (UNEP) level. In future analyses, it will be important to explore the extent to which those interests have also become entangled in domestic politics across national borders. The British complaint that US environmental groups were trying to influence British politics is one example of this. Another area of interest is to explore the extent to which industries lobby outside their own countries to garner support in the international arena for their position – especially if it is weakened by countervailing domestic forces.

Analysis of the Montreal Protocol negotiations also suggests that economic interests of large oligopolistic producers are strengthened when environmental issues move from the domestic to international arena. There is some evidence to suggest that both the United States and the United Kingdom helped push discussions about the regulation of ozone depleting substances into the international arena to protect the competitive position of the world's two largest CFC manufacturers, ICI and DuPont, and not simply to protect the ozone layer.

In the United States, industry successfully persuaded the US government to push regulatory issues into the international arena. By using the argument of the broader global public interest, the industries were successful in advancing their policy position. Pushing discussion of regulations forward in the international arena essentially removed it from the more volatile political arena of the US Congress, which the Alliance for Responsible CFC Policy considered vulnerable to the influence of more extreme environmental interests and the support they were able to rally from American voters. In the international arena, the US industrial position was reflected in the stance of many of the European countries. In this political but less volatile climate, the corporations and industry associations with significant scientific and technological resources were able to play a more central role in defining the issue than would have been possible had they operated domestically only.

Finally, the shift in emphasis in environmental problem-solving from the national to international and, indeed, to the global arena has led and will continue to lead to some surprising and unintended consequences which will need further exploration and analysis. International forums for consensus-building provide unusual opportunities for competing industries to participate in and contribute to the construction of knowledge on the subject issue and to share information that may facilitate cartelization. At the same time, industry participation at this level provides direct channels of communication to corporate decision-makers who are generally reluctant to accept outside assessments regarding the nature and seriousness of the problem.

At the national level, the increasing intensity of global environmental negotiations is contributing to structural changes within national governments. The creation of new offices and divisions within bureaucracies to deal specifically with the highly technical and scientific issues related to global environmental change is a recent phenomenon. In the United States, these offices, located within the EPA, appear to have developed working relationships with industry that are far removed from the traditional adversarial approach more common in dealing with domestic environmental regulation and enforcement. At the same time, their counterparts in the United Kingdom have also become more open to input from other forces outside of their traditional business/government arrangements.

Ultimately, the Montreal Protocol suggests that reconciliation of narrow economic interests with provision of a collective good and little coercion from the state is possible. This paper begins an exploration of the conditions under which such reconciliation is likely to occur. Market structure matters. Firms that are part of a strong oligopolistic core industry stand to benefit from regulation that limits market penetration by smaller firms. Other forces, however, also had to be present to overcome inherent resistance to change. In particular, the synergistic relationship between industry, government, and science created the critical mass necessary to move firms and governments beyond narrow self interest to contribute to the collective good.

The lesson of the Montreal Protocol is not that it is a model for other negotiations on global environmental problems. Rarely, perhaps, will all the conditions – especially the potentially favorable economic conditions – be present in other cases. Our ability to predict the outcomes, however, will be enhanced through better understanding of the conditions under which industries and firms are likely to recognize their own self-interest in international regulations.

Notes

1. Support for research in the development of this chapter was provided by the VOLVO/MIT Award for Environmental Research and grants from the MacArthur Foundation and the Center for International Studies, Massachusetts Institute of Technology, and is gratefully acknowledged.
2. Oran Young, *International Cooperation: Building Regimes for Natural Resources and the Environment* (Ithaca: Cornell University Press, 1989); Oran Young, "Global Environmental Change and International Governance," *Millenium: Journal of International Studies* 19:3 (1990), 337–346; Lynton K. Caldwell, *International Environmental Policy: Emergence and Dimensions* (Durham, NC: Duke University Press, 1984).
3. Sebenius, "Designing Negotiations Toward a New Regime: The Case of Global Warming," *International Organization* 43 (1989), 349–375.
4. UNEP, Montreal Protocol on Substances that Deplete the Ozone Layer, 1987.
5. Philip Shabecoff, "DuPont to Halt Chemicals that Peril Ozone," *The New York Times*, 24 March 1989.
6. James Maxwell and Sanford Weiner, "Green Consciousness or Dollar Diplomacy? An Analysis of the British Response to the Threat of

Stratospheric Ozone Depletion." Case-study for the Center of Technology, Policy and Industry Development, Massachusetts Institute of Technology, Cambridge, MA, 1991.

7. Because of high transoceanic shipping costs involved in transporting CFCs, relatively little trade in proportion to overall production occurred between the three primary regional markets – the United States, Europe, and Japan. Only DuPont produced CFCs in all three. In 1986, only 8 percent of US consumption was imported from Europe (mostly from ICI in Britain), and only small quantities moved between Europe and Japan or Japan and the United States. Forest Reinhardt, "DuPont Freon@ Products Division (A) and (b)," case study for the National Wildlife Federation, Washington, DC, p. 4.

8. Lydia Dotto and Harold Schiff, *The Ozone War* (Garden City, NY: Doubleday & Co., 1978).

9. For an excellent account of the public relations battle for control of US policy, see Dotto and Schiff, *The Ozone War.*

10. Dotto and Schiff, *The Ozone War.*

11. For a review of the media coverage of the first phase of the ozone depletion issue in the 1970s, see Dotto and Schiff, *The Ozone War.*

12. An excellent analysis of the marketing impacts of the US action is to be found in Reinhardt, "DuPont Freon."

13. Alternative Fluorocarbons Environmental Acceptability Study (AFEAS), "Production Sales and Atmospheric Release of Fluorocarbons through 1994" (Washington, DC: AFEAS Program Office, 1995).

14. Richard Elliott Benedick, *Ozone Diplomacy: New Directions in Safeguarding the Planet* (Cambridge, MA: Harvard University Press, 1991), p. 26.

15. Ibid.

16. Maxwell and Weiner, "Green Consciousness."

17. Reinhardt, "DuPont Freon," p. 12; Maxwell and Weiner, "Green Consciousness," p. 12.

18. Peter M. Morrisette, "The Evolution of Policy Responses to Stratospheric Ozone Depletion," *Natural Resources Journal* (Summer 1989), 793–820.

19. UNEP, The Vienna Convention on Substances that Deplete the Ozone Layer: Final Act, 1985.

20. Author interview with Kevin Faye, Executive Director of Alliance for Responsible CFC Policy, Washington, DC, 18 November 1991.

21. Author interview with J. P. Glas, 1995.

22. Reinhardt, "DuPont Freon."

23. Ibid., exhibit 15.

24. Ibid. p. 23.

25. Maxwell and Weiner, "Green Consciousness."

26. For an excellent analysis of the formulation of the EC position and the control exercised by industry in the United Kingdom and France, see Markus Jachtenfuchs, "The European Community and the Protection of the Ozone Layer," *Journal of Common Market Studies* 28:1 (March 1990), p. 263.

27. For an analysis of the strategic importance of this, see the testimony by Stephen Anderson of the EPA and a letter to Congressman Jim Bates from David Doniger and David Wirth of the Natural Resources Defense Council submitted to Hearings before the Subcommittee on Health and the Environment on Ozone Layer Depletion, 9 March 1987, US Government Printing Office.
28. Kiki Warr, "Ozone: The Burden of Proof," *New Scientist* 27 (October 1990), 36–40.
29. Shabecoff, "DuPont to Halt Chemicals that Peril Ozone."
30. There is doubt today about the quality and availability of high quality substitutes for some important uses.
31. See UK Department of the Environment, Stratospheric Ozone Research Group (SORG) Second Report, "Stratospheric Ozone" (London: HMSO, 1988).
32. Jachtenfuchs, "The European Community"; Morrisette, "The Evolution of Policy Responses."
33. Like the findings in Kal Raustiala's contribution to this volume regarding the positions of the United Kingdom and United States on the convention on biological diversity, I found that the environmental-interest community plays an important role in focusing domestic attention on an issue. The ozone policy outcomes, however, are better explained through analysis of the political economics of CFC controls.
34. Montreal Protocol on Substances that Deplete the Ozone Layer, 16 September 1987, art. 6, 26 I.L.M. at 1556.
35. Kiki Warr, "Ozone: The Burden of Proof."
36. This was particularly surprising in light of the fact that only eleven days before the Ozone Trends Panel report became public, the DuPont Chairman, in a letter to three Senators, had claimed: "At the moment, scientific evidence does not point to the need for dramatic CFC emission reductions." See Reinhardt, "DuPont Freon".
37. Benedick, *Ozone Diplomacy*, ch. 11.
38. Jachtenfuchs, "The European Community," p. 286.
39. Interview with ICI.
40. Quoted in Martin Jacques, "Why Thatcher Turned Green," *The Sunday Times* [London], 2 October 1988.
41. Throughout the early 1980s British policy emphatically emphasized improving economic performance over environmental interests. In addition to dragging its feet in the CFC negotiations, the British government also fought vigorously in the EC for the least restrictive limits on emissions of sulfur (vis-à-vis acid rain) and radiation in food.
42. Michael Oppenheimer, "The Greening of Mrs. Thatcher," *The New York Times*, 10 May 1989.
43. Eurobarometer.
44. Ronald Inglehart, Jacques-René Rabier, and Helene Riffault, *European Communities Studies, 1973–1984: Cumulative File* [machine readable data file]

in Interuniversity Consortium for Political and Social Research (ICPSR) codebook, Ann Arbor, MI, 1991.

45. Jacques, "Why Thatcher Turned Green."
46. *The Times*, 3 and 31 July 1989.
47. *The Sunday Times*, 2 October 1988.
48. Norman J. Vig and Michael E. Kraft, *Environmental Policy in the 1990s: Toward a New Agenda* (Washington, DC: Congressional Quarterly Press, 1990).
49. Ibid.
50. Jachtenfuchs, "The European Community," p. 271.
51. Ibid.
52. Dale S. Bryk, "The Montreal Protocol and Recent Developments to Protect the Ozone Layer," *Harvard Environmental Law Review* 15:1 (1991), 275–298.
53. Faye interview.
54. See Elizabeth DeSombre and Joanne Kauffman, "The Multilateral Fund of the Montreal Protocol," in Robert Keohane (ed.), *Financial Transfers for Global Environmental Protection* (Cambridge, MA: MIT Press, 1996).
55. Edward A. Parson, "Protecting the Ozone Layer," in Peter M. Haas, Robert O. Keohane, and Marc A. Levy (eds.), *Institutions for the Earth: Sources of Effective Environmental Protection* (Cambridge, MA: MIT Press, 1993), pp. 27–73.
56. Jachtenfuchs, "The European Community."
57. This is not unique to environmental policy. Jack Snyder, *Myths of Empire: Domestic Politics and International Ambition* (Ithaca: Cornell University Press, 1991) examines these phenomena with respect to security issues.

5 The internationalization of environmental protection in the USSR and its successor states

Robert G. Darst

Until its collapse in 1991, the USSR was one of the world's most heavily industrialized countries, and one of its largest producers of environmental pollution. Yet despite the USSR's enormous scientific and technological prowess, and its leaders' oft professed commitment to human health and welfare, Soviet environmental policies stubbornly lagged behind those in Western Europe and North America – a gap that steadily widened throughout the course of the 1970s and early 1980s. When the Soviet regime finally joined its predecessors on the dustheap of history, this distinction was passed on to its successor states – heirs not only to an environmental crisis of almost unimaginable proportions, but also to the facilities and practices that had generated that crisis in the first place.[1]

This environmental crisis threatened not only the citizens of the USSR itself, but also their neighbors abroad. Even though the vast inner spaces of the USSR could contain environmental problems that would quickly have attained transboundary dimensions elsewhere in the world, a significant portion of the air, water, and radioactive pollution generated within the Soviet Union inevitably crossed its outer borders – whether in a slow steady trickle, or in sudden explosions like the Chernobyl disaster. Indeed, long before the Chernobyl accident, environmental specialists and officials in northern and western Europe recognized that they could not solve their own environmental problems without the cooperation of the USSR and its socialist allies. Accordingly, Western scientists and diplomats labored to persuade the Soviet government to adopt more vigorous policies towards environmental protection. This campaign is best characterized as one of "international socialization" – in intent, if not always in effect – for it was nothing less than an effort to transmit to the USSR the increasingly comprehensive and intrusive international environmental agenda that was then taking shape in the West.[2]

At the same time, there was also growing pressure for improved environmental protection from actors *within* the USSR and, later, the successor states. The cast of characters changed over time, in response to domestic political change within the former Soviet Union: initially confined to a handful of scientists and prominent cultural figures, the internal advocates of environmental protection later expanded to include citizen activists and popularly elected officials. With very few exceptions, these actors were concerned primarily with internally generated environmental problems. Where internal and external concerns overlapped, however, the domestic advocates of environmental protection in the USSR and the successor states consistently sought to draw upon external economic, political, and scientific resources in order to further their cause. Thus, over time, the struggle against environmental degradation in the USSR and its successor states increasingly became a transnational campaign.

Over the past quarter-century, this transnational campaign has been played out against a dramatic backdrop of internal and international political upheaval. When organized East–West environmental cooperation first began in the late 1960s, the Soviet political and economic order differed sharply from that of the other major industrialized powers, from whom it was divided by a rigid barrier of military and ideological hostility. By the time of the Chernobyl accident in 1986, a new Soviet leader had embarked upon an unprecedented and breathtaking campaign to radically reform domestic and international politics. Then, in 1990–1991, everything changed once again: the Cold War came to an abrupt end, the USSR disintegrated, and the Soviet order gave way (at least in the European successor states) to economic marketization and political pluralism: uneven, weakly institutionalized, and decidedly imperfect, to be sure, but recognizable nonetheless.

How did these revolutions in the internal and international context affect transnational efforts to promote environmental protection? At first glance, we might expect that the end of the Cold War and genuine democratization throughout much of the former USSR would be positively associated with substantive progress in the solution of the region's environmental ills. During the Cold War period, international environmental cooperation was hampered by the hostility and secrecy that accompanied the rigid bipolar division of the European continent; to make matters worse, internal efforts to address environmental degradation within the USSR were sharply constrained by the totalitarian character of the Soviet political system and the leadership's determination to pursue military and industrial development at any cost. By contrast, in the wake of the dramatic events of 1989–1991, the barriers associated with the Cold War vanished, and domestic political power increasingly devolved to the people most likely to benefit from improved environmental quality – the ordinary citizens of Russia and the other successor states.

In fact, the end of the Cold War and the collapse of the Soviet Union have not proved as unalloyed a boon for international environmental cooperation as we might have initially expected. First, although the totalitarian political system did indeed constrain the advancement of environmental protection in the USSR, successive Soviet leaders – including the dour Brezhnev – did respond positively, if not always fervently, to Western calls for East–West environmental cooperation. Secondly, the period of greatest enthusiasm for East–West environmental cooperation began well *before* 1990, at a time when the top-heavy Soviet political order was still firmly in place. Finally, while there have been remarkable advances in international environmental cooperation since 1990, this has for the most part occurred only when concerned Western governments and international lending organizations have been willing to foot a considerable part of the bill – and even then progress has typically been slow and laborious.

How can we account for these anomalies? First, while the extremely hierarchical structure of the Soviet political system excluded popular participation and thus sharply constrained the advancement of environmental protection prior to 1986, that same political system also provided Gorbachev and his fellow reformers the means necessary to engineer an abrupt "greening" in Soviet foreign and domestic policy in the late 1980s. By contrast, the subsequent conjunction of democratization with political and economic crisis led to the virtual evaporation of popular and official support for aggressive environmental protection, despite the fact that environmental advocates were now free to publicize their cause. Secondly, the East–West tensions of the Cold War – itself in large part the product of the aggressive policies pursued by the USSR – led successive Soviet leaders, including Gorbachev, to devote *more* attention to environmental issues of interest to the West than they did to those that were purely domestic in scope, for this was seen as a relatively harmless way to placate Western anxiety. With the end of the Cold War, this link between environmental cooperation and "high politics" was broken. The successor states subordinated international cooperation to the pursuit of local environmental and economic objectives, and thus began to respond more selectively to the environmental agenda advanced by their Western neighbors. Moreover, the rigid Cold War division of Europe was replaced by a more porous (but no less real) "poverty curtain" separating East from West.[3] This situation induced the Western states to subsidize environmental protection measures in the East, and encouraged the successor states to demand external financing for any costly measures to address international environmental concerns.

Domestic structure and international environmental cooperation

Recent work in the field of "transnational relations" has concluded that the opportunities open to transnational actors are in large part a function of the domestic political structure of the target state.[4] Domestic structure refers to the enduring framework within which political conflict takes place: the nature and autonomy of state institutions, the extent of autonomous societal organization and the distribution of resources among various social groups, and the character of the intermediate institutions or "policy networks" that link societal actors to the state.[5] Prior to the late 1980s, the USSR was the epitome of what Thomas Risse-Kappen has identified as a "state-controlled" structure: one in which a strong, centralized state apparatus squared off against a weak, fragmented society, and one in which all intermediate organizations (or "policy networks") linking the state and society were geared primarily toward the mobilization of the populace on behalf of official goals, rather than the aggregation of societal interests and demands. Risse-Kappen hypothesizes that while transnational actors attempting to wield influence within such structures face considerable hurdles in gaining initial access to the political agenda, they stand to gain enormous influence if their programs are adopted by the state leadership, thanks to the tremendous autonomy which the latter is able to exercise in pursuit of its chosen goals.[6] This proposition is borne out by Matthew Evangelista's study of the changing fortunes of the transnational scientific groups that attempted to moderate Soviet national security policies during the postwar era.[7]

The contrast with the subsequent period could not be more pronounced. In 1990–1991, the Soviet state disintegrated, and with it the state-controlled structures inherited from the Stalinist period; the successor states that emerged fell at the opposite end of the domestic-structural spectrum. Despite the survival of a political culture that emphasized the role of the state as the caretaker of its citizens, the post-Soviet states were weak and badly fragmented. In each of the successor states, the transition from Soviet rule was accompanied by considerable conflict within the central institutions of the state, and among the national, regional, and local authorities – the latter phenomenon being especially pronounced in the Russian Federation. Moreover, the weakness and fragmentation of state institutions was complemented by an extremely low level of societal organization. There was variation among the successor states, to be sure (by the mid-1990s, for example, the Baltic states had begun to recover a modicum of organizational coherence), but the similarities remained as striking as the differences.

The problems facing transnational actors attempting to exert influence in such a political environment are exactly the opposite of those confronted in state-controlled structures. On the one hand, the barriers to entry are considerably lower. Given the fragmentation of the state, it is relatively easy for transnational actors to canvass state officials and societal actors in support of their policy goals. On the other hand, the greater level of political competition within such a system and the greatly reduced ability of state leaders to mobilize resources on behalf of official goals make it correspondingly more difficult for transnational actors to build winning coalitions in support of their programs.[8] This leads to what Evangelista describes as "the paradox of state power": given a receptive political leader, a closed, authoritarian political system may be more conducive to the success of transnational lobbying than an open, pluralist one.[9]

These insights provide a start for our investigation into the ups and downs of transnational efforts to promote better environmental protection in the former Soviet Union, but many key questions remain unanswered. First, it is one thing to argue that the leaders of state-controlled political systems *may* implement the programs advanced by transnational actors if they so choose; it is quite another to explain why the receptivity of the leadership of such a state might change over time, independent of any major change in domestic political structure. Why was the leadership of the USSR so resistant to energetic international environmental cooperation prior to 1986, and subsequently so enthusiastic? An analogous problem arises when we examine policy outcomes in the early post-Soviet period: despite the greater barriers to the construction of winning coalitions, there has been considerable environmental cooperation between the successor states and their Western neighbors, although the speed and scope have varied from case to case. How can we explain these variations?

In order to answer these questions, we must turn to a more detailed examination of international environmental cooperation in the Soviet and post-Soviet periods. From the initial emergence of environmental protection as a major international issue in the late 1960s, the domestic political milieu in the former Soviet Union has passed through three distinctive phases: (1) the pre-reform period ("the period of stagnation"), which stretched from the late 1960s to 1985; (2) perestroika, Gorbachev's attempt to reform the Soviet system, which emerged in 1986 and ended, for all practical purposes, in 1990; and (3) the post-Soviet period of political and economic transition, which began somewhat in advance of the formal dissolution of the USSR and continues to unfold. I will illustrate the developments during each of these periods with reference to three specific international environmental issues: pollution in the Baltic Sea, transboundary air pollution, and nuclear power safety.[10]

These three issues were chosen because from the Soviet and post-Soviet perspective, the problems of international collective action associated with them are relatively minor. In each case, the activities giving rise to concern on the part of the former USSR's neighbors have caused even greater damage within the former Soviet Union itself, typically in the immediate vicinity of the sources of the pollution. By comparison, transboundary emissions emanating from outside the former Soviet Union's borders have had a much smaller effect. Consequently, the USSR could have taken unilateral steps at any point to reduce the internal damage associated with these problems. Focusing on these three issues thus allows us to hold the effects of the international contractual environment more or less constant and direct our attention more squarely onto the effects of domestic politics.

Brezhnev, détente, and subterranean learning

Due to the extremely hierarchical and centralized structure of the Soviet political system prior to late 1989, environmental policy during the Soviet period was above all a function of the coalition-building strategy pursued by the reigning Soviet leader. Although no aspiring Soviet politician could hope to become or remain General Secretary without cultivating his own base of personal power and appealing to powerful interests within the ruling elite, political outcomes at the apex of the Soviet hierarchy were not simply the mechanical result of clashing vectors of political power or group interests. Instead, rival candidates for the position of General Secretary also sought to demonstrate that they offered innovative and distinctive solutions to the USSR's most pressing problems. Thus, each leader's coalition-building strategy was a product of political entrepreneurship as well as the constellation of parochial interests within the Soviet elite.[11]

Political entrepreneurship at the apex of the Soviet hierarchy had a twofold effect upon environmental protection. First, the leader's strategy defined the *domestic* context of environmental politics by determining the priority of environmental protection relative to other goals, and by molding the institutional framework within which environmental regulation took place. Secondly, the General Secretary's coalition-building strategy also determined the permissible scope of *international* environmental cooperation by establishing the relative importance of cooperation versus confrontation in East–West relations. The coalition-building strategies pursued by the two dominant Soviet leaders during the period under consideration, Leonid Brezhnev and Mikhail Gorbachev, set strikingly different parameters along both of these axes. Indeed, the differences are so profound that the transition from one leadership strategy to the next marks a distinct historical dividing line, despite the fact that fundamental structural changes took place only quite late in the perestroika period.

In late 1964, the pugnacious Nikita Khrushchev was unceremoniously ousted from his position as General Secretary of the CPSU after his increasingly radical assaults on the institutional legacy of Stalinism alienated the most powerful constituencies within the Soviet political elite. His successor, Leonid Brezhnev, advanced a much less confrontational coalition-building strategy.[12] Brezhnev sought to conciliate the elite by eschewing fundamental political and economic reforms and by basing his economic strategy upon ambitious programs of capital investment in the sectors of greatest interest to conservative groups: agriculture, energy, heavy industry, and defense. At the same time, Brezhnev also sought to extend his appeal to the rapidly growing urban stratum of well-educated professionals, scientists, and technocrats, a group hitherto courted by his rivals. Thus, beginning in late 1969, Brezhnev increasingly spoke of the importance of specialist participation in policy-making and expanded economic ties with the capitalist West, although he was careful to stress the need for increased vigilance in order to minimize the danger of attendant ideological contamination. This pattern of domestic coalition-building set the parameters for environmental protection in the USSR until the emergence of perestroika.[13]

At first glance, it is difficult to see why environmental protection should have proved so intractable a problem in Brezhnev's Soviet Union. In comparison with its Western neighbors, the USSR was blessed with a number of putative advantages when it came to pollution control and natural resource conservation. The consumption and distribution of scarce resources was dictated by central planning, almost down to the last detail, so the wasteful competition of self-interested, profit-maximizing firms, the scourge of environmentalists in the West, was entirely absent. Moreover, state ownership of almost everything implied that externalities would almost immediately be internalized. And indeed the USSR was among the very first countries to pass environmental protection legislation and to set highly restrictive standards on the disposal of industrial, agricultural, and municipal wastes. By the late 1960s, Soviet environmental standards were comparable to those in the leading Western countries, and they remained so throughout the Soviet period.

In practice, however, implementation of these noble goals proved to be highly problematic. Environmental protection and natural resource conservation in the USSR suffered from all of the defects of the Soviet planning system, as well as the ideological burden of Marxism–Leninism, the weakness and fragmentation of the environmental regulatory agencies, the impenetrability of the central economic ministries, and the absence of an autonomous public arena in which the advocates of more aggressive environmental protection might mobilize support for their cause.[14] These structural obstacles were compounded by the comparatively low political priority attached to environmental protection by the Soviet leadership before Gorbachev. Although professing to support environmental protection, and even willing to devote significant sums of money toward that purpose, the leadership was rarely willing to expend the *political* capital necessary to ensure that its good intentions were realized. And, indeed, it could hardly have been otherwise: a genuine attempt to implement these goals would not only have alienated Brezhnev's most influential supporters, but would also have meant forgoing short-term economic gains at a time when the Soviet economy was already stumbling – quite inadvertently – toward "zero growth."

As a consequence of these domestic political constraints, the USSR made relatively little progress in environmental protection during the two decades preceding the emergence of perestroika. The state-controlled domestic structure of the Soviet regime, in combination with the leadership's emphasis upon military procurement and heavy industrial development, generated a domestic political milieu in which effective environmental regulation was exceedingly difficult. The advocates of environmental protection could only rarely expand the scope of conflict beyond the very narrow limits prescribed by the Soviet leadership, yet within these limits military and industrial interests reigned supreme. These same political impediments also stymied the growth of environmental knowledge: Soviet environmental specialists found it difficult either to measure the amount of pollution generated within their own country or to learn about the latest advances in the West.

Paradoxically, however, the very same coalition-building strategy that frustrated environmental protection at home also provided an external window of opportunity. By the end of the 1960s, it had become increasingly apparent that Brezhnev's ambitious economic policies would fail without additional investment capital. The only way to accomplish this without further redistribution of the domestic budgetary pie was to attract Western capital, which Brezhnev hoped to achieve through the selective relaxation of Cold War tensions.[15] For this strategy to work, the Soviet leadership had to offer the West some evidence of its good intentions, but it had to do so in such a way that the key interests of the ruling coalition – which favored a rapid arms buildup and aggressive competition in the developing world – were not threatened. As it happened, this shift in Brezhnev's coalition-building strategy coincided with the emergence of environmental protection as a prominent international issue. After some initial fumbling – most notably, the decision to boycott the 1972 Stockholm Conference in protest against the UN's failure to accord East Germany full membership – the Soviet leadership realized that it could express its cooperativeness by engaging in international environmental cooperation: a concession that posed a relatively small threat to the internal or external security of the Soviet state, yet one of considerable interest to its Western counterparts. In these discussions, the Soviet Union tended to respond almost automatically to the issues raised by the Western countries, for the substance of this cooperation was far less important than the appearance of cooperativeness itself.

The proximate motivations which led the Soviet government to engage in East–West environmental cooperation varied from case to case. The conclusion in 1973 of the Helsinki Convention to combat pollution in the Baltic Sea was a product of Brezhnev's initial campaign to improve East–West relations – an approach reinforced by the fact that Baltic Sea cooperation placed additional pressure on West Germany to recognize its eastern neighbor, one of the last major stumbling blocks to the advancement of détente. The USSR's support for the conclusion of the 1979 Convention on Long-Range Transboundary Air Pollution (LRTAP) was part of Brezhnev's unsuccessful effort to forestall the subsequent unravelling of détente, and Soviet acceptance of the LRTAP sulfur protocol in 1984 was intended both as an olive branch to Western Europe and as a diplomatic coup against the recalcitrant United States, which refused to sign the protocol. In both cases, the Soviet leadership had no particular interest in the environmental issues under discussion; it simply went along with Western concerns in order to advance its broader political and economic objectives.

The proof of the Soviet government's substantive disinterest lay in the limitations which it placed upon environmental cooperation with the West. In the Baltic Sea case, the Soviet government insisted that all international activities be restricted to the open waters of the Baltic; since the narrow sea's coastal waters constituted not only its most polluted part but also a considerable portion of its area, this was hardly evidence of serious environmental concern. Likewise, in international discussions of transboundary air pollution, the USSR refused to release any raw data about the size or content of its industrial emissions – the military feared that such data could be used by clever Western intelligence agents to map the layout of the Soviet industrial complex – and the geographical scope of Soviet participation was limited to the western portion of the USSR. Even the USSR's acceptance of the sulfur protocol was not a compelling demonstration of official concern about acidification or long-range air pollution, since the Soviet government expected to meet the agreed targets anyway as a result of changes in its energy policies.[16]

Yet having agreed to cooperate with the West on these issues, the Soviet government could not avoid devoting greater scientific, economic, and political resources to them. To begin with, East–West environmental cooperation stimulated changes in domestic legislation and regulation, although the practical results of these reforms uniformly fell short of the Soviet government's declared intentions. More importantly, East–West environmental cooperation expanded and strengthened the position of the Soviet specialists interested in the solution of these problems, providing them with otherwise unavailable opportunities to interact with their Western counterparts. Although most of the knowledge which Soviet specialists gained in the process could not be immediately put into effect, their experience did constitute an important reservoir of "subterranean learning" that could quickly be brought to bear once domestic political circumstances changed.[17]

Ironically, the most marked behavioral change of the pre-reform period occurred in the area of nuclear power safety, precisely that area in which East–West interaction was subjected to the tightest restrictions. Had it not been for the construction of two Soviet reactors in Finland – part of the effort to balance trade between the two countries – it is doubtful that there would have been any meaningful interaction at all. Yet Soviet participation in the construction of the Loviisa nuclear power plant led to the adoption of more aggressive safety standards and techniques, and the overall safety of the Soviet nuclear industry was unquestionably improved as a result. Unfortunately, these improvements were primarily limited to the pressurized-water wing of the nuclear engineering industry, the only group to participate directly in the project. The lessons learned at Loviisa were not absorbed by the more influential group committed to the design and exploitation of the graphite-moderated pressure-tube reactor, or RBMK – the type that was later to explode at Chernobyl.

Gorbachev and the greening of the USSR

Shortly after midnight on 26 April 1986, the no. 4 reactor at the Chernobyl nuclear power station erupted. The force of the blast flung the roof off the reactor housing – there was no outer containment shell – and hurled the contents of the reactor core into the atmosphere. As Soviet firefighting teams and military units fought to bury the burning reactor under thousands of tons of sand, lead, and concrete – efforts which, despite the enormous human costs incurred, may have done little to mitigate the disaster – tens of millions of curies of radioactive material were released into the atmosphere. A considerable portion of this material coalesced into a giant plume which drifted over much of the Northern Hemisphere as it settled. In the end, scores of people were dead, hundreds of thousands had been evacuated, and millions more, both within the USSR and abroad, had been exposed to elevated levels of radiation.[18]

That the Chernobyl accident occurred just as a new General Secretary,

Mikhail Gorbachev, was launching an audacious effort to reform the Soviet system is one of history's great conjunctures. It is impossible to know how history might have been altered if the Chernobyl accident had been averted at the last minute, or if it had occurred two years earlier, or two years later. But it is surely safe to say that the Chernobyl disaster, by exposing the corruption, ineptitude, and callousness of the Soviet system, provided a crucial impetus to Gorbachev's fledgling reform campaign at a time when he needed it most; and it is equally indisputable that the conjunction of the accident and Gorbachev's reform effort fundamentally transformed the domestic and international context of environmental politics in the USSR.[19]

Environmental protection figured prominently in Gorbachev's reform strategy from the very outset, even prior to the Chernobyl disaster. This was due in part to genuine concern; by the early 1980s, environmental degradation in many areas of the USSR had reached critical levels, with deleterious consequences for both the economy and public health. Equally important from the point of view of Gorbachev and his advisers, however, were the political gains to be made by calling attention to the Soviet Union's environmental woes. At home, criticism of the Soviet Union's past environmental record implied criticism of the Brezhnev regime, and, by extension, of the surviving conservative opponents of Gorbachev's reform program.[20] Environmentalism was also seen as a politically safe way to encourage pressure from below upon a recalcitrant bureaucracy; accordingly, environmentalism was one of the first popular movements permitted to flourish openly as political controls were selectively relaxed.

Environmental protection also played a prominent role in Gorbachev's foreign policy. International ecological interdependence became a watchword of the "new political thinking," the radically revisionist view of international relations personified by Gorbachev and Foreign Minister Eduard Shevardnadze.[21] This new-found interest in international environmental cooperation was dictated less by environmental concerns than by broader political considerations. Neither the political leadership nor the specialist community believed that the solution of the USSR's environmental woes depended upon the reduction of transboundary pollutants emanating from outside its borders, nor, at this stage, did either group view international cooperation primarily as a promising source of large-scale financial assistance. Rather, this shift was a continuation and intensification of the basic pattern which prevailed under Brezhnev: the Soviet leadership sought to use environmental cooperativeness to advance its overall foreign policy goals, while environmental specialists and officials took advantage of the opportunities thus created to advance the cause of *domestic* environmental protection – albeit now with the full blessing of the top leadership.[22]

From a political standpoint, this "greening" of Soviet foreign policy served a dual purpose. First, it helped to discredit the foreign policy platform of the old guard Communists, who, in order to maintain their privileged political positions, continued to argue that class conflict must remain the dominant consideration in international politics. In order to undermine this claim, and therefore the political grip of the conservatives, the reformers had to find convincing arguments in support of their contention that the common interests of humanity superseded class divisions and differences in social systems.[23] What more convincing evidence could there be of this counterclaim – especially in the wake of Chernobyl – than a looming global ecological catastrophe that threatened capitalists and socialists alike?

The second target of the new emphasis upon international environmental cooperation was Gorbachev's audience abroad. The reformers believed that a necessary (although clearly not sufficient) condition for the success of perestroika was a major reduction of the Soviet Union's military spending and its commitments abroad, as well as the integration of the USSR into the world capitalist economy. Since the reformers would be politically vulnerable at home if they were seen to be deliberately and unilaterally weakening the USSR's international position, they had to find some way to convince Western leaders to join the USSR in the disarmament process. The emphasis upon the global environment served this goal by promoting the image of a reformed, activist, humanitarian Soviet leadership and by raising the specter of a common problem that could only be averted by jointly reassigning military expenditures to environmental protection.

In terms of its underlying political logic, then, Gorbachev's approach to international environmental policy was remarkably similar in many ways to that pursued by his predecessors – but the practical consequences were quite different. Due to the fundamentally more radical character of the coalition-building strategy pursued by Gorbachev, his "peace offensive" was complemented by a serious effort to revamp domestic environmental policy-making, and indeed domestic politics in general. Moreover, in comparison to Brezhnev, Gorbachev was far less constrained by the need to cater to the interests of the military–industrial complex and the guardians of Marxist–Leninist purity; on the contrary, his whole strategy depended upon the circumvention of the disproportionate influence of those groups. As Gorbachev fought to expand press freedoms, popular political participation, and international transparency, the ability of these entrenched interests to confine political conflict within the sovereign confines of the traditional policy-making structures was gradually whittled away.

As a result, Soviet policies toward international environmental co-operation were increasingly dominated by the activist specialists and diplomats whose efforts had been frustrated during the "years of stagnation." In each of the three cases under consideration, Soviet policy shifted dramatically as these officials sought to bring their country's practices in line with those advocated by their Western counterparts. In the wake of the Chernobyl accident, the Soviet government released a flood of information relating to the disaster and Soviet nuclear power in general, and the USSR began to participate much more actively in the safety programs of the International Atomic Energy Agency. Even bolder positions were taken with regard to pollution in the Baltic Sea and transboundary air pollution. In both cases, the barriers to the free exchange of information were gradually eliminated (although monitoring within the USSR continued to be obstructed by persistent technical and bureaucratic obstacles), and the Soviet government agreed to ambitious targets for reductions in its emissions of transboundary pollutants. Unlike the sulfur protocol, to which the USSR had agreed in 1984, the new commitments undertaken in 1988–1989 (namely a freeze in transboundary emissions of nitrogen oxide by 1994, a 50 percent reduction in the discharge of harmful substances into the Baltic Sea by 1995, and a 50 percent reduction in sulfur dioxide emissions in the north-western USSR, also by 1995) would have involved enormous capital investments and the fundamental restructuring of the entire industrial base of the north-western USSR.

It is important to keep in mind that this ambitious "greening" was not the result of any fundamental change in domestic political structure. The centralized, hierarchical political system that Gorbachev had inherited from his predecessors remained largely intact until 1989, and it was this fact, in combination with the change in leadership strategy at the top, that allowed Soviet environmental specialists to "capture" the levers of policymaking and institute the programs advocated by their respective international epistemic communities. Thus, the initial changes in the USSR's positions toward these issues were the result not of a more general expansion of the scope of political conflict within the Soviet Union, but rather of a redistribution of power within the elite, brought about by a change in the top political leadership.

However, this idyllic interlude of enlightened technocracy was fated to be short-lived. As Gorbachev met with growing elite opposition to his reform campaign, he responded by redefining his strategy in an increasingly radical direction, encouraging ever greater political pluralism and pressure from below. The result was an unprecedented explosion of environmental activism and pressure for self-determination at the local, regional, and republican levels. The first manifestation of this shift was the formation of a large number of "informal" (i.e., non-governmental) environmentalist clubs and organizations throughout the USSR. Some of these organizations, like the various groups formed in Leningrad to oppose the completion of the nearby dam across the Gulf of Finland, were limited to a specific locality or environmental issue, and could claim only a handful of members; others, like Zelenyy Svit ("Green World") in Ukraine and the Estonian Green Movement, were considerably larger republic-wide organizations. The power of "environmentalism from below" was strengthened still further in 1989–1990 by a series of increasingly competitive elections at the federal, republic, and local levels. Upon assuming office, these newly elected politicians – many of whom had run on "green" platforms – moved quickly to establish new legislative organs to oversee environmental protection at the federal, republican, regional, and local levels. This wave of environmentalism from below peaked in the summer and fall of 1990 when the various local, regional, and republican Soviets voted to halt a long string of environmentally contested projects, including the Leningrad dam and a large number of nuclear power units under construction throughout the USSR.

As the permissible scope of environmental politics expanded, the centralized policy-making elite increasingly lost control over the formulation of environmental policy. In some cases, this structural change reinforced the new policies that had been instituted by the specialist elite; elsewhere, those positions were challenged or ignored. In the Baltic Sea case, the demands of local officials and environmental activists in the Baltic republics and Leningrad meshed quite well with the policies advocated by the environmental epistemic community associated with the Helsinki Commission (HELCOM), the international organization established to oversee cooperative efforts to clean up the sea. It thus appeared that the devolution of environmental policy-making authority to the local level could only enhance the prospects for effective international cooperation. By contrast, the spread of popular environmentalism had no such effect in the transboundary air pollution case. To the extent that local activists and environmental officials were concerned about air pollution, they focused their attention primarily on the short-range deposition of particles and heavy metals rather than the long-range pollutants of concern to the specialists and diplomats involved in international cooperation. The "localization" of environmental protection thus did not appear to bode well for the fulfillment of the USSR's LRTAP obligations.

The expansion of the scope of environmental politics had the greatest impact in the case of nuclear power safety. Although the Chernobyl disaster did increase sensitivity to the problems of nuclear power safety in both the USSR and the West, the Gorbachev leadership did not undertake a major re-evaluation of the Soviet nuclear power program. Local activists took a different view, however, and in 1988–1990 public opposition to the further expansion of nuclear power spread like wildfire. In response, the Soviet government and top nuclear power officials sought to use their carefully cultivated international contacts to *combat* domestic environmental protest, inviting sympathetic teams from the IAEA to inspect several contested plants and to review the Soviet government's handling of the Chernobyl disaster – a strategy made possible by the fact that the international epistemic community in the nuclear safety case was essentially pro-nuclear, and its members less alarmed by the problems of Soviet nuclear engineering than they would subsequently become. Nevertheless, these efforts were unsuccessful, and by mid-1990 it appeared that further expansion of nuclear power in the USSR was extremely unlikely.

But just as suddenly as this storm of public activism had overwhelmed environmental politics in the USSR, it even more suddenly died away. First of all, the public and official attention available for environmental protection was sapped by the chaos into which the USSR plunged in 1990–1991. The political revolution unleashed by Gorbachev's reform effort did not stop with the devolution of political power to the republican, regional, and local levels; instead, the entire political and economic system came apart at the seams. Rationing for basic goods was introduced in individual cities, regions, and republics as territorial officials sought autarkic solutions to the collapse of the Soviet economic system. Soviet-era political institutions provided a poor guide in this new era of pluralist political competition, and so as the Soviet Union split up along regional and republican lines, intense conflict (generally peaceful, but sometimes quite violent) erupted among the various territorial units and between the legislative and executive organs at each level. By December 1991, when Ukraine's vote for independence delivered the *coup de grâce* to the still shuddering corpse of the USSR, interest in environmental protection at both the official and popular levels had already plummeted to a record low.

Secondly, it is clear in retrospect that the burst of popular environmentalism in 1987–1990 was artificially amplified by the peculiar structure of domestic politics during the perestroika period. Thanks to a lifetime of familiarity with the command economy, ordinary citizens and local and regional officials were unused to the notion that there might be a trade-off between environmental protection on the one hand, and employment and the provision of basic services such as heat and electricity on the other. Thus, when local activists and officials demanded the closure of a polluting factory or the halt to the construction of a nearby nuclear power plant, they assumed that Moscow would provide a substitute at no cost to the local economy. Moreover, since environmentalism was one of the earliest forms of independent political activity to receive the imprimatur of the Soviet authorities, it attracted many activists who were actually more interested in the advancement of much broader goals, such as republican independence or the overthrow of the Soviet regime. Environmentalist protest thus initially served as a surrogate for broader political demands. Once these broader goals could be pursued openly, popular mobilization around environmental issues declined precipitately.[24]

Thus, in the end, the tidal wave of popular and elite environmental consciousness that swept the USSR between 1986 and 1990 was overtaken by events. Gorbachev's reform campaign gave way to economic collapse, political chaos, and the disintegration of the Soviet Union; Gorbachev himself retired in disgrace. To the extent that the ambitious international environmental obligations taken on by the Gorbachev regime were fulfilled, this was due almost entirely to the catastrophic downturn in economic and agricultural production that accompanied the collapse of the USSR. While this inadvertent reduction in emissions provided some solace to Western environmentalists, it was hardly the outcome that Gorbachev and his advisers had envisaged during the heady summer days of perestroika.

Bribery and blackmail: international environmental politics in the post-Soviet era

The disintegration of the Soviet regime ushered in an even more fundamental revolution in the domestic and international context of environmental protection. Internally, the breakup of the USSR was accompanied by the further decentralization of political and economic decision-making, both among and within the fifteen Newly Independent States, and (in the European successor states) by the spread and institutionalization of democratic political institutions, non-governmental organizations, and freedom of speech and the press. Internationally, the demise of the Soviet Union marked the end of the East–West rivalry that had reigned for forty years, and the virtual evaporation of the political barriers that had frustrated earlier efforts at international environmental cooperation. Official controls on foreign participation in the collection and dissemination of environmental information were dramatically relaxed – though by no means eliminated entirely – and a flood of foreign officials, advisers, activists, and lobbyists now poured into the easily accessible successor states, seeking internal allies and pressing for long-awaited reforms in environmental policy.

However, this new era of democratization and international cooperation did not lead automatically to the speedy solution of the successor states' environmental problems. First, the post-Soviet period was characterized not only by accelerating democratization, but also by persistent administrative and economic crisis, and by a sharp drop in popular pressure for aggressive environmental protection. This combination of indifference and instability made it difficult for external actors to find willing and able partners in the successor states. Secondly, the end of the Cold War removed the strategic incentives for environmental cooperation that had motivated the USSR. As a result, the environmental priorities of the successor states ceased to accord so neatly with those of their Western neighbors. Western activists and officials were interested primarily in environmental problems with transboundary implications, while their counterparts in the successor states were interested primarily in projects which promised local environmental and economic benefits – and even then they were typically unwilling to contribute much to the cost.

In the face of this unexpected resistance, Western governments and international lending organizations increasingly resorted to bribery:

offers to subsidize specific environmental protection measures within the Newly Independent States. However, this tactic proved to have several undesirable and unavoidable side-effects. First, it encouraged the successor states to pass the costs of environmental protection on to their more affluent neighbors wherever possible. Secondly, the successor states realize that if they continued to operate risky or "dirty" factories and power plants, external actors would feel pressured to step in to minimize the associated environmental dangers – funding modernization projects that would, in the process, make those facilities more profitable and reliable. Finally, the successor states now had an incentive to blackmail their more wealthy neighbors by threatening to engage in highly visible and environmentally threatening activities – such as the modernization of the Chernobyl nuclear power plant – while promising that these activities could be halted with sufficient quantities of Western assistance.[25]

The first and most obvious effect of the collapse of Soviet socialism was the radical fragmentation and decentralization of political and economic power. Throughout 1990, the Soviet government increasingly lost ground in its battle with the peripheries, and at the end of 1991 the USSR was formally partitioned into fifteen independent successor states. Moreover, political and economic power within these states themselves was generally far less centralized than it had been in the USSR. While it was not always easy to detect signs of genuine political pluralism in post-Soviet Central Asia, most of the European successor states were characterized by quite lively (if not always peaceful) political competition. In addition, the collapse of Soviet rule was also accompanied by a shift of power from the central government to regional and local officials, a process that was particularly pronounced in the badly fragmented Russian Federation. This was not an orderly or planned process – the immediate result was near anarchy throughout much of the former USSR – but by and large this decentralization of power was gradually institutionalized as political authority was fitfully and unevenly reconstituted in the successor states. At the same time, the governments of the successor states loosened their hold on economic activities within their borders, giving the directors of individual plants and public utilities ever greater leeway to negotiate directly with the representatives of foreign organizations. This increasing autonomy was due both to the continuing weakness of national, regional, and local governments, and to accelerating efforts to privatize state enterprises, or at least to increase their share of self-financing. As a result, responsibility for environmental protection was now dispersed among a far wider cast of characters than had been the case during the Soviet period, ranging from national governments (of which there were now many more) to the directors of individual factories and power plants.

The successor states also continued to be racked by economic and political crises that drained their administrative capacities and diverted popular and elite attention from environmental protection. Industrial production and real wages plummeted, and for the first time millions of workers faced the prospect of genuine unemployment. Even when workers' names remained on the books, they often failed to receive their pay for many months at a time. Under these circumstances, it was not surprising that many ordinary people subscribed to the motto, "Better dirty bread than no bread at all." Popular and elite attention was also sapped by skyrocketing crime rates and the continuing political turmoil that accompanied the disintegration of the USSR, its effects ranging from smoldering ethnic tensions in Ukraine and the Baltic states to open warfare in the Caucasus, Central Asia, and the streets of Moscow. Environmental specialists and officials in the successor states thus found themselves virtually bereft of support from either above or below – indeed, many found themselves bereft of employment, due to plummeting state support for science.

This revolution within the former USSR was accompanied by an equally dramatic revolution in the broader international political environment, and hence in international environmental politics. First, the collapse of Soviet socialism led to the end of the Cold War, and thus to the link between the "high politics" of East–West relations and receptivity to Western environmental concerns. During the Cold War, the Soviet government shifted its environmental priorities in the direction of the issues raised by its Western neighbors, since it was more interested in the appearance of cooperativeness than in the substance of the issues under discussion. By contrast, decision-makers in the post-Soviet period felt little need to engage in cooperation for cooperation's sake. Instead, they approached international environmental cooperation from the perspective of their own (usually local) environmental and economic priorities – priorities that were not necessarily identical to those of their prospective Western partners.

Secondly, the ongoing political and economic turmoil in the former USSR compelled Western actors to become far more directly involved in environmental policy-making in the successor states. Prior to the disintegration of the Soviet political and economic order, most environmental specialists and officials (both in the USSR and abroad) had assumed that the Soviet government was capable of autonomously implementing appropriate environmental protection measures, provided that it could be convinced of the desirability of doing so. By late 1990, this was manifestly no longer the case; the flailing USSR was clearly in no condition to resolve its environmental problems on its own. Consequently, Western governments and international organizations became increasingly involved in identifying, planning, and subsidizing environmental protection projects in the former USSR. Thus, as the 1990s progressed, environmental protection increasingly became an international project, taking place as much in foreign capitals and international organizations as in the successor states themselves.

The Western decision to subsidize environmental protection in the East – typically through some combination of grants and loans – was not an altruistic gesture. By the late 1980s, all of the Soviet Union's Western neighbors had undertaken expensive measures to reduce industrial and municipal emissions and improve nuclear power safety within their territories. Further measures to reduce those emissions could only lead to diminishing marginal returns, especially when compared to the much greater improvements in Western environmental quality which could be obtained by investing in more basic and less expensive environmental protection measures in the former Soviet Union and Eastern Europe. (In most cases, Western donors refused to pay the entire cost; instead, they attempted to subsidize the desired measures just to the point at which the ecological self-interest of the Eastern states would lead them to cover the residual costs: after all, the citizens of these countries were suffering far more from the activities in question than were their Western neighbors.) Moreover, Western subsidization projects were also designed to serve Western economic interests, since the provision of large amounts of aid was typically tied to the purchase of equipment and consulting services from the donor countries.

In practice, it was not always an easy task to piece together successful international projects in the post-Soviet period. Cooperation could proceed only when there was a propitious fit between internal and external environmental and economic interests, and when actors in the target states and regions were able to assemble the administrative, financial, and scientific resources necessary for participation in joint projects. Generally speaking, successful environmental cooperation depended upon two conditions: the economic interests of polluting enterprises or public utilities had to be directly engaged, and there had to be a government at some level of the territorial hierarchy with both the will and resources to guarantee the repayment of credits or otherwise smooth the way for joint projects.

Of the three issues under consideration, international cooperation proceeded most swiftly in the area of Baltic Sea pollution. Even after the breakup of the USSR, self-inflicted inland and coastal water pollution remained the single most pressing environmental problem facing the heirs to the Soviet Baltic coast – the Baltic states and the Russian regions of Kaliningrad and Leningrad/St. Petersburg.[26] Moreover, since much of this pollution ultimately found its way into the open Baltic and the coastal waters of the other littoral states, the successor states' Western neighbors shared an interest in its abatement, particularly since further investment in their own environmental controls had grown prohibitively expensive. The result of this happy confluence of interests was the Baltic Sea Joint Comprehensive Environmental Action Programme (JCP), drawn up in 1990–1992 under the aegis of HELCOM. Perhaps the most ambitious international environmental program in human history, the JCP identified more than 100 municipal, industrial, and agricultural "hot spots" in the Baltic Sea basin, and also included programs designed to strengthen national regulatory systems and institutions, applied research, and public environmental awareness. The total cost of the program over twenty years was projected to be about 18 billion ECU, of which 10 billion would be used to address the "hot spots." Funding for these projects was pieced together through elaborate co-financing schemes which brought together grants and credits from individual Western countries and the European Union, loans from international lending institutions such as the World Bank, EBRD, and Nordic Investment Bank, and contributions from the recipient states themselves. By early 1995, one-quarter of the total investments envisaged by the program had been allocated or reserved; of this, approximately 820 million ECU were earmarked for investment projects in the former socialist states.[27]

Although the HELCOM program achieved an astonishing degree of progress over quite a short period, international cooperation did not move ahead with uniform speed across the ex-Soviet Baltic seaboard. First of all, progress was primarily achieved through investment in public infrastructure (primarily in municipal waste-water treatment) as opposed to the regulation of industrial emissions or non-point sources such as agriculture and transportation. Non-point sources were not amenable to the primary tool favored by external donors – technology-intensive, easily monitored capital investment projects – and while industrial sources were amenable to such an approach, donors were less certain that investments in these facilities would be repaid. Secondly, successful cooperation depended upon the political, scientific, and economic resources commanded by the relevant decision-makers across the post-Soviet Baltic seaboard. Implementation of the HELCOM program moved forward most rapidly in the three Baltic republics, which were now independent masters of their own fates; by contrast, progress was much slower in Kaliningrad and St. Petersburg, which remained part of the much more vast Russian Federation, and thus had to compete with many other claimants for Moscow's attention. Finally, the successor states were interested only in projects that would reduce pollution in their own inland and coastal waters; they were considerably less eager to contribute to the cost of measures that would primarily benefit the open sea, such as enhanced nitrogen removal at municipal waste-water treatment plants.

Unlike the comprehensive program pursued in the Baltic Sea case, international cooperation to reduce long-range transboundary air pollution in the post-Soviet period proceeded on a fairly limited and ad hoc basis. Despite efforts to draw up a comprehensive investment plan to reduce long-range air pollution throughout Europe, Western countries had relatively little interest in subsidizing the reduction of air pollution in most parts of the former USSR – for the very simple reason that the prevailing winds blow from west to east, and thus carry most of that pollution further into the successor states' own territories. Consequently, most areas in the former Soviet Union, including those where the local effect of air pollution was most severe, could not count upon significant amounts of external aid. The exceptions to this rule were those areas sufficiently close to the Nordic countries (mainly Estonia and the border areas of north-western Russia)to generate transboundary air pollution problems despite the prevailing west-to-east wind pattern. Of particular concern were a pair of aging nickel smelters on the Kola Peninsula, whose emissions had already destroyed much of the surrounding environment on the Russian side of the border and were now blamed for the deteriorating quality of the forests in the adjacent regions of Finland, Sweden, and Norway. Particularly worrisome was the Pechenganikel smelting combine, located a scant few kilometers from the Norwegian border. Indeed, as more information about these plants became available in the late 1980s and early 1990s, passions in the Nordic countries grew so inflamed that some Norwegian environmentalists even called for the bombing of the Pechenganikel plant.[28]

In order to reduce transboundary air pollution from the adjacent areas of the former USSR, the Nordic states launched a variety of subsidization proposals, including the modernization of the production processes of major industrial polluters – such as an iron pellet plant in Karelia and the Pechenganikel combine – and the promotion of cleaner thermal power, whether through the installation of modern flue gas scrubbers or (as in St. Petersburg) through participation in the construction of cleaner gas-fired plants. Although the reduction of long-range air pollution was of relatively little interest to local decision-makers – after all, most of it wound up in some other republic or oblast – these projects successfully appealed to local and national officials' interest in the continued operation of major industrial employers, reliable energy production, and the reduction of local air pollution. And, of course, this cooperation received support from factory and power plant directors, whose immediate economic interests were served by the modernization programs. Even so, negotiations over the modernization of the Pechenganikel combine dragged on for several years, due to the extremely large costs involved. In March 1996, Russia and Norway finally reached a formal agreement to proceed with the project – but only after persistent pressure from the Nordic countries and the selection of an alternative tender which brought the projected costs down from $640 million to $260 million.[29]

Of the three issues under consideration, nuclear power safety proved to be the most difficult and controversial problem for international cooperation in the post-Soviet period. Within two years of attaining independence, the governments of the four successor states that had inherited the Soviet Union's nuclear power plants – Russia, Ukraine, Lithuania, and Armenia – had decided to maintain, restart, or expand those facilities, despite the fact that many of these same politicians had strenuously objected to the technology during their earlier rise to power. Unfortunately, this change of heart was not a response to any improvement in the safety of these facilities; on the contrary, as the consumers of electric power increasingly refused to pay their bills, nuclear power plants found themselves unable to pay for routine maintenance, fuel, or even wages, much less for extensive modernization plans.[30] Rather, the return to nuclear power was dictated by more immediate political and economic concerns: Lithuania, Armenia, and Ukraine quickly learned that imports of fossil fuels could easily be disrupted as a result of warfare, unpaid debts, or political conflicts with Russia, while the Russian government itself (encouraged by the powerful oil, gas, and nuclear power lobbies) sought to free up its valuable fossil fuel reserves for export.

Ironically, the evaporation of the indigenous anti-nuclear power movement coincided with a sharp increase in *external* concern about the safety of Soviet-built nuclear power plants. Despite the shock of the Chernobyl accident, Western fears really began to mount only in 1990–1991, when Western nuclear experts finally gained relatively free access to nuclear facilities in the former Soviet Union and Eastern Europe; the alarming conclusions of these inspections were underscored by a string of disturbing accidents at the Chernobyl, Leningrad, and Kola nuclear power plants between 1991 and 1993. International concern was particularly aroused by Ukraine's decision in late 1993 to keep the Chernobyl nuclear power plant in operation – overturning an earlier decision to close the plant as soon as possible – despite the fact that the facility continued to be plagued by safety problems: the plant's second unit had been shut down after a major fire in October 1991, and the condition of the "sarcophagus" covering the highly contaminated remains of the destroyed fourth unit continued to deteriorate, threatening the integrity of the entire complex.

Faced with the successor states' determination to proceed with the exploitation of nuclear power (and the lack of any popular anti-nuclear opposition that could prevent them from doing so), concerned Western governments had little choice but to offer to subsidize safety improvements at Soviet-built nuclear plants in the former Socialist bloc – even at those installations which they would have preferred to see shut immediately, such as the older VVERs and the Chernobyl-type RBMKs. The proffered assistance took a variety of forms, ranging from twinning programs with nuclear power plants in the West to large-scale modernization projects channeled through a Nuclear Safety Account set up within the EBRD. External attention naturally focused first of all on the plants nearest to Western Europe, such as the Kola and Leningrad plants in Russia and the Ignalina plant in Lithuania. However, the 1986 Chernobyl disaster had demonstrated that a nuclear accident anywhere would be a disaster for nuclear power everywhere, and since most of the major Western states continued to rely upon nuclear power for some portion of their energy needs, their efforts were by no means confined to nearby facilities.

Despite the clear coincidence of environmental interests between the successor states and the West in this case – even having decided to proceed with the development of nuclear power, the successor states had no more wish to relive the experience of Chernobyl than did their Western neighbors – progress was often slow and frustrating. To a considerable extent, this was the result of the ubiquitous economic and administrative confusion that also hampered cooperation to combat air and water pollution: donated safety equipment was held up in customs for months at a time, and the indebtedness of electricity consumers to nuclear power producers sapped the resources available for safety improvements. However, progress was also slowed by several factors peculiar to the nuclear safety issue itself.

First, Western penetration was resisted by the nuclear power industry in Russia and Ukraine, where it had emerged from the wreckage of the USSR with much of its clout and most of its perquisites intact. True, the post-Soviet nuclear power complex was not as monolithic as it once had been; the facilities in Ukraine, Lithuania, and Armenia were no longer under the direct control of the Russian Ministry of Atomic Energy (although personal and organizational links remained strong), and even in Russia individual plants and R&D institutes now had far greater autonomy that they had prior to the disintegration of the USSR. Nevertheless, the leaders of the nuclear power complex in Russia and Ukraine (where the development of nuclear power had been most extensive) retained a powerful veto over the shape and extent of cooperation with the West. Spokesmen for the nuclear industry painted Western safety complaints as a Machiavellian campaign to capture the supply of nuclear power equipment to Eastern Europe and the former USSR, thereby removing a potent international competitor. While industry leaders were not opposed to wide-ranging cooperation with the West, they resolutely opposed any agreements that would undermine the viability of the indigenous nuclear power industry, such as the wholesale import of Western components or the construction of Western nuclear power plants on a turnkey basis. These sentiments were shared by many of the directors of individual nuclear power plants – particularly those equipped with RBMK reactors, which could not be brought up to Western safety standards in any case – and by sympathetic political leaders already suspicious of Western intentions.

Secondly, the successor states were slow to adopt national legislation that would absolve participating Western firms from liability in the event of an accident. This legislation was required to bring the successor states' laws in line with the Vienna Convention on Third Party Liability, which assigns sole liability to the operators of nuclear installations, not to their suppliers, and was an essential prerequisite for substantial foreign assistance. Progress on this issue was slowed both by ongoing internal upheaval – the Russian parliament had been on the verge of considering nuclear power legislation when it was forcibly dissolved in October 1993 – and by reluctance to incur any further international financial obligations. Lithuania and Armenia joined the Vienna Convention in 1992 and 1993, respectively, clearing the way for Western participation in their nuclear power programs. As of mid-1996, however, neither Ukraine nor Russia had acceded to the Vienna Convention – although Russia announced its intention of doing so at the nuclear safety summit in Moscow in April 1996. Western governments and the EBRD sought to circumvent this obstacle through various ad hoc agreements exempting foreign suppliers from liability in specific instances, but Russian and Ukrainian intransigence remained a severe sticking point in nuclear safety cooperation.

Finally, the governments of the successor states found themselves in a stronger bargaining position relative to nuclear safety than they were in the other two cases. First, decision-making power in the nuclear field tended to be concentrated at the very top of the political hierarchy. Regional and municipal officials had very little influence over decisions concerning the facilities within their territories and could not strike international deals on their own. Secondly, Western states could not easily offset failure to achieve safety improvements at one nuclear facility with greater progress elsewhere. This was in sharp contrast to the "substitutability" characteristic of most air and water issues: since the goal of reducing the overall level of pollutants in the Baltic Sea or of sulfur deposition in the Nordic countries could be achieved through various combinations of local projects, frustration on one front could usually be offset by greater success elsewhere – a consideration not lost on local decision-makers, who had an incentive to secure external funds for their own local problems before that money moved elsewhere. (The main exception to this rule was the protracted bargaining over the modernization of the Pechenganikel smelting combine, whose emissions could not be offset by reductions elsewhere.) By contrast, safety improvements at one nuclear plant would not reduce the risks of an accident at another: the one was not substitutable for the other. Consequently, officials in the successor states felt little pressure to rush to agreements.

In some cases, the successor states' aggressive bargaining tactics were tantamount to outright blackmail. This was nowhere more evident than in the dispute over the fate of the Chernobyl nuclear power plant. Following the Ukrainian government's decision in late 1993 to keep the plant open, Western governments demanded that the station be closed as previously planned. After two years of diplomatic wrangling, the Ukrainian government agreed in principle to close Chernobyl by the year 2000, but only if the West agreed to contribute $4.5 billion toward the decommissioning of the plant, the reconstruction of the ailing sarcophagus (the hastily constructed "tomb" surrounding the destroyed fourth unit), the resettlement of the plant's workforce, and the construction of new generating facilities to replace the electricity produced at Chernobyl.[31] Plant director Serhiy Parashyn helpfully suggested that the EU and G-7 countries might raise this sum by contributing a mere $200 million each, noting that "this price is not very high for an advanced country that would like to solve an enormous task and rid its own people of worries."[32]

In December 1995, Ukraine, G-7 members, and the European Commission signed a memorandum of understanding which called for assistance of $2.3 billion in exchange for the closure of Chernobyl: approximately $500 million in grants for short-term safety improvements and decommissioning, and $1.8 billion in credits for the modernization of existing hydroelectric and thermal power plants and the completion of two unfinished nuclear reactors.[33] However, progress toward implementation of this agreement stalled in early 1996. Ukraine complained that the grant proportion was too small, and that the amount Ukraine itself was expected to contribute (approximately $1 billion) was too large. Ukraine also pointed out that the G-7 package did not constitute genuinely "new" money, since it included a number of projects that were already underway when the Chernobyl negotiations began. Finally, Ukraine refused to accede to the Vienna Convention on nuclear liability, insisting that it lacked the resources to back such a commitment.[34] In April 1996, Ukraine announced that the plant's first unit – an aging "first generation" RBMK – would be removed from operation by the end of the year, and that its fuel channels would not be replaced as originally planned.[35] However, the Ukrainian government did not rule out a restart of the only slightly less antiquated second unit, and in any case the "second generation" third unit could conceivably continue to operate until well into the twenty-first century.

Conclusion: the perils of pluralism

In many respects, the collapse of the USSR was a blessing for environmental protection. The environment was freed from the heavy hand of Soviet-style socialism, which consistently subjugated public health and environmental protection to the voracious demands of military might and heavy industrial development, while squashing the free flow of information and debate necessary to deal effectively with the terrible ecological consequences of this behavior, either internally or at the international level. All of the protestations of Soviet ideologists aside, the USSR and its Eastern European satellites performed astonishingly badly in their efforts to cope with the ecological side effects of industrialization and urbanization, certainly far worse than their rivals in Western Europe and North America. In retrospect, then, it would seem that effective action to resolve Europe's environmental problems ultimately hinged upon the emergence of political pluralism in the USSR and Eastern Europe – a development that necessarily entailed the demise of Soviet totalitarianism, even if its trappings could somehow have been maintained.

Yet, ironically, the emergence of genuine political competition in the USSR was followed by a precipitous decline in official and popular support for aggressive environmental cooperation, whether at home or in collaboration with the West. The initial opening of the Soviet political system was attended by an impressive burst of environmentalist activism, but this phenomenon was artificially stimulated by patterns of political conflict peculiar to the perestroika period: the assumption that the central government in Moscow would bear all of the economic costs of improved environmental protection, and the possibility of exploiting environmentalist protest as a surrogate for broader forms of political dissent. After the victory of the peripheries over the center, this enthusiasm dissipated. Although demands for improved environmental quality could now be voiced freely and openly, the political salience of environmental problems decreased, as did the administrative and economic wherewithal for addressing them. In some cases, the territorial fragmentation of the Soviet Union also exacerbated the problems of collective action; to the extent that the USSR's heirs could export their pollution problems to neighboring republics and oblasts, the incentive to take precipitant action to control internal emissions was correspondingly reduced.

The demise of the USSR had an equally paradoxical impact upon international efforts to promote environmental protection in the successor states. On the one hand, the demise of totalitarianism opened up vast new opportunities for Western specialists and officials to ascertain the precise level of danger emanating from the former socialist states and to insert themselves into the policy-making processes of those states. On the other hand, the collapse of the Soviet regime destroyed the very combination that had fueled past receptivity to the Western environmental agenda: the existence of a highly centralized and authoritarian regime whose leaders were capable of orienting the nation's environmental priorities as they saw fit, and an atmosphere of international hostility (itself largely the product of the expansionist policies pursued by the USSR) that gave those leaders an incentive to project a more cooperative image abroad. Once that combination was gone, receptivity to the Western environmental agenda inevitably grew more selective – especially given the political and economic chaos that accompanied the collapse of the USSR – and dependent upon large influxes of money from abroad.

It is one of the most bitter ironies of the late twentieth century that a reform movement fueled by ecological tragedy and dedicated to the transformation of global environmental politics should have ended with the virtual evaporation of domestic support for environmental protection. Yet the internal advocates of environmental protection in the successor states are now more dependent upon external political, economic, and scientific resources than they were before 1986. In some areas, particularly those situated most closely to Western Europe, the domestic proponents of environmental protection have found sufficient support from external actors to make substantial headway against the obstacles that confront them. However, most of the territories of the former Soviet Union have thus far been left to their own devices, and to a dangerous cycle of economic distress and environmental crisis.

Ultimately, the prospects for effective environmental protection in the former Soviet Union will hinge upon the solution of the superordinate political and economic difficulties that currently absorb popular and official attention. The psychologist Abraham Maslow has argued that human needs may be arranged in a hierarchy in which the "highest" needs, such as self-actualization and interpersonal affection, are dependent upon the fulfillment of "lower" or more basic needs, such as food, shelter, and personal safety. If these more basic needs are not gratified, then individuals will tend to set the pursuit of higher-order concerns aside.[36] Building upon Maslow's insight, Ronald Inglehart has argued that environmental protection is a "postmaterialist" value: one that flourishes primarily in those societies (and among those members of society) that have already made considerable progress in addressing the more basic problems of economic scarcity and human welfare.[37] This argument has been borne out by public opinion surveys in advanced industrial societies, which have found that environmental concerns are more often associated with a broad "postmaterialist" outlook than with self-interested reactions to particular episodes of local environmental degradation.[38]

From this perspective, the obstacles to aggressive environmental protection in the successor states appear formidable. Given the widespread unemployment, low wages, skyrocketing inflation, rising violence and crime, and widespread ethnic conflict endemic to all of the successor states, it is not surprising that most ordinary citizens have very little attention left over for environmental protection – even in those areas where the ecological situation is extremely critical. This preoccupation with more basic concerns, more than any fact of domestic political structure or coalition-building, explains the low level of political support for environmental protection and the fact that the environmentalist movement in the former USSR is now utterly dependent upon external financial and organizational assistance.

Of course, there is no reason to expect that the current political and economic crisis will continue indefinitely. To the extent that the successor states succeed in establishing stable and effective state institutions and in introducing viable economic reforms, many of the concerns that now divert attention from environmental protection may be alleviated. Indeed, this is likely to happen sooner rather than later in the areas nearest to Western Europe, particularly the relatively more developed Baltic states – perhaps adding an internal environmentalist "push" to the external "pull" generated by Western penetration and subsidization. But changes in political institutions and economic policies will lead only slowly to a significant improvement in living standards, and the lag between changes of this sort and increased popular support for environmental protection is likely to be longer still. Broad public support for environmental protection in the much more affluent states of Western Europe and North America did not materialize overnight, and there is no reason to expect a radically more rapid blooming of environmental consciousness amid the ruins of the USSR.

Notes

1. For comprehensive reviews of the current state of the environment in the former Soviet Union, see Murray Feshbach, *Ecological Disaster: Cleaning Up the Hidden Legacy of the Soviet Regime* (New York: Twentieth Century Fund Press, 1995); Murray Feshbach and Alfred Friendly, Jr., *Ecocide in the USSR: Health and Nature Under Siege* (New York: Basic Books, 1992); and, D. J. Peterson, *Troubled Lands: The Legacy of Soviet Environmental Destruction* (Boulder: Westview Press, 1993).
2. The concept of "international socialization" (and its relationship to domestic regime change) is analyzed at further length by G. John Ikenberry and Charles A. Kupchan, "Socialization and Hegemonic Power," *International Organization* 44:3 (1990), 283–315.
3. See Jyrki Käkönen (ed.), *Dreaming of the Barents Region: Interpreting Cooperation in the Euro-Arctic Rim* (Tampere, Finland: Tampere Peace Research Institute, 1996).
4. See especially Thomas Risse-Kappen, "Public Opinion, Domestic Structure, and Foreign Policy in Liberal Democracies," *World Politics* 43:4 (1991), 479–512; Thomas Risse-Kappen, "Bringing Transnational Relations Back In: Introduction," in Thomas Risse-Kappen (ed.), *Bringing Transnational Relations Back In: Non-State Actors, Domestic Structures and International Relations* (Cambridge: Cambridge University Press, 1995); and Thomas Risse-Kappen, "Structures of Governance and Transnational Relations: What Have We Learned?" in Risse-Kappen, *Bringing Transnational Relations Back In*. According to the seminal work on the subject, "transnational relations" consist of those "contacts, coalitions, and interactions across state boundaries that are not controlled by the central foreign policy organs of governments." See Robert O. Keohane and Joseph S. Nye, Jr. (eds.), *Transnational Relations and World Politics* (Cambridge, MA: Harvard University Press, 1972), p.xi. This category includes much of the behavior typical of "epistemic communities," transnational networks of specialists united by common causal beliefs and an associated policy program. See ch. 1, fn 8 for relevant works. Although Western efforts to socialize the USSR and the successor states do not conform precisely to the ideal type of transnational relations – these efforts have been mounted by loose coalitions of government officials, independent specialists, and public and private firms, typically operating under the aegis of formal intergovernmental agreements and backed by Western diplomacy – the findings of this work are directly applicable to the cases at hand.
5. For representative discussions of domestic structure and applications of domestic structural analysis to environmental politics see chapter 1 in this volume.
6. Risse-Kappen, "Bringing Transnational Relations Back In," pp. 3–33, and Risse-Kappen, "Structures of Governance," pp. 280–313. Risse-Kappen's approach draws heavily upon previous comparative studies of Western

democracies, most of which defined domestic structure in terms of state autonomy and the relative strength of state and society (hence the famous weak state/strong state distinction). See, for example, Stephen D. Krasner, *Defending the National Interest: Raw Materials Investment and U.S. Foreign Policy* (Princeton: Princeton University Press, 1978). See also chapter 1, fns 3 and 13. Similar points about the relatively greater capacity of the Soviet government to introduce innovative policies have been made by Zbigniew Brzenzinski and Samuel P. Huntington, *Political Power: USA/USSR* (New York: Viking Press, 1965), p. 413 and Donald R. Kelley, Kenneth R. Stunkel, and Richard R. Wescott, *The Economic Superpowers and the Environment: The United States, the Soviet Union, and Japan* (San Francisco: W. H. Freeman, 1976), pp. 290–293.

7. Matthew Evangelista, "The Paradox of State Strength: Domestic Structure, Transnational Relations, and Security Policy in Russia and the Soviet Union," *International Organization* 49:1 (1995), 1–38.

8. Risse-Kappen, "Bringing Transnational Relations Back In" and Risse-Kappen, "Structures of Governance."

9. Evangelista, "The Paradox of State Strength."

10. For a more detailed account of the history of these issues, see Robert Darst, "Leninism, Pluralism, and International Cooperation: The Internationalization of Environmental Protection in the USSR and its Successor States, 1968–1993," Ph.D. dissertation, University of California, Berkeley (1994).

11. This coalition-building perspective draws heavily upon George W. Breslauer, *Khrushchev and Brezhnev as Leaders: Building Authority in Soviet Politics* (London: Allen and Unwin, 1982); George W. Breslauer, "Soviet Economic Reforms Since Stalin: Ideology, Politics, and Learning," *Soviet Economy* 6:3 (1990), 252–280; George W. Breslauer, "Evaluating Gorbachev as a Leader," in Ed A. Hewett and Victor H. Winson (eds.), *Milestones in Glasnost and Perestroika: Politics and People* (Washington, DC: Brookings Institution, 1991); Jack Snyder, "The Gorbachev Revolution: A Waning of Soviet Expansionism?" *International Security* 12:3 (1987/88), 93–131; and Jack Snyder, *Myths of Empire: Domestic Politics and International Ambition* (Ithaca: Cornell University Press, 1991).

12. This interpretation of Brezhnev's coalition-building closely follows Breslauer, *Krushchev and Brezhnev.*

13. For all practical purposes, the leadership coalition crafted by Brezhnev underwent no significant change during the brief Andropov–Chernenko interregnum. That being said, there is ample evidence to suggest that Andropov did plan to introduce more far-reaching domestic reforms. On this see Georgi Arbatov, *The System: An Insider's Life in Soviet Politics* (New York: Times Books, 1992). Even during his brief tenure as General Secretary, some liberalization of state controls over transnational scientific contacts did filter down to the specialists engaged in East–West environmental cooperation. However, Andropov died before undertaking any fundamental changes in either domestic or foreign policy.

14. The secondary literature includes many excellent studies of the politics of environmental protection in the USSR before perestroika. See, for example, Marshall I. Goldman, *The Spoils of Progress: Environmental Pollution in the Soviet Union* (Cambridge, MA: MIT Press, 1972); Philip R. Pryde, *Conservation in the Soviet Union* (New York: Cambridge University Press, 1972); Philip R. Pryde, *Environmental Management in the Soviet Union* (New York: Cambridge University Press, 1991); John Martin Kramer, "The Politics of Conservation and Pollution in the USSR," Ph.D. dissertation, University of Virginia (1973); Donald R. Kelley, "Environmental Policy-making in the USSR: The Role of Industrial and Environmental Interest Groups," *Soviet Studies* 28(1976), 570–589; Boris Komarov, *The Destruction of Nature in the Soviet Union* (White Plains, NY: M.E. Sharpe, 1980); Thane Gustafson, *Reform in Soviet Politics: Lessons of Recent Policies on Land and Water* (Cambridge: Cambridge University Press, 1981); Joan DeBardeleben, *The Environment and Marxism-Leninism: The Soviet and East German Experience* (Boulder and London: Westview Press, 1985); Barbara Jancar, *Environmental Management in the Soviet Union and Yugoslavia* (Durham, NC: Duke University Press, 1987); Charles E. Zeigler, *Environmental Policy in the USSR* (Amherst, MA: University of Massachusetts Press, 1987); and Eric Green, *Ecology and Perestroika: Environmental Protection in the Soviet Union* (Washington, DC: American Committee on U.S.-Soviet Relations, 1990). For a spirited account of the vicissitudes of Soviet conservation from the Russian Revolution until the death of Stalin, see Douglas R. Weiner, *Models of Nature: Ecology, Conservation, and Cultural Revolution in Soviet Russia* (Bloomington: Indiana University Press, 1988).

15. This analysis follows Breslauer, *Krushchev and Brezhnev*; Harry Gelman, *The Brezhnev Politburo and the Decline of Detente* (Ithaca: Cornell University Press, 1984); Snyder, "The Gorbachev Revolution"; and Snyder, *Myths of Empire.* This strategy of "offensive detente" (a term coined by Snyder, not the Soviet leadership) combined a massive military buildup and vigorous competition in the developing world with sufficient East–West cooperation to codify Soviet gains, diminish the risks of uncontrolled escalation, and ensure access to the external goods and capital needed to bolster the faltering Soviet economy. In the long run, of course, these goals proved to be incompatible, just as environmental protection at home could not be squared with the need to pump further growth out of an unreformed command economy, but that conflict would not be officially recognized until the advent of Mikhail Gorbachev.

16. In the late 1970s, the Politburo had opted to shift much of the country's domestic fuel balance toward greater use of natural gas and nuclear power. The primary motivation for this shift was the need to free up oil production for hard-currency export. The politics of Soviet energy policy in the 1970s and 1980s is analyzed in detail in Thane Gustafson, *Crisis Amid Plenty: The Politics of Soviet Energy Under Brezhnev and Gorbachev* (Princeton, NJ: Princeton University Press, 1989).

17. The notion of "subterranean learning" is drawn from Breslauer, "Soviet Economic Reforms," 270–271.
18. A. R. Sich, "Chernobyl Accident Management Actions," *Nuclear Safety* 35:1 (1994), 1–24, argues that the measures taken to manage the accident during the first ten days were generally ineffective. Most notably, he argues that the aerial bombardment missed the reactor core altogether, because the heli-copter crews mistakenly dumped their loads upon a different glowing mass (perhaps burning graphite or tar from the roof) located to the side of the damaged core. If so, the total radioactive release may have been much greater than the "official" figure of 50 million curies.
19. The literature on the Chernobyl accident and its aftermath is extensive and continues to grow. See, for example, David R. Marples, *Chernobyl and Nuclear Power in the USSR* (New York: St. Martin's Press, 1986); David R. Marples, *The Social Impact of the Chernobyl Disaster* (New York: St. Martin's Press, 1988); Grigori Medvedev, *The Truth About Chernobyl* (New York: Basic Books, 1991); Zhores Medvedev, *The Legacy of Chernobyl* (New York: W. W. Norton, 1990); and William C. Potter, "The Impact of Chernobyl on Nuclear Power Safety in the Soviet Union," *Studies in Comparative Communism* 24:2 (1991), 191–210.
20. The environmentalist message attracted not only members of the liberal intelligentsia but also influential public figures, such as the Russian nation-alist writers, who disliked the Soviet regime but otherwise did not share perestroika's Westernizing spirit. See Robert Darst, "Environmentalism in the USSR: The Opposition to the River Diversion Projects," *Soviet Economy* 4:3 (1988), 223–252.
21. For broad overviews of the new political thinking in Soviet foreign policy, see V. Kubálková and A. A. Cruickshank, *Thinking New About Soviet "New Thinking"* (Berkeley: Institute of International Studies, 1989); Robert Legvold, "War, Weapons, and Soviet Foreign Policy," in Seweryn Bialer and Michael Mandelbaum (eds.), *Gorbachev's Russia and American Foreign Policy* (Boulder: Westview Press, 1988); Robert Legvold, "Soviet Learning in the 1980s," in Breslauer and Tetlock (eds.), *Learning in US and Soviet Foreign Policy* (Boulder: Westview, 1991), pp. 684–732, and Steven Kull, *Burying Lenin: The Revolution in Soviet Ideology and Foreign Policy* (Boulder: Westview, 1992). Soviet political writings on international environmental cooperation during and in the years preceding the new thinking are analyzed by Barbara Welling Hall, "Soviet Perceptions of Global Ecological Problems: An Analysis Based on Simulated Interviewing", Ph.D. dissertation, Ohio State University (1987) and Walter C. Clemens, Jr., *Can Russia Change? The USSR Confronts Global Interdependence* (Boston: Unwin Hyman, 1990).
22. The primacy of these broader political aims in the new thinking's emphasis on international ecological interdependence was reflected in the vague character of the references to international environmental problems made by the Soviet leadership. Gorbachev, Shevardnadze, and other prominent "new thinkers" seldom referred to specific international environmental

problems, and even the Chernobyl disaster itself was usually invoked only in the same breath as nuclear disarmament. The Soviet government's chief international environmental initiative – the creation of an international environmental "rapid deployment force" under the aegis of the United Nations – was a rather modest and generic proposal, unconnected to any particular environmental concern.

The generic character of the new thinkers' interest in ecological interdependence is not surprising, for the advisers who initially promoted the new political thinking were not environmental scientists. They tended instead to be cultural figures, progressive ideologists, and specialists in international political affairs. These individuals moved in entirely different circles from the specialists involved in concrete questions of international environmental cooperation, such as the Baltic Sea or nuclear power safety, and the various groups were only vaguely aware of one another's activities. Gorbachev's environmental advisers were only a tiny subset of the broader intellectual community that developed and promoted the "new thinking"; for more on the composition and entrepreneurial efforts of this broader community, see Sarah Mendelson, "Internal Battles and External Wars: Politics, Learning, and the Soviet Withdrawal from Afghanistan," *World Politics* 45:3 (1993), 327–360, and Jeff Checkel, "Ideas, Institutions, and the Gorbachev Foreign Policy Revolution," *World Politics* 45:2 (1993), 271–300.

23. This interpretation agrees with Snyder, "The Gorbachev Revolution" and Snyder, *Myths of Empire*.

24. Jane I. Dawson, *Eco-nationalism: Anti-nuclear Activism and National Identity in Russia, Lithuania, and Ukraine* (Durham, NC: Duke University Press, 1996).

25. These phenomena are explored in greater detail in Robert G. Darst, "Bribery and Blackmail in East-West Environmental Politics," *Post Soviet Affairs* 13:1 (1997), 42–77.

26. The city of Leningrad was renamed St. Petersburg in June 1991, but the surrounding region retained its Soviet-era name of "Leningrad Oblast."

27. HELCOM, *The Baltic Sea Joint Comprehensive Environmental Action Programme*, Baltic Sea Environment Proceedings, no. 48, 1993 and *HELCOM News*, no. 1, 1995.

28. *International Environmental Reporter*, 27 January 1993, pp. 38–39.

29. *Mining Journal*, 29 March 1996, 326:8371. Most of these arrangements had been ironed out almost a year earlier (*Rossiyskaya gazeta*, 13 July 1995, p. 4/FBIS-SOV-95-144-S), but the final agreement was delayed until Russian president Boris Yeltsin could complete a long-awaited and repeatedly postponed state visit to Norway. For more details on the current proposal, see "Modernization of the Nickel Smelter in Pechenga: Status of the Project, and the Financing Arrangements," PM 31.03.95, Ministry of the Environment, Oslo, Norway.

30. It is emblematic of the post-Soviet period that the only two groups engaged in visible public protest against the state of the nuclear power industry in the Russian Federation after 1991 were Greenpeace International and the

nuclear power plant operators themselves – the latter staging several demonstrations, work stoppages, and hunger strikes (both at their plants and in Moscow) to protest the fact that they had not been paid in many months and could not carry out necessary maintenance. However, even this did not arouse any palpable public concern.

31. For official pronouncements along these lines, see: Nur Nigmatulin, deputy chairman of the State Committee for Atomic Energy (Interfax, 21 April 1994/FBIS-SOV-94-078); Ukrainian President Kravchuk (ITAR-TASS, 25 April 1994/FBIS-SOV-94-082); Mykhaylo Pavlovskyy, chairman of the Parliamentary Committee for nuclear issues (Paris AFP, 13 February 1995/FBIS-SOV-95-030); Mykhailo Umanets, head of the State Committee for Atomic Energy (Intelnews 30 March 1995/FBIS-SOV-95-061); Foreign Minister Hennadiy Udovenko (ITAR-TASS, 20 April 1995/FBIS-SOV-95-077); Ukrainian President Kuchma (ITAR-TASS, 24 April 1995/FBIS-SOV-95-079); Yuriy Kostenko, Minister of Environmental Protection and Nuclear Safety (*Vseukrainskiye vedomosti*, 13 September 1995, p. 6/FBIS-SOV-95-181); Prime Minister Yevheniy Marchuk (*Uryadovyy kuryer*, 25 November 1995/FBIS-SOV-95-229).

32. *Holos Ukrayiny*, 19 April 1995, p. 4 (FBIS-SOV-95-077).

33. "Memorandum of Understanding between the Governments of the G-7 Countries and the Commission of the European Communities and the Government of Ukraine on the Closure of the Chernobyl Nuclear Power Plant" (Ottawa, 20 December 1995). By this time, Ukraine had already brought the sixth unit at the Zaporozhzhya nuclear power plant on line, making it the largest nuclear power plant in Europe (*Nuclear News* 38:9, August 1995, p. 87).

34. All of these complaints were voiced after the nuclear safety summit in Moscow by Viktor Tatarynov, head of the International Department of the Ukrainian Ministry of Environmental Protection and Nuclear Safety (Infobank, 5 June 1996/FBIS-SOV-96-109).

35. ITAR-TASS, 20 April 1996 (FBIS-SOV-96-078).

36. Abraham Maslow, *Motivation and Personality*, 2nd edition (New York: Harper and Row, 1970).

37. Ronald Inglehart, *Culture Shift in Advanced Industrial Society* (Princeton: Princeton University Press, 1990).

38. Robert Rohrschneider, "Citizens' Attitudes Toward Environmental Issues: Selfish or Selfless?" *Comparative Political Studies* 21:3 (1988), 347–367, and Robert Rohrschneider, "The Roots of Public Opinion Towards New Social Movements: An Empirical Test of Competing Explanations," *American Journal of Political Science* 34:4 (1990), 1–30.

6 Domestic institutions and international environmental agendas in Japan and Germany

Miranda A. Schreurs

As regional leaders and economic heavyweights, Japan and Germany are important actors in global environmental politics. Yet Japan and Germany responded quite differently to the emergence of global environmental risks in the 1980s. Whereas Germany was relatively pro-active in response to the emergence of global atmospheric pollution problems, Japan was relatively reactive. New ideas about international environmental problems reached the German policy agenda more quickly than they did the Japanese. Acid rain, for example, was an issue on the German policy agenda in the early 1980s, yet it did not surface as a political concern in Japan until the end of the 1980s, even though it was a scientific concern before this time. In the mid-1980s, Germany emerged as a leader within the European Community (EC) pushing for the establishment of international regulations on ozone-depleting substances. In contrast, there was almost no mention of stratospheric ozone depletion in Japan prior to the fall of 1987, just months before states met to draw up the Montreal Protocol on Substances that Deplete the Ozone Layer. Similarly, in the case of global warming, Germany was one of the first countries to propose the establishment of international targets for the reduction of greenhouse gas emissions and announced an ambitious domestic target as a starting point. The pillar of Germany's climate change policy was its target to reduce CO_2 emissions by 25 percent of 1987 levels by 2005. Japan, on the other hand, initially joined the United States, Russia, and China in objecting to an international target, and instead called for more research into climate change. Domestically, there was very little public, scientific, or political pressure for action.

By the end of the 1980s, Germany was widely perceived as an international environmental leader, while Japan's image was that of a state that was good at cleaning up its own pollution problems but relatively unconcerned with international environmental protection initiatives. This chapter examines the linkages between domestic political factors and international scientific and political developments that help explain the reactive nature of the Japanese response and the more proactive nature of Germany's approach to international environmental policy formation during the 1980s. It also attempts to explain why, despite Japan's reluctance to take up global environmental concerns in the 1980s, it emerged in the early 1990s as a prominent international player – addressing such problems as global climate change, loss of bio-diversity, and environmental degradation in the developing world. In the late 1990s, global environmental protection issues have a prominent place on the political agenda in both Japan and Germany.

This work is concerned with how differences between states in their environmental policy communities can influence their responses to early scientific warnings about environmental threats. Within the decision-making literature, there is considerable interest in the question of how issues reach policy agendas.[1] Why international environmental issues reach domestic political agendas when they do and in the form they do are questions with considerable practical significance.

In the environmental area, international communities of environmental experts may play a particularly important role in exchanging information on new scientific discoveries and building international consensus about the seriousness of an environmental risk.[2] Epistemic communities and international institutions clearly play important roles in diffusing scientific and policy-relevant knowledge. Yet, domestic institutions and political cultures influence how those ideas are brought into the policy-making process. Institutions are important because they structure interactions among actors, influence their relative power within society, and affect their strategies of action. They also have ideas about policy issues embedded within them. Institutions, therefore, exert a strong, if indirect, influence on the policy-making process.[3]

Institutions are likely to influence which societal actors are available as potential policy sponsors.[4] The position of potential policy sponsors within a political system, whether they are in a ruling or opposition party, in a strong or weak bureaucratic agency, in a powerful or weak social movement, will impact their chances of getting new ideas about policy problems and solutions onto the domestic political agenda.[5]

This chapter argues that a major reason behind Japan's reactive responses and Germany's relatively more proactive responses to international environmental problems in the 1980s lies in the different shapes their environmental policy communities took in the preceding decade. Differences in institutional structures and political processes between Japan and Germany produced very different environmental policy communities, which in turn influenced how international environmental issues were perceived and acted upon. The chapter also suggests, however, that once new ideas are sponsored by domestic actors and make it to the domestic political agenda they can lead to changes in norms and institutions that can influence policy-making over the long term.

The Japan–Germany comparison

In terms of their political, economic, and environmental histories, Japan and Germany share much in common, which explains why they are commonly chosen for cross-national comparison.[6] Both states are highly industrialized parliamentary democracies with the second and third largest economies in the world respectively. Their economic activities have considerable direct and indirect impacts on the environment, both regionally and globally. Their energy structures are similar. By the end of the 1980s, Japan was the world's fourth largest emitter of carbon dioxide, while Germany was fifth.

There are also important institutional differences between these countries. The German political system is federalist while the Japanese is unitary. In essence what this means is that politics in Germany are more decentralized than in Japan. In Germany, environmental policy formation and implementation are made more complex because of the power of the Länder vis-à-vis the federal government. In addition, the German state is required to contend with an additional level of policy negotiation and coordination which stems from its membership in the European Union (formerly the European Community [EC]). This has provided Germany with both opportunities and constraints in its efforts at environmental policy formation.

In comparing Japan and Germany, one of the most striking differences between the two countries lies in the shape of their environmental policy communities. The environmental policy community in Japan is characterized by numerous small, local, informally organized, single-issue citizens' movements. There are few nationally organized environmental groups, and the ones that do exist are small in terms of membership and budget. The Japanese Environment Agency is weak, and its jurisdiction is limited. In environmental policy-making, the agency is often overshadowed by larger, older, and more powerful ministries – the Ministry of International Trade and Industry (MITI), the Ministry of Construction, the Ministry of Foreign Affairs, and the Ministry of Transportation. Until recently, there were only a handful of politicians who showed any interest in the environment.

Germany's environmental policy community, in contrast, is best known for its strong Green Party. The existence of the Green Party guarantees that environmental interests have a direct voice in parliament. It also ensures that politicians in other parties remain sensitive to environmental concerns. In addition to the Green Party, there are strong local, federal, and international environmental groups based in Germany. These groups are relatively well financed, and many boast large memberships. In Germany, the Federal Ministry for the Environment by no means dominates the German bureaucracy, but it is strong compared with its Japanese counterpart, as suggested by the fact that it was elevated to ministerial status in 1986. These differences between Japan and Germany emerged only in the 1970s. Prior to this, the Japanese environmental movement may have been even stronger than the German. It is important to consider why these differences in the environmental policy communities of Japan and Germany emerged in order to begin to explain more subtle differences in the timing, content, and effectiveness of Japanese and German global environmental policy decisions.

The emergence of environmental policy communities in Japan and Germany

The Japanese case

Japan was one of the first countries where citizens organized against the state to protest its lack of attention to the environment. For Japan, after defeat in World War II, the 1950s and 1960s were spent trying to "catch up" economically with the West. In the state's fervor to double its national income in ten years (a plan envisioned by Prime Minister Ikeda in 1960), a national consensus was built around the idea of rapid economic growth. By the late 1960s Japan had surpassed this goal and become the third largest economy in the world. These economic growth policies, however, so completely ignored the environment that by 1970, Japan was considered to be one of the most polluted countries in the world. The horror of Minamata mercury poisoning, Yokkaichi asthma, and *itai-itai byô* (literally, "ouch, ouch sickness," from cadmium poisoning) vividly spoke of the tragedy of environmental neglect.[7]

The severity of pollution problems in Japan and the government's failure to take action, slowly, but then with a domino-like effect, convinced citizens of the need to organize against local industries and governments, and eventually the state, in demanding policy change. The first groups were formed with the aid of environmental, academic, and scientific experts from within Japan as well as from abroad. Initially these groups turned to traditional forms of protest, seeking recognition of their demands in the forms of petitions, consultation, and eventually demonstrations. But with the national government and industry refusing to acknowledge the severity of the problems or the need for major policy change, these groups turned in desperation to the courts. In Japan, where litigation is seen as a means of last resort, these initiatives had a profound impact, attracting widespread public attention domestically and abroad. With the courts siding in favor of pollution victims, other groups were encouraged to form, and by the early 1970s, there were an estimated 1,500–3,000 citizens' groups organized largely around local environmental problems.

The initial policy response of the national government was to pass a Basic Law for the Environment in 1967. But this law, with its infamous harmony clause (stating that the preservation of the living environment should occur in harmony with the healthy development of the economy) lacked any emission standards and did not provide any measures for the relief of pollution victims. It failed to lead to noticeable environmental improvements or to satisfy citizens' demands. The failure of this initial concession by the government to stem the swelling environmental movement posed a serious threat to the Japanese state. Frank Upham has argued that use of the courts and the media attention this attracted opened what was normally an informal, closed, and particularistic decision-making process to public and judicial scrutiny. The national government was forced to consider anti-pollution legislation or risk the possibility that fragmented local citizens' groups would merge into a nationally-based movement that might concern itself not only with environmental issues, but with other issues as well, thereby weakening state authority.[8]

Equally important was the fact that these events occurred just as international attention was turning to the environment. The mid-1960s saw the emergence of a strong environmental movement in the United States, a country from which Japan borrowed many policy ideas.

Furthermore, in 1968, the United Nations adopted a resolution to convene a conference on the problems of the human environment in Stockholm in 1972. The resolution pointed to a "need for intensified action at the national, regional, and international level in order to limit and, where possible, to eliminate the impairment of the human environment ..."[9] The objective of the conference was to focus the attention of governments and public opinion on the need for action to protect the environment. Preparation for this conference gave international legitimacy to the cries of citizens' groups for action. It is certainly no coincidence that most of the industrialized countries formed environmental agencies and passed major environmental laws around this time.

Faced with strong domestic pressures for environmental protection, as well as with the elevation of the environment to the international policy agenda, the ruling Liberal Democratic Party (LDP) was forced to take action. In December 1970, in what is popularly referred to as "the Pollution Diet," fourteen major anti-pollution amendments and laws were passed, making Japan's environmental laws among the toughest in the world. Successful implementation of these new laws won Japan recognition from the Organization for Economic Cooperation and Development (OECD). A 1977 appraisal by the OECD of Japanese environmental conditions found that trends in environmental quality were on the whole as good as or better than in other countries.[10] As a result of policy changes made in the late 1960s and early 1970s, Japan rapidly established one of the world's most successful air pollution control programs. In this process, the government also managed to take the steam out of the environmental movement. By responding to many of its concerns and routinizing environmental policy formation within the bureaucracy, the government coopted the movement's agenda. Furthermore, any efforts by Japanese citizens' groups to form national environmental groups were made difficult by tax laws that greatly restrict the formation of new non-profit organizations. The movement, therefore, remained local in focus.

The German case

The first wave of environmental policy change in Germany also occurred around 1970, but lacked the dynamism of the movement in Japan. In contrast to the bottom-up pressures for policy change in Japan, policy change in Germany was largely a top-down process. In 1969, when the new Social Democratic Party/Free Democratic Party (SPD/FDP) coalition came into power, ending twenty years of political dominance by the Christian Democratic Union and its Bavarian sister party, the Christian Social Union (CDU/CSU), it initiated a reformist policy package that included pollution control as a central element. This took concrete form in 1971 when a federal environmental program was established. There was growing awareness of environmental issues among the German public in the 1960s, spurred by such events as the 1969 poisoning of fish in the Rhine and the popularity of books such as Rachel Carson's *Silent Spring*.[11] Still, the impetus for policy change appears to have come largely from the Federal Executive – from Chancellor Brandt, his senior aide, Horst Ehmke, and Interior Minister Hans-Dietrich Genscher.[12] In their search for new ideas for their reformist policy package, they borrowed from the United States, where a strong environmental movement in the mid-1960s led to the establishment in 1969 of a National Environmental Policy Act. Edda Müller argues that the new environmental laws in Germany cannot be explained by domestic environmental crises or strong public pressure. Rather, they were essentially imported from the United States into the Federal Republic.[13]

The early 1970s appeared promising for the development of a strong environmental program. In 1969 the Ministry of the Interior won an interministerial battle and succeeded in largely taking over responsibility for pollution control from the Ministry of Health. Under the leadership of its activist minister, and with the support of the chancellor, a progressive Federal Environmental Program was established in 1971 based upon three principles: the polluter pays, precaution, and cooperation. With a supportive coalition in power, numerous laws pertaining to air, water, and noise pollution control were enacted in the following years. In 1974, a Federal Environment Agency was established to conduct research into environmental issues.

This promising beginning for environmental protection in Germany resembled developments in Japan. When Helmut Schmidt succeeded Willy Brandt as chancellor in 1974 and appointed a new Minister of the Interior, however, the environmental movement lost two prominent supporters. After the 1973 oil shock and the recession of the mid-1970s, industrial opposition to environmental initiatives became more vocal. In 1975, in a closed meeting of industry and trade unions organized by the Chancellor's Office, it was decided to relax environmental standards which were viewed as an obstacle to industrial investment.[14] Although in the end most of the new standards were left in place, there was no mistaking the SPD's change in attitude toward environmental protection in the face of an economic recession.

Moreover, in contrast with the relatively successful implementation of new environmental laws in Japan, implementation efforts were less successful in Germany.[15] The 1971 Federal Environmental Program was more concerned with research than with implementation. While the program contained many goals, it had few testable standards, thus making implementation difficult. Another factor often cited for the failure of these laws to improve noticeably the quality of the environment was the limited attention given to implementation in some Länder. Under the Federal Emissions Control Act, industries were required to use "appropriate" or state-of-the-art technology in pollution control. The ambiguity of this requirement led to long negotiations between the government, industry, and the public over construction plans. The legislation was primarily targeted at assuring that state-of-the-art technology was employed in new facilities, but it did not provide sufficient incentive for existing companies to improve pollution control measures, and enforcing improvements in existing plants proved difficult. Companies could avoid measures aimed at reducing emissions in existing plants by reference to technical difficulties or the "excessive" economic costs that would be involved. The Länder and municipal governments had only limited means at their disposal to force existing plants to adopt measures to reduce emissions. It was difficult to withdraw permits from existing plants unless it could be proved that the public would require protection from potentially severe damage. Injunctions, moreover, could be appealed in court, leading to lengthy delays in implementation.[16]

While the 1970s saw a decline in environmental activism in Japan, in Germany citizens' action groups (*Bürgerinitiativen*) gained in force. *Bürgerinitiativen* first emerged in the 1960s around local urban planning issues, highway development, and the environment, and eventually banded together to form an umbrella organization, the *Bundesverband Bürgerinitiativen Umwelt* (BBU), in 1972.[17]

By the mid-1970s, there were an estimated 15,000 to 50,000 *Bürgerinitiativen*, with somewhat under half of them involved with environmental issues. The environmental movement was emerging as a serious political force. Closed out of the cooperative policy circle that existed between government and industry, environmentalists and anti-nuclear activists organized major protests against the construction of both coal-burning and nuclear power plants. Particularly prominent were the protests against the building of nuclear power plants in Baden-Württemburg and Schleswig-Holstein. When these protest efforts failed to produce major policy changes, the citizens' initiatives also began to consider other means of influencing government policy. Green lists and parties were formed in the Länder. The Greens won their first government seats in two Länder in 1979, and increased their representation at the Länder level in subsequent elections. In the 1983 federal election, they passed the 5 percent vote barrier required to win seats in the Bundestag, Germany's Lower House.[18] The success of the Greens is probably the main reason why other parties, including the CDU/CSU-led coalition which took over control of the government in 1982, became active in the following years in addressing environmental issues. By the end of the next decade, Germany was considered to have some of the most progressive environmental laws in the world.

The environmental movement in Germany subsequently became centered around the Green Party. In Japan, the movement remained fragmented. When international environmental issues like stratospheric ozone depletion and transboundary air pollution began to receive international political attention in the late 1970s, Japan's environmental movement was weak; Germany's was strong. The implications for these states' respective responses to international environmental pressures were substantial.

The emergence of global environmental risks

The shift in environmental awareness from the local or regional scale to the global scale has been a gradual one. Two important issues that reflect this growing scientific and political focus on international environmental issues are those of stratospheric ozone depletion and global climate change.

As already discussed in chapter 4, there were two waves of policy activity at the international level related to ozone layer protection. The first began in the mid-1970s after the US government, pushed by an unusual coalition of environmentalists, scientists, and producers of chlorofluorocarbons (CFCs), introduced the issue in UNEP. Several states either banned the use of ozone destroying chemicals in aerosol spray cans (where they were most widely used) or placed a freeze on production capacity of those chemicals. A second wave began in the period leading up to the formation of the Montreal Protocol in 1987 and subsequent amendments to this international agreement. The formation of the Montreal Protocol was a major success for those seeking to further international efforts to protect the environment. The amended Montreal Protocol essentially calls for a complete phase out of CFCs and some other ozone depleting substances. This was a remarkable achievement considering that CFCs were used in such products and processes as aerosol sprays, refrigerants, in air conditioning, as solvents for cleaning circuit boards, and in styrofoam packaging.

Throughout the 1970s Japan and Germany showed only limited interest in theories linking CFCs to stratospheric ozone depletion. Neither country was very involved in stratospheric science; nor were there strong environmental lobbies calling for policy action on ozone layer protection. An internationally oriented environmental movement had yet to develop in either country. Still, Germany was somewhat more responsive than Japan to US and international pressures for coordinated international policy action. This was primarily because the German Interior Ministry became a sponsor for policy change within Germany. At its initiative the German government in 1977 negotiated an informal agreement with industry to reduce CFCs in aerosols by 30 percent of 1975 levels. This made Germany one of the first countries to take some kind of action. The Interior Ministry was also instrumental in making Germany the host to the second international conference on CFCs in 1978 where a general agreement among participating states was reached to take measures at the national level to reduce the release of CFCs. Germany was also affected by subsequent decisions of the Commission of the European Community. In 1978, the Commission recommended that the production of two kinds of CFCs not be expanded and that research into alternatives be encouraged. Then, under growing international pressure, in the spring of 1980 the EC heads of state went beyond their 1978 decision and agreed to a freeze on production capacity of CFC-11 and CFC-12, and to a reduction in the use of these chemicals by at least 30 percent in aerosol sprays by the end of 1981.

In Japan there was little awareness of the theory linking CFCs to stratospheric ozone depletion. The Environment Agency did not consider ozone layer protection a major issue and thus allocated few resources to this area. It was only after the EC announced its regulatory goals and Japan became isolated within the OECD that MITI announced that it similarly would use administrative guidance to freeze production capacity and reduce CFC use in aerosol sprays. This occurred in December 1980.

Still, at this time, it is perhaps only in comparison with Japan that Germany appeared relatively proactive in its policy response. Neither in Japan nor Germany were domestic pressures for policy action as strong as they were in the United States. Despite US and Canadian efforts to get stronger legislation passed internationally, the German government took no new policy initiatives outside of those made within the EC in 1980. This EC initiative, moreover, was largely symbolic since the provisions to reduce the use of CFCs had already been achieved when the law was established. During the first wave of international policy activity, Germany was more proactive than Japan, but it was certainly not an international leader. Some have even argued that in the early 1980s, Germany used its EC membership as a way of reducing domestic and international pressure on it to take any additional policy measures beyond those established within the EC. The Dutch Environmental Minister Winsemius, argued that it was the most advanced states within the EC, and in particular Germany, France and the United Kingdom, which clung to the 1980 EC policy on CFCs as a way of protecting their domestic chemical industries.[19] Stratospheric ozone depletion was not a particularly big political issue in Japan or Germany at this time.

The Montreal Protocol

The efforts made in several states to reduce CFC use in aerosols in the late 1970s, combined with changing consumer preferences, led to a drop in world CFC production by almost 25 percent by 1982 over 1974 levels. The problem of CFCs in the environment, however, was not solved. The drop in worldwide production of CFCs was short lived. By 1982, production levels were again rising because of the growing importance of CFCs as cleaning solvents, in foam, and as refrigerants. Thus, despite low levels of interest in the issue in any country at this time, at the international level negotiations for an international agreement to protect the ozone layer were initiated within the UNEP. Between 1982 and 1985 there were seven meetings related to the formation of a framework convention on stratospheric ozone depletion.

As a result of these preparatory meetings, in March 1985 an international meeting was convened in Vienna to draw up an ozone convention. Because of differences among participating states over what kind of measure to adopt – a worldwide ban on the non-essential use of CFCs in aerosols or a production-capacity freeze – the Vienna Convention created no concrete targets and instead simply created a general obligation for signatories to take "appropriate measures" to protect the ozone layer. Germany signed the convention; Japan did not. Not recognizing the importance of the meeting, the Environment Agency of Japan failed to send a representative. Japan's formal justification for its decision not to sign was that the agreement lacked any concrete measures.[20]

International efforts to form a protocol were accelerated by subsequent scientific findings and in particular the discovery by British scientists of a "hole" in the ozone layer over Antarctica. This finding was quickly confirmed by the work of Chubachi Shigeru, a Japanese scientist working for the Meteorology Agency. He had made a similar discovery in 1982 of an unprecedented decline in the ozone layer over Japan's Showa Observatory in Antarctica, but his findings had gone largely unnoticed both within Japan and internationally.[21] This new scientific evidence and the development of a growing consensus about the seriousness of the problem within an international expert community helped to move international negotiations forward. It was not sufficient, however, to alter the position of national governments until sufficient domestic support for policy action was achieved. This occurred in Germany more quickly than in Japan.

Germany's evolving leadership

After the discovery of the "ozone hole," Germany became more supportive of policy action. The shift in the German government's international stance reflected the greening of the domestic political landscape after the election of the Green Party to the Bundestag in 1983. The Green Party entered the Bundestag on a platform that focused on the SPD-led government's failure to take air pollution and acid rain seriously enough. The Green Party also criticized the government's support of nuclear power. Responding to these pressures, the newly elected CDU-led government greatly strengthened Germany's air pollution control laws. The 1985 Chernobyl nuclear accident further heightened domestic awareness of the international nature of many environmental problems. With this change in the domestic political milieu, the German government's position within the EC became markedly more proactive than it had been earlier in the decade. With environmental issues high on the German political agenda, Chancellor Kohl proposed in June 1986 that a Federal Ministry for Environment, Nature Protection, and Reactor Safety be created by combining the environmental divisions in the Ministry of the Interior, nature protection activities of the Ministry of Agriculture, and radiation hygiene and control of food contamination from the Ministry of Health. Kohl did this in an effort to show his support for environmental initiatives in the post-Chernobyl period and to respond to calls by the SPD and the Greens for an immediate halt to Germany's nuclear energy program. This institutional change also strengthened the position of those in the bureaucracy calling for a stronger regulatory position on ozone layer protection.

After the discovery of the ozone hole and the formation of the Vienna Convention, in early 1986, the German government amended its clean-air regulations, including a minor provision which defined emission limits for CFC emitting installations. Pressures quickly grew, however, for more substantial action. Calls for a total CFC ban in aerosols came from numerous directions, including environmentalists and the opposition parties.[22] Reacting to these domestic pressures, the Bundesrat (Upper House) adopted a resolution in March 1986 calling for a general ban on the production and marketing of CFCs. A few months later, the Bundestag adopted a similar proposal for the immediate ban of CFC-containing aerosol cans and sharp reductions of the use of CFCs in other areas. Chancellor Kohl added his voice to the growing domestic demand for action in March 1987 when he called for national and international action to address the growing global threats to the Earth's atmosphere.[23]

Within a year of the discovery of the "ozone hole," protection of the ozone layer was clearly on the political agenda in Germany. The SPD proposed a motion in August 1987 calling for a ban on CFC use and the following month the Green Party proposed a program designed to protect the climate by taking immediate action on ozone layer protection. In October 1987 the German Bundestag unanimously approved the establishment of a study (Enquete) commission on Preventive Measures to Protect the Earth's Atmosphere, with the mandate to study the ozone problem and make proposals for action.[24]

Initially, the German government relied completely on informal agreements with industry to reduce the emissions of CFCs. The need to negotiate with other EC members on a joint plan for action prior to formulating domestic policy regulations slowed domestic policy formation. In contrast with the situation in 1980, however, this time Germany was actively pushing other EC member states to agree to regulations.

Importantly, the change in Germany's stance shifted the balance of pro- and anti-regulatory views within the European Council of Ministers in the direction of stricter regulations and allowed for agreement between the EC and the United States on a proposal to take an initial step to reduce CFC production and consumption by 20 percent.[25]

By February 1987, Germany was advocating unilateral cuts of 50 percent and urging other EC members to follow suit. Germany took over the EC presidency in 1987, and put ozone layer protection on the top of the EC agenda.[26] In May 1988, the German Federal Cabinet approved the Montreal Protocol, and a month later under German presidency, the EC Council of Ministers for the Environment also signed the Montreal Protocol into force.

Japan's reactive policy formation

Japan also signed the Montreal Protocol but this was not the result of domestic policy pressures. Despite the important findings about ozone layer depletion over Antarctica made by Chûbachi in 1982, only a small handful of Japanese scientists were working on stratospheric ozone issues. Working within their scientific community, they were largely isolated from political activities. These experts had no way to push stratospheric ozone depletion onto the political agenda in Japan.

There was generally little awareness of the ozone layer issue among the public or even within the environmental policy community. CFCs were the domain of the CFC-producing and consuming industries and MITI. Since the early 1980s MITI had monitored international developments, but it remained opposed to the formation of an international agreement largely because of its fears that regulation of CFC-113, which was used as a cleaning solvent, would have serious implications for Japanese producers of semi-conductors at a time when Japan dominated the semi-conductor market worldwide. Without a lobby calling for regulatory action in Japan, the position of MITI and the CFC-producing industries was only challenged from outside Japan. Politically, MITI's position was relatively safe as long as other major CFC producers, such as the United Kingdom and France, opposed regulations. Once these countries' positions began to change, however, it became harder for Japan to remain opposed to the establishment of an international agreement.

After the discovery of the "ozone hole," the United States mounted a bilateral effort to get Japan to change its position. Without Japanese support, any international treaty on CFCs would be considerably weakened since Japan produced over 10 percent of the global total of CFCs. In early 1987, US experts on ozone depletion traveled to Japan to exchange information on the problem with Japanese specialists and to lobby the Japanese government. As a result of such activities, a few actors slowly began to enter the debate in Japan. From 1987, for example, a few Kômeito and Socialist party members began to raise questions about

Japan's stratospheric ozone policy in the Diet. The Environment Agency also stepped up its research activities in this area. Yet, it was not a swell of grassroots support for policy change that led to Japan's acceptance of the idea of an international agreement for ozone layer protection; rather, it was primarily economic interests that determined Japan's policy position.

Once Du Pont, the world's largest producer of CFCs supplying about 25 percent of the world market, announced its intentions to completely phase out CFCs by early next century, pressure built up for Japanese CFC producers to do the same. Also important was that at several points in the on-going international negotiations for the formulation of a legally binding protocol, the United States introduced specific proposals to restrict trade in CFCs and other controlled substances to countries that failed to become parties to an international agreement.

In June 1987, just months before the convening of the Montreal Convention, Environment Agency director-general Inamura announced at the UNEP's annual General Council meeting that Japan would agree to the establishment of an international treaty. Japan agreed to the protocol after a compromise was made that gave Japan some flexibility in its use of CFC-113 by allowing countries to shift consumption among CFCs, so long as a given total ozone depleting potential was not exceeded.[27]

The global climate change debate

It was only months after the meeting in Montreal over CFCs that the greenhouse effect became the top issue on the international environmental agenda. The greenhouse effect is a natural phenomenon that makes life on earth possible. The fear of many scientists is that industrial and agricultural activities are increasing concentrations of certain greenhouse gases, including carbon dioxide (CO_2), CFCs, methane, and nitrous oxides, in the atmosphere above natural levels and that this will cause unnatural rates of temperature change.[28] CO_2 is the main greenhouse gas. As of 1989, Japan was responsible for about 4.7 percent of total global CO_2 emissions and the former West Germany for about 3.4 percent, putting them, respectively, a distant fourth and fifth place behind the United States (24.2 percent), the Soviet Union (18.7 percent), and China (9.7 percent).

Despite years of scientific research on global climate change and various international meetings on the subject, it was not until the record hot summer in the United States in 1988 that the issue suddenly received widespread public and political attention. In an effort to ascertain the state of the science and to make policy proposals, the UNEP and the World Meteorological Organization established an Inter-governmental Panel on Climate Change (IPCC) in November 1988. The recommendations of this international expert group, which included a call for international action on greenhouse gases, were released at the second World Climate Conference in Geneva in November 1990.

In November 1989 the Dutch government organized an international ministerial conference on climate change at which they proposed that as a first step to addressing climate change industrialized countries should agree to the stabilization of CO_2 emissions by the year 2000. In line with this, the Netherlands was the first country to announce a domestic CO_2 reduction target in its 1989 National Environmental Plan. Germany followed suit in June 1990 with a Cabinet Resolution which established a target to reduce CO_2 emissions by 25 percent over 1987 levels by the year 2005. As a result, Germany became an international leader in calling for dramatic and quick "precautionary" action on a potentially serious environmental issue. In contrast, at the 1989 Noordwijk meeting, Japan joined the United States and the Soviet Union in opposing international regulatory action as premature given the state of climate change science. This stance was similar to the one that Japan had taken in the case of stratospheric ozone depletion. Scientific uncertainty was used to justify policy inaction.

In this case, however, the Japanese position quickly became more proactive. Within a few weeks of Germany's announcing a concrete reduction target, the Japanese Cabinet announced that Japan would come up with its own target in time for the November 1990 World Climate Conference. This occurred even though the IPCC had yet to release its first major report on climate change. There was still no real scientific "consensus" about the nature of the problem and the United States, which in the past had been the primary state pushing Japan on various international environmental issues, was itself still opposing international regulatory action and the establishment of a concrete domestic reduction target. How can we explain this more proactive environmental position in Japan?

As with the case of stratospheric ozone depletion, there was initially little domestic pressure for any kind of regulatory action on global warming in Japan and little media interest in international environmental issues prior to 1989. Only a handful of groups were working on international environmental issues and these were focused largely on refugee issues, indigenous peoples, and tropical deforestation. The global environment was rarely brought up in Diet deliberations and relatively little climate change research was undertaken.

Developments leading up to the Montreal Protocol, however, had proved a learning experience for many environmental actors in Japan. After its weak performance in the CFC case, the Environment Agency began to strengthen its research and policy-making capacities related to climate change and other global environmental issues. In 1987 global climate change research was initiated at the Environment Agency's National Laboratory of Pollution (now the National Institute for Environmental Studies). In 1988 the Environment Agency issued an Environmental White Paper entitled *Japan's Contributions Toward the Conservation of the Global Environment* addressing such issues as ozone depletion, desertification, deforestation, loss of biodiversity, and global warming.[29] Also in May 1988 the Agency set up a Research Group on Global Warming, which produced its first report six months later. By July 1989, the Agency had established a Global Environment Protection Room, which was elevated to the status of a division in 1990.[30] The Environment Agency began to push for a CO_2 stabilization target as was being done in the Netherlands and Germany. On its own, however, the Agency would have had little success in winning support for regulatory action over the opposition of MITI to a concrete stabilization target. Importantly, however, the Environment Agency found a coalition partner in unexpected quarters.

In the late 1980s, the LDP, which had largely ignored environmental issues in the 1980s, suddenly turned more supportive of the environment. Some of the strongest voices for policy action on global climate change came from the LDP and the leader of its largest faction, Noboru Takeshita. Although then Prime Minister Takeshita was not much of an environmentalist, he played a crucial role in getting international environmental issues onto the agenda in Japan. The environment became a big international issue at a time when Japan was being criticized for not contributing to solving global problems at a level consistent with its status as an economic superpower. Moreover, for a man tainted by political scandal the environment was a "clean" issue.[31] Thus, Takeshita found it in his interest to turn green. The shift in stance by Takeshita and a few other key LDP politicians within his faction was a boon for environmentalists. In the absence of strong pressure for policy change from the grassroots, the emergence of a powerful politician as a policy sponsor was important in getting climate change onto the policy agenda.[32] In a coup for the Agency, Prime Minister Uno appointed the Environment Agency's director-general as Global Environmental Minister in July 1989, despite opposition from MITI and the Ministry of Foreign Affairs. The Ministerial Council on Global Environmental Protection was to play a central role in the formulation of Japan's "Action Plan to Arrest Global Warming."[33]

The greening of the LDP helped to get global climate change onto the Japanese policy agenda and strengthened the position of the Environment Agency. This does not mean, however, that other ministries and agencies did not exert considerable influence over the shape of Japanese policy. With LDP support for environmental policy, the environment budget began to grow. Japan's ministries and agencies each began to find ways to link their own policy interests to the climate change debate. Thus, there quickly emerged support for an Action Plan, but there were important differences among ministries over what the shape of the plan should be. As will become clearer below, MITI was in a stronger bargaining position vis-à-vis environmental interests in Japan than was its German counterpart in the Economics Ministry vis-à-vis environmental interests in Germany in shaping climate change policies.

Representatives from the Environment Agency supported the idea of international cooperation and the establishment of a CO_2 reduction target called for by the Dutch in Noordwijk. They also wanted to introduce a carbon tax to ensure that a reduction target could be met. MITI officials also expressed some concern about possible climate change, but like their German counterparts, they were more concerned about the economic implications of "premature action" and the division that existed between the US and European positions on CO_2 stabilization. Instead of a concrete target, MITI sought a plan that would promote energy conservation, nuclear power, the transfer of energy efficiency know-how, and R&D in new technologies. Energy efficiency and the promotion of alternative energies fit in well with MITI's existing interests in energy supply diversification and improving energy security. Moreover, MITI felt that Japan's past successes in improving energy efficiency warranted some recognition and that a growth in CO_2 levels was inevitable if economic growth was to continue at late 1980s levels.[34] Thus, MITI supported action on climate change as long as regulatory targets and the introduction of carbon taxes could be avoided.

Interestingly, the differences between the positions of MITI and the Environment Agency were never completely bridged. At the 23 October 1990 meeting of the Ministerial Council on Global Environmental

Protection two plans for CO_2 stabilization were announced. The first was MITI's plan calling for stabilization of CO_2 emissions at 1990 levels by 2000 on a per capita basis – a plan that actually allowed for a 6 percent increase in CO_2 levels based on projected increases in the population. The Action Plan then went on to say that if technological developments in new energies and CO_2 fixation went faster than predicted, the Environment Agency's plan would be put into effect.[35] Japan officially announced its CO_2 stabilization plan at the Second World Climate Conference in November 1990 and signed the Framework Convention on Climate Change in Rio de Janeiro in 1992.

Since this time, the Environment Agency has had to back away from the idea of a flat stabilization target because of its failure to date to push through a tax on CO_2 emissions. Instead, MITI is using the global climate change issue to improve energy efficiency, to justify the building of more nuclear power plants, and to encourage the development of new pollution control industries.

The German response to theories of global climate change

In Germany calls for action to address global warming built on the preceding two years of intense public concern for the global environment that stemmed from the Chernobyl nuclear accident and the discovery of the hole in the ozone layer above Antarctica. At the political level a strong linkage was made between ozone layer depletion and global climate change in the major reports to the Bundestag prepared by the Enquete Commission on Preventive Measures to Protect the Earth's Atmosphere. The Enquete Commission completed its first report, which reviewed the state of scientific knowledge on the earth's atmosphere and made regulatory proposals to deal with ozone layer depletion, in September 1988. This report included three chapters on the greenhouse effect and climate change and another on tropical deforestation.[36] In building a consensus on the need for action, this Commission, made up of politicians from Germany's four main parties and of expert witnesses, was aided by the support provided by Chancellor Kohl. Kohl had signaled his concern about climate change in a March 1987 policy speech.

The environment was big on the German political agenda, and thus despite scientific uncertainties related to climate change the need for precautionary action was taken seriously. Moreover, as was the case in Japan, most relevant actors could find ways to link their interests to the issue. For the pro-nuclear CDU/CSU, for example, it was seen as important to its domestic image in the post-Chernobyl period, but was also a way to gain support for the embattled nuclear energy industry and to justify reducing subsidies to the German coal industry. After the Chernobyl nuclear accident, the nuclear industry and the CDU tried to promote nuclear energy as a solution to global warming. Interestingly, with support for the Green Party growing, an official in the Economics Ministry also suggested that the CDU hoped that by taking a strong stance on climate change, they would be able to drive the Green Party out of the Bundestag.[37] For the opposition SPD support of the climate change issue was a means to pursue a green image through promotion of energy conservation and promotion of alternative energies.

The initiative to establish a national CO_2 reduction target officially originated in the Federal Chancellery. Officials working in the Ministry of the Environment lobbied colleagues in the Chancellor's Office on the advisability of the German government preparing a statement of its intentions to establish a reduction target, since such targets were already being discussed in international meetings. As in Japan, where support came from Takeshita, the Chancellor's Office was very influential in winning over other ministries to the idea of a reduction target.[38]

Again like the situation in Japan, the Ministry for the Environment was made responsible for formulating the outline of a climate change policy. This was to be done in consultation with other relevant ministries, including the Ministry of Transport; the Ministry for Regional Planning, Building, and Urban Development; the Ministry of Economic Affairs; and the Ministry of Food, Agriculture, and Forests. The Environment Ministry seized upon the political support coming from the Chancellor's Office and with its right of first draft prepared a proposal calling for an ambitious plan to reduce Germany's CO_2 emissions. In June 1990, it produced a report for discussion outlining CO_2 reduction potentials.[39] This report served as a working proposal for the 13 June Cabinet resolution announcing that Germany intended to reduce its CO_2 emissions by 25 percent of 1987 levels by 2005 – a goal that went significantly beyond the 20 percent reduction figure urged upon the international community at the Toronto World Conference on the Changing Atmosphere more than a year earlier. The report was based on materials prepared by the Energy Commission and in consultation with members of the Enquete Commission.

As with the case in Japan, there were differences between ministries in Germany over the advisability of a CO_2 reduction plan. The Economics Ministry argued that a reduction in CO_2 emissions was a worthy goal, but that a 25 percent reduction target was a political decision that did not take into consideration economic cost calculations. In an article critical of the plan, Dr. Knut Kübler of the Economics Ministry wrote: "In Toronto a reduction in global CO_2 emissions of around 20 percent of 1988 levels by 2005 was proposed. It is important to know that this '20 percent figure' was the outcome of negotiations among conference participants – mainly scientists and journalists. In other words: the reduction figure was what was ecologically necessary, not what is economically feasible ..."[40] The more ambitious German target underlines the greater strength of the German environmental policy community vis-à-vis economic interests compared with that of Japan.

The 13 June 1990 Cabinet Resolution also established a Climate-Gas Reduction Strategies Inter-ministerial Working Group. The Environment Minister, Klaus Töpfer, was appointed chairperson, and five study groups, each headed by a separate ministry, were established to determine the potential for greenhouse gas reduction in the areas of energy supply, transportation, the building sector, agriculture and forest management, and new technologies. Both this working group and the Enquete Commission produced reports related to the implementation of Germany's climate change policy and reviewed the reduction target in light of German reunification in late 1989.

In October 1990, the Enquete Commission for Preventative Measures to Protect the Earth's Atmosphere produced its third report to the Bundestag entitled *Protecting the Earth: A Status Report with Recommendations for a New Energy Policy*. In this report, in light of unification and the potential to rapidly reduce greenhouse gas emissions in the former East Germany, the Commission proposed a reduction that went beyond that already proposed by the German government under Environment Minister Töpfer. The Commission supported a call for a 30 percent reduction in CO_2 emissions in Germany by 2005; a 20–25 percent reduction for the European Community, and a 5 percent reduction worldwide.

In November 1990, the Climate-Gas Reduction Strategies Inter-ministerial Working Group released an interim report for submission to the Cabinet that took into account added energy reduction potentials in the former East Germany. Acting on this report, the federal cabinet altered its reduction target to a 25 percent reduction in CO_2 emissions by 2005 over 1987 levels for the old Länder, and to "a considerably higher extent" in the new German Länder. One year later, the Inter-ministerial Working Group produced a second interim report. On the basis of this report, the Federal Government confirmed its previous resolutions and decided on a reduction of CO_2 emissions for the whole of Germany of 25 to 30 percent of 1987 levels by 2005. This goal was reconfirmed by Chancellor Kohl in Rio de Janeiro.

In producing these reports, there was inter-ministerial agreement on many measures, such as those that dealt with energy saving and the promotion of new energy efficient technologies. As in Japan, there were conflicts, however, over support for nuclear energy, the idea of a carbon/energy tax, and possibilities for reductions in the transportation sector. While the Ministry of Research and Technology argued strongly for the inclusion of a sentence stating that nuclear energy was necessary to meet a reduction target, the Environment Ministry was against it. On this particular issue, the Environment Ministry won support from the Chancellor's Office (probably because of the sensitive pre-election timing – the first elections within a unified Germany were scheduled for 2 December 1990). Thus, nuclear energy remained an alternative, but not a "necessary" one. The Environment Ministry, however, was unable to push through a national CO_2 tax over the Economic Ministry's contention that such a tax should only be introduced if it were done at the EC level. The SPD was also unwilling to have the tax turned into an energy tax since this would raise costs for the coal industry, a key supporter of the SPD. Thus, although the Environment Ministry had the support of manufacturers of energy technologies, the German energy sector and energy-intensive industries had made it clear that they were opposed to an energy/CO_2 tax because the financial burden would reduce capital resources for investments to promote energy efficiency and because of concerns of international competitiveness. Instead, measures focused on improving energy efficiency became the mainstay of the report's proposals.

The Ministry of the Environment was not in as strong a position to push forward its goals once discussions moved to questions of implementation. This reflected in part the fact that the Environment Ministry has no jurisdiction over the energy and transportation sectors where primary measures for greenhouse gas reductions would have to take place. It also reflected a change in the political milieu. Because of the many problems plaguing the economic infrastructure in the former East Germany, and the rapid rise in unemployment, German unification drained government coffers. In post-unification Germany, these new problems quickly rose to the top of the political agenda. Also, for the first time since 1983, the West German Green Party was not represented in parliament because its opposition to unification was viewed negatively by voters.

In this changing political milieu, the Ministry of the Environment found that it could not push through important items on its agenda such as the introduction of a carbon tax at the national level. The more powerful ministries, in particular the Ministries of Economics, Research and Technology, Agriculture, and Housing, ironed out the details of policy measures for meeting Germany's reduction targets.

Conclusion

Differences in institutional structure and political culture between Germany and Japan clearly influenced their respective responses to the emergence of international environmental problems. In Japan, throughout the late 1970s and much of the 1980s, the Environment Agency was weak and inwardly focused, and both government and environmentalists remained on the periphery of international environmental networks. Thus, in contrast to the late 1960s and early 1970s, when citizens' groups helped pressure the Japanese government into making sweeping environmental policy reforms, there were no domestic actors concerned with pushing the state into action when stratospheric ozone depletion and other global environmental issues emerged as areas of international concern.

In Germany, by contrast, a strong environmental movement emerged just as more international attention was being directed toward transboundary and global environmental concerns. The importance of the green movement in Germany was not its direct sponsorship of international environmental issues, but rather the pressure it placed on other political and economic actors to become more sensitive to environmental issues. Concern with international issues such as acid rain bolstered the success of the domestic movement, thus encouraging a much stronger overall international outlook.

International scientific bodies, international organizations (especially UNEP), and international environmental groups helped foster awareness of new environmental issues. They also exerted strong pressures on states to participate in international environmental agreements once consensus was obtained internationally on the seriousness of a problem. International pressures were not very effective in promoting policy change, however, until those pressures were successfully linked, positively or negatively, to the interests of key domestic policy actors.

As was evident in the initial ten years of near non-response in Japan to international activities concerning stratospheric ozone depletion, the lack of domestic actors sponsoring the problem or offering their own policy solutions meant that the Japanese government took little notice of the international debate. Concern was confined to a small group of actors, specifically MITI and relevant industries, which continued to monitor international developments but did not act upon them until relatively late in the process. The decision to use administrative guidance to limit production capacity in 1980 came only because non-action was assessed as being potentially more damaging to Japanese foreign relations than a largely symbolic gesture to freeze production capacity of CFCs.

In Germany during the 1970s concern about ozone layer depletion remained similarly unfocused, and hence policy change was also limited. Membership within the EC, furthermore, was used by the German government to legitimize the less aggressive stance taken on CFCs in aerosols in Germany than in the US. This changed, however, once the Green Party had come to power and focused the attention of the established parties in Germany on environmental issues. By the mid-1980s, Germany was rapidly becoming a leader within Europe in pursuing more stringent domestic and international environmental protection measures. By the mid-1980s, Germany had become a primary force pushing the EC into action on stratospheric ozone depletion. Germany also became a leader in the climate change case.

Until the emergence of global climate change as an issue, Japan was a reactive state in the area of international environmental policy-making. This was largely because of the lack of domestic scientific research into global environmental issues, the absence of strong environmental interest groups, and the weakness of the Environment Agency. As the case of stratospheric ozone depletion has suggested, lack of information and resources made it difficult for domestic groups to sponsor ideas about global environmental problems emanating from abroad. Thus, powerful interests content with maintaining the status quo were able to shape Japan's international environmental policies, keeping them largely off the agenda.

Internationally, scientific and political developments defined global climate change as a policy problem. In Japan it was not pressure from the grassroots but the greening of Prime Minister Takeshita and a general change in stance on the part of business, the LDP, and the economic ministries that made environmental policy change possible on a scale not seen since the early 1970s. In many ways, this was rather similar to the top-down policy process that put environmental issues onto the political agenda in Germany twenty years earlier when the SPD under Willy Brandt saw in environmental protection a way to fulfill promises that the SPD would be a party of reforms.

Internationally, new ways of viewing the potential threat that economic activities were having on the environment were critical to the process of domestic policy change. The surge in environmental policy activity in Japan in recent years came largely because powerful domestic actors found ways to link their own interests to the global climate change debate and other environmental issues. Prior to the "greening" of Takeshita, the Environment Agency had started to push for global environmental policy change but it did not have the resources necessary to get environmental issues onto the agenda on their own. They could not count on NGOs as coalition partners because Japanese NGOs were too weak to be much of a political force.

The rise of global climate change and other environmental problems to the domestic policy agenda has brought major changes to Japan's environmental policies and institutions, much as occurred in Germany after the institutionalization of the environmental movement in the Green Party. The surge in environmental policy activity in Japan just prior to UNCED occurred because international events opened a window of opportunity to link Japanese interests – which were not necessarily primarily environmental – to this issue area. Now that the environment is on the agenda, however, institutional and normative changes are occurring that are likely to make Japan take increasingly proactive stands on environmental issues. Today in Japan there is a growing NGO community, strong public awareness of the environment, and interest in becoming a regional environmental leader.

Notes

1. See, for example, John Kingdon, *Agendas, Alternatives, and Public Policies* (Boston: Little, Brown, and Co., 1984) and Frank Baumgartner and Bryan D. Jones, *Agendas and Instability in American Politics* (Chicago: The University of Chicago Press, 1993).
2. For a discussion of work dealing with epistemic communities see chapter 1, fn 8.
3. See Peter Hall, *Governing the Economy: The Politics of State Intervention in Britain and France* (Washington, DC: The Brookings Institution, 1993) for an excellent case-study that links institutions, ideas, and policy change.
4. On policy sponsors see Kingdon, *Agendas, Alternatives, and Public Policies*; John C. Campbell, *How Policies Change: The Japanese Government and the*

Aging Society (Princeton, NJ: Princeton University Press, 1992); Peter Hall, "Policy Paradigms, Social Learning, and the State: The Case of Economic Policymaking in Britain," *Comparative Politics* (April 1993), 275–296; and Hugh Heclo, *Modern Social Politics in Britain and Sweden* (New Haven: Yale University Press, 1974).

5. This discussion draws on theoretical arguments made in Miranda A. Schreurs, "Domestic Institutions, International Agendas, and Global Environmental Protection in Japan and Germany," Ph.D. Dissertation, University of Michigan, August 1996.

6. See, for example, Haruhiro Fukui (ed.), *The Politics of Economic Change in Japan and Postwar Germany* (New York: St. Martin's Press, 1993); Ian Buruma, *The Wages of Guilt: Memories of War in Germany and Japan* (New York: Farrar, Straus, and Giroux, 1994); Jeffrey Bergner, *The New Superpowers: Germany, Japan, the United States, and the New World Order* (New York: St. Martin's Press, 1991). There are also some important comparative works in the environmental area. Helmut Weidner's 700–page dissertation on Japanese environmental policy includes detailed descriptions of air and water pollution control policies and various instruments for monitoring and enforcement of these policies. It also includes comparisons with the German approach to similar environmental problems. Helmut Weidner, *"Basiselemente einer erfolgreichen Umweltpolitik: Eine Analyse der Instrumente der japanischen Umweltpolitik unter Berücksichtigung von Erfahrungen in der Bundesrepublik Deutschland,"* Ph.D. Dissertation, *Fachbereich Politikwissenschaft der Freien Universität Berlin*, October 1992. In another piece he argues that the European Community nations have done better than Japan in addressing global environmental problems and that Japan's responses have been more symbolic than substantive. Helmut Weidner, *"Globale Umweltherausforderungen,"* in Hanns W. Maull (ed.), *Japan und Europa: Getrennte Welten?* (Frankfurt and New York: Campus, 1993). Another important work that deals with Japanese, German, and US environmental technology development is Alan Miller and Curtis Moore, *Green Gold: Japan, Germany, the United States and the Race for Environmental Technology* (Boston: Beacon Press, 1994).

7. This section draws on the research of the following works: Julian Gresser, Koichiro Fujikura, and Akio Morishima, *Environmental Law in Japan* (Cambridge, MA; MIT Press, 1981); Norie Huddle, Michael Reich, and Nahum Stiskin, *Island of Dreams* (New York: Autumn Press, 1975); Helmut Weidner and Shigeto Tsuru (eds.), *Environmental Policy in Japan* (Berlin: Ed. Sigma Bohn, 1989); Margaret McKean, *Environmental Protest and Citizen Politics in Japan* (Berkeley: University of California Press, 1981); T. J. Pempel, *Policy and Politics in Japan: Creative Conservatism* (Philadelphia: Temple University Press, 1982); and Susan Pharr and Joseph Badarracco, "Coping With Crisis: Environmental Regulation," in Thomas K. McCraw (ed.), *America vs. Japan* (Boston: Harvard Business School Press, 1986).

8. Frank Upham, *Law and Social Change in Postwar Japan* (Cambridge, MA: Harvard University Press, 1987).

9. Quoted in Lynton Caldwell, *International Environmental Policy* (Durham and London: Duke University Press, 1990), p. 50.

10. Organization for Economic Cooperation and Development, *Environmental Policies in Japan* (Paris: OECD, 1977).

11. Edda Müller, *Innenwelt der Umweltpolitik: Sozial-liberale Umweltpolitik – Ohnemacht durch Organisation?* (Opladen: Westdeutscher Verlag GmbH, 1986); and Jochen Hucke, "Environmental Policy: The Development of a New Policy Area," in Manfred Schmidt and Klaus von Beyme (eds.), *Policy and Politics in the Federal Republic of Germany* (New York: St. Martin's Press, 1985), pp. 156–173.

12. Douglas Barnes, "Established Parties and the Environment in the Federal Republic of Germany: The Politics of Responding to a New Issue," paper presented at the American Political Science Association Annual Meeting, The Palmer House Hilton, Chicago, Illinois, 3–6 September 1992.

13. Müller, *Innenwelt*, p. 5.

14. Helmut Weidner, "The Capability of the Capitalist State to 'Solve' Environmental Problems: The Examples of Germany and Japan," paper presented at the XVth World Congress of the International Political Science Association, Buenos Aires, Argentina, 21–25 July 1991.

15. Renate Mayntz, "Intergovernmental Implementation of Environmental Policy," in Kenneth Hanf and Fritz W. Scharpf (eds.), *Interorganizational Policy Making: Limits to Coordination and Central Control* (Beverly Hills: Sage Publications, 1978).

16. Gabriele Knôdgen, "The STEAG Coal-Fired Power Plant at Voerde or Changing German Clean Air Policy," paper from the International Institute for Environment and Society of the Science Center Berlin, November 1981, p. 60.

17. See Lutz Mez, "*Von den Bürgerinitiativen zu den GRÜNEN: Zur Entstehungsgeschichte der 'Wahlalternativen' in der Bundesrepublik Deutschland*," in Roland Roth and Dieter Rucht (eds.), *Neue soziale Bewegungen in der Bundesrepublik Deutschland* (Frankfurt and New York": Campus Verlag, 1987); and Dieter Rucht, "*Von der Bewegung zur Institution? Organisationsstrukturen der Ökologiebewegung*," in Roth and Rucht, p. 253.

18. For a discussion of the challenge the Greens posed to Germany's "semi-sovereign" state, see Peter J. Katzenstein, *Policy and Politics in West Germany: The Growth of a Semi-Sovereign State* (Philadelphia: Temple University Press, 1987), pp. 353–360.

19. Markus Jachtenfuchs, "The European Community and the Protection of the Ozone Layer," *Journal of Common Market Studies* 28:1 (1990), 265.

20. Imura Hidebumi and Kobayashi Hikaru, "Kagakuteki Fukakujitsusei no moto ni okeru Ishi Kettei: Ozonsô o Megutte no Kôsatsu," *Kankyô Kenkyû* 68 (1988), 27–28.

21. Kawahira Koji and Makino Yukio, *Ozon Shoshitsu* (Tokyo: Yomiuri Kagakusensho, 1989).

22. German Bundestag, *Protecting the Earth's Atmosphere: An International*

Challenge (Bonn: German Bundestag, 1989). See also Tim O'Riordan and Jill Jaeger (eds.), *Politics of Climate Change: A European Perspective* (New York: Rouledge, 1996).

23. German Bundestag, *Protecting the Earth's Atmosphere.*
24. Ibid.
25. Jachtenfuchs, "The European Community," p. 266.
26. Ibid., p. 267.
27. Karen Litfin, *Ozone Discourses: Science and Politics in Global Environmental Cooperation* (New York: Columbia University Press, 1994), p. 114.
28. See for instance, Stephen Schneider, "The Greenhouse Effect: Science and Policy," *Science* 243, 771–781.
29. Environment Agency of Japan, *Quality of the Environment in Japan*, 1988.
30. Kankyôcho, *20 Shunen Kinen Jigyô Jikkô Iinkai* (Tokyo: Gyôsei, 1991), pp. 112–116.
31. Interview with Asahi newspaper reporter Takeuchi Ken, 19 April 1991.
32. Peter Hall, *Governing the Economy: The Politics of State Intervention in Britain and France* (New York: Oxford University Press, 1993).
33. "Naikaku ni Chikyû Kankyô Tanto," *Asahi Shimbun*, 8 July 1989.
34. OECD, *OECD Environmental Performance Review:Japan* (Paris: OECD, 1994), p. 144.
35. Naikaku Sôri Daijin, "Chikyû Ondanka Bôshi Kôdô Keikaku," 10 February 1990.
36. German Bundestag, *Protecting the Earth's Atmosphere.*
37. Interview with an official of the German Economics Ministry, 8 June 1993.
38. Interview, Federal Environment Ministry, 18 May 1993.
39. Bundesministerium für Umwelt, Naturschutz and Reaktorsicherheit, "Bericht des Bundesministers für Umwelt, Naturschutz und Reaktorsicherheit zur Reduzierung der CO_2-Emissionen in der Bundesrepublik Deutschland zum Jahr 2005: Erster Bericht auf der Grundlage des Beschlusses der Bundesregierung zu Zielvorstellungen für eine erreichbare Reduktion der CO_2-Emissionen 13 Juni 1990," (Bonn, 13 June 1990).
40. Dr. Knut Kübler, "Die Energiepolitik zum Schutz der Erdatmosphäre," *Energiewirtschaftliche Tagesfragen*, vol. 41, 1991, p. 21.

7 Zimbabwe and CITES: illustrating the reciprocal relationship between the state and the international regime

Phyllis Mofson

This chapter considers Zimbabwe and the changes it has undergone as a member of the Convention on International Trade in Endangered Species of Wild Fauna and Flora (CITES). This is done using the listing of the African elephant under CITES as a case-study. Zimbabwe is a range state, meaning it is rich in many of the wildlife species that CITES protects, including the African elephant. Zimbabwe is also a leader in the developing world, the non-aligned movement, and in broader North–South dynamics. Its self-defined political and economic interests are often antithetical to CITES strategies. Thus, although Zimbabwe has entered into the CITES agreement, it has often been opposed to the behavior changes that the regime has expected.

CITES, an established and widely recognized international environmental agreement, was formed in 1973 and, as of 1995, had 128 national signatories.[1] CITES' purpose is to regulate international trade in animals, plants, and their products in order to prevent or mitigate species extinction, where international trade plays a major role in threatening that species. While CITES regulations are formulated at the international level, they are implemented nationally. Zimbabwe became a party to CITES in 1981.

CITES regulates trade in threatened and endangered species through listings in its three appendices. Appendix I lists species considered to be endangered, and generally bans commercial trade in those species. Appendix II includes threatened species, and subjects their trade to a system of permits and quotas. A third appendix is used by member states to list species threatened only in their particular jurisdictions; the protection of these species requires the cooperation of their trading partners.[2]

Fear of the decimation of the African elephant population led to initial moves to list the African elephant under CITES under Appendix II in 1978, and a quota system on ivory was established in 1985. The population of African elephants across the continent fell from an estimated 1.3 million to 600,000 during the 1980s.[3] Although southern Africa sustained large losses, the range states of east Africa accounted for the majority of the elephants lost. It is difficult to determine exact elephant populations in southern Africa. Elephants travel freely between wilderness areas on the borders of Zimbabwe, Botswana, Mozambique, Zambia, and South Africa. All five of Zimbabwe's national parks are in border areas. Government statistics on the Zimbabwe elephant population range from 60,000 to 70,000, with officials claiming that 45,000 is a "comfortable number."[4]

Initially, the ivory export quota and ivory tusk marking systems that were introduced by CITES in 1985 were heralded with cautious optimism by CITES, its members, and NGOs. The CITES secretariat proclaimed in July 1986 that the quota program was off to a "very promising start."[5] But less than two years later, the quota system was declared a failure. After just two years, TRAFFIC, a CITES watchdog group and a sub-division of World Wildlife Fund, concluded that the system had "succeeded in controlling the movement of only 20 to 40 percent of the total amount of ivory produced annually in Africa."[6] Furthermore, the quota system allowed for government-regulated trade of confiscated ivory. TRAFFIC estimated that because of this loophole, up to 70 percent of the so-called legal ivory trade came from poached elephants.[7]

After the elephant was listed in Appendix II, the illegal ivory trade swamped the legal trade in quantity, due to rampant poaching and smuggling. This was tied to the introduction of sophisticated assault weapons in Africa and a period of economic growth in east Asia, the largest market for ivory consumption. Poaching and smuggling was compounded by the political and military instability that has characterized the region since the 1970s. Zimbabwe's war of independence in the late 1970s and civil wars in Angola and Mozambique in the 1980s were not fully contained within their respective borders and the military forces of neighboring countries became involved in each of these conflicts. During this chaotic period, the armed forces of Zimbabwe, South Africa, Angola, and Mozambique were prime offenders in institutionalizing poaching and an illegal ivory trade across borders.[8]

In response to the failure of the CITES ivory quota and marking system to control the poaching of elephants, the United States unilaterally adopted the African Elephant Conservation Act in the autumn of 1988; this allowed it to impose a moratorium on imports of ivory from any country which participated in the ivory trade or which was not a member of CITES.[9] As a major ivory market, implementation of the new law had immediate impact. This action, combined with an NGO-driven campaign to change consumer attitudes about ivory, resulted in a significant drop in the worldwide demand for ivory and set the stage for other countries to follow suit. By May 1989, the United States, Canada, the European Community, and Australia had banned the commercial importation of ivory.[10] In the following year, the African elephant was given Appendix 1 listing within CITES.

Zimbabwe and several other African states opposed the Appendix 1 listing. Zimbabwe had an economic interest in ivory trade. From 1979 to 1988, Zimbabwe exported about 100 tons of ivory to the international market.[11] Much of the ivory industry in Zimbabwe was supplied from elephants in neighboring countries. While the domestic market remained active, supplied largely by culling by wildlife officials, ivory retail sales had reportedly fallen by 75 percent from 1989 to 1991 and many ivory carvers lost their jobs.[12] In addition, Zimbabwe's population of elephants was actually stable or rising in the 1980s. Thus, Zimbabwe felt its interests were threatened by the ban. Nevertheless, Zimbabwe has abided by the ivory trade ban imposed by the regime.

This case points to two conclusions. First, CITES, as an international regime, has made a difference in policy decisions taken by a member state. CITES membership induced changes in Zimbabwe's trading behavior, despite serious initial resistance. Zimbabwe has abided by the 1989 ivory trade ban established by CITES, even though it feels the ban is inappropriate and misguided. This change in behavior was primarily precipitated by an alteration in Zimbabwe's calculations of the costs and benefits of participation in the regime.[13] The perceived costs of continued trade in ivory increased because of the likelihood that Zimbabwe would be viewed as an international "outlaw." The benefits of trade, moreover, had decreased because the lucrative ivory export market was virtually eliminated, and prices had plummeted after the regime went into effect.

Second, this case study suggests that a member state's relationship to a regime can evolve over time. Zimbabwe has learned to pursue change from within the CITES system both to promote its domestic economic and political goals and to maintain popular support in the international community. Zimbabwe's approach to CITES and CITES' rules has evolved from a position of angry protest, signified by threats of with-drawal, to the assumption of a leadership role in debates about the organization's future. Zimbabwe is now actively working from within the CITES power structure to alter the nature and strategies of the organization. This leadership role was recognized by the parties to the convention when Zimbabwe's offer to host the next CITES meeting was accepted in November 1994. Zimbabwe's current and future efforts to initiate changes in regime procedures and principles have the potential to influence the future of CITES in far more permanent ways than the more visible and politically charged battles over individual species which characterized its previous involvement in the regime.

The findings of this study also suggest that regime membership, rather than requiring the surrender of some degree of national sovereignty and power, can in some cases enhance sovereignty and other national interests in the international arena. Through learning to become an inside player in the CITES system, Zimbabwe has empowered itself as an international actor.

CITES

CITES holds a Conference of the Parties (COP) every two to three years. These conferences serve as venues for amending the CITES appendices, discussing and adopting new resolutions, clarifying existing regulations, reviewing implementation by member states, making recommendations for improving the effectiveness of the treaty, and conducting budgetary and administrative business.

The Lausanne COP

The Appendix I listing for the African elephant was proposed at CITES' seventh COP held in Lausanne, Switzerland in 1989 by Austria, Gambia, Hungary, Kenya, Somalia, Tanzania, and the United States.[14] The proposal, based on recommendations from the CITES African Elephant Working Group and studies commissioned by the specially-convened Ivory Trade Review Group, was adopted over the objections of eleven countries, including Botswana, Mozambique, Zambia, South Africa, and Zimbabwe.[15] Four countries, including Japan, abstained from the vote. All remaining southern African countries and the People's Republic of China registered reservations to the listing within the prescribed 90-day period. Zimbabwe officially entered a reservation to the listing before the meeting ended.[16]

The Appendix I listing virtually ended what remained of the international commercial ivory trade.[17] Despite predictions in *The Economist* and elsewhere that the ban would result in increased ivory demand and rising prices, prices fell following the listing, and the major pre-ban markets for ivory largely disappeared.[18] The ivory trade ban was considered unfair by Zimbabwe because during the 1980s the population of elephants in Zimbabwe and Botswana had not decreased but was stable or rising, a fact that was even recognized by US CITES officials. Even before the Lausanne COP, it was acknowledged that a total commercial ivory trade ban would have adverse effects on conservation programs in certain countries. US CITES officials readily admitted that "Zimbabwe really does have a legitimate problem. It's intractable."[19]

Without an effective means to distinguish legal from illegal ivory, nor an effective means to keep tight control on the legal trade, however, the international consensus maintained that any relaxation in the ivory trade would only open the door to the large illegal trade that existed before 1989. Nevertheless, convinced by the arguments of Zimbabwe and other southern African countries that not all of Africa's elephant herds were endangered, the COP adopted a Somali proposal to review specific range state populations prior to the next COP to allow the downlisting of elephants in certain countries back to Appendix II.[20]

In an attempt to gain greater control over their ivory exports, which they assumed would resume after the next COP, Zimbabwe, Botswana, Zambia, and Malawi formed an organization called the Southern African Center for Ivory Marketing (SACIM). This was designed to be the "sole exporting agency of ivory from members."[21] In August 1991, Zimbabwe hosted a SACIM workshop on the future of CITES.[22] Although designed primarily as a forum for airing grievances, several influential documents emerged from the workshop, including a set of recommendations for new criteria for listing species in CITES Appendices and a report entitled "The Case for a New Convention on International Trade in Wild Species of Flora and Fauna," which argued in very confrontational language that CITES is full of "major defects," does not work, and needs to be replaced.

The Kyoto COP

At the eighth COP, held in Kyoto, Japan in March 1992, the SACIM countries submitted a proposal to downlist their elephant herds to Appendix II. There was, however, almost universal opposition to downlisting at the conference. Only two SACIM members, Zimbabwe and

Botswana, met the Somali Amendment conditions.[23] Moreover, because of the highly publicized success of the ivory trade ban in reducing elephant poaching in the previous two years, most of the delegations and NGOs which came to Kyoto were strengthened in their resolve to oppose any resumption of trade or the downlisting of any elephant populations. There was a pervasive belief that any downlisting, even one which included a moratorium, would send a message to poachers and smugglers that it would be only a matter of time before the trade resumed; this was particularly true for the east African range states, which had seen their tourism industries revive since the ban.

In the face of this opposition, the SACIM countries amended their proposal during the conference to include a zero-quota on ivory sales at least until the next COP, a removal of their standing reservations, and an automatic return of their elephant populations to Appendix I at the next COP if they could not present acceptable plans for ivory marketing and elephant management by that time.[24] Despite these concessions, however, opposition remained overwhelming, and the proposals were finally withdrawn.[25] In his speech withdrawing the SACIM resolution, Botswana's Minister of the Environment said, "We are extremely perplexed … It seems to us that the goalposts have been moved … We will review our participation in CITES as soon as we have reported to our respective governments."[26]

The assumption that a downlisting of Zimbabwe's elephants would be adopted at Kyoto was logical and reasonable, based on the Lausanne discussion. Indeed, Rowan Martin, Assistant Director of Terrestrial Research in the Department of National Parks and Wildlife Management (DNPWM) in Zimbabwe since 1989, maintained that Zimbabwe's implementing legislation went farther than CITES required. He further claimed that Zimbabwe's domestic controls have always been more stringent than CITES requirements, making CITES largely "irrelevant."[27]

Zimbabwean officials were extremely upset with the politicization of the elephant protection issue, which they felt resulted in a climate in which they have not been permitted to explore and present plans that might meet ivory identification and trade control requirements. In protest of CITES' handling of the African elephant earlier in the COP, Zimbabwe introduced a proposal to list the northern Atlantic herring in Appendix I.[28] The proposal, which had no scientific grounding, was withdrawn after discussion allowed Zimbabwe to make its point that CITES listings were increasingly being used for political purposes and not grounded in any scientific criteria. The herring was chosen because it is an important commercial commodity for many European countries, just as, Zimbabwe argued, the elephant is for many African range states.

This dispute was only a precursor to a larger debate that was emerging internationally over the appropriate environmental conservation paradigm to be employed by the CITES regime – sustainable use or preservation.[29] Zimbabwe emerged as a leading proponent of the sustainable use paradigm. The sustainable use paradigm, which has been discussed in wildlife conservation circles since the 1980 publication of the "World Conservation Strategy," by the IUCN and World Wildlife Fund, emphasizes the goal of using living resources to meet both human and ecological needs.[30] The principle asserts that in many cases wildlife can best be conserved by exploiting it for economic gain. Zimbabwe would like to see a sustainable use ethic replace the existing "preservationist" ethic. Zimbabwe's "pro-use" allies in CITES include Japan, Canada, Norway, southern African elephant range states, and increasingly, developing country range states of commercial timber species such as Malaysia, which has also played a very active role in the last two COPs. Pro-use advocates stress that the economic profit that can be gleaned from use of wildlife is seen as giving value to that wildlife and thus provides a genuine motive for people to manage and conserve the resource. Such use might range from eco-tourism to selling hunting rights to marketing products from culled wild or ranched animals. Some in the US government and NGO communities, however, are suspicious of what they see as a "political" application of the sustainable use concept in CITES. These skeptics use the term "sustainable use" as a synonym for a "pro-trade" position in CITES, regardless of the effect of such policies on wildlife conservation.[31]

Pushing the sustainable use approach in CITES was one way Zimbabwe began to link its economic interests in trading ivory to an environmental idea that was gaining popularity elsewhere. The 1992 United Nations Conference on Environment and Development (UNCED), held in Brazil three months after the Kyoto CITES COP, had as its theme "sustainable development," a closely-related concept introduced in the 1987 publication *Our Common Future*, by the UN-appointed World Commission on Environment and Development. The prevailing rhetoric at the UNCED was that environmental protection and economic development must go hand in hand if either is to be achieved. The Biodiversity Convention, signed at UNCED by some 150 countries, states that natural resources belong to the range states in which they are found. Some southern African delegations wondered then how that philosophy would fit in to the CITES regime, which they saw as taking a fundamentally different approach.[32]

The Kyoto Conference initiated what can only be called a constitutional crisis for CITES. At Kyoto, attention was focused on species which represented large-scale commercial industries for range states and consumer states alike; the African elephant represents only one of these species – others include the Bluefin Tuna and several tropical timber species. Countries with high economic stakes in these species include Japan, Canada, and the United States in the tuna case, and Malaysia in the tropical timber case. In the tuna case, the lobbying against listing was so strong that the proposal never reached the floor. Should CITES assume a larger role in regulating commercial species, the economic stakes of CITES participation will be raised for many member states. This is another important factor pushing Zimbabwe to strengthen its position within the regime.

After the Kyoto COP, participants and observers worldwide began speaking of the "politicization" of CITES, a development which many believed would herald the organization's demise. TRAFFIC's analysis of the conference included the following assessment: "Many conference decisions were made without regard for scientific data … with the results reflecting political expediency rather than practical conservation …"[33]

When its downlisting proposal was rejected at Kyoto, Zimbabwe threatened to withdraw from the organization. After the Kyoto COP, an unofficial document known as CITES II was floated informally to CITES delegations of several countries. Its stated purpose was to transform "the present CITES to a new convention which rectifies some of the perceived defects and is more closely aligned with modern conservation concepts."[34] These "perceived defects" included claims that CITES' protection had not measurably improved the status of any listed species; that CITES was founded in outdated conservation principles that are inconsistent with the goal of sustainable development; and that it was an imperialist treaty, codifying "the entrenched dominance of Western importing states … [which] is a source of political irritation to developing countries."[35]

In responding to a questionnaire about CITES in October 1992 (about the time CITES II was being floated), Martin wrote:

[Question: What have been the advantages and disadvantages for Zimbabwe in participating in CITES? On balance, which dominate?]

a) *Advantages*: It is very difficult to think of any. In a nihilistic sense we have needed to be members of CITES to ensure that some wildlife products (e.g. crocodile skins) find their best markets. Certainly, there have been no conservation advantages.

b) *Disadvantages*: They are legion. Without considering the obvious case of listing elephant on Appendix I (to which it could be argued that we would be no worse off as non-Parties), there are a number of cases where the bureaucracy surrounding CITES business seriously prejudices our attempts to promote wildlife as a general form of land use in Zimbabwe ...

c) Without a doubt, the disadvantages of CITES totally outweigh any benefits attached to being Parties. It would be accurate to state that we are forced to remain in the CITES forum if only to protect our interests ...

DNPWN director Willie Nduku, however, was later quoted as saying that Zimbabwe would seek an agreement with any country interested in buying its ivory stockpiles if CITES failed to lift the ivory ban at the Fort Lauderdale COP in 1994.[36]

The Fort Lauderdale COP

Only two proposals relating to elephants were brought to the Fort Lauderdale COP – South Africa proposed downlisting its elephants to Appendix II to permit only trade in hides, hair, and meat, with a continued ban on ivory trade; and Sudan asked for a one-time downlisting of its elephant population to allow it to sell its ivory stockpile. The Sudanese proposal received no support from any party, neither Africans nor others, primarily because Sudan has virtually no elephants of its own, and its entire ivory stockpile came from poached elephants from other countries. Sudan acknowledged that its proposal did not meet the Lausanne criteria and had not been reviewed by the Panel of Experts. After a decision was taken that the range states would meet to review the issue of stockpiles before the next COP, Sudan withdrew the proposal.[37] Zimbabwe and the other SACIM countries did not offer any downlisting proposals because they believed that getting approval "was not possible" at Fort Lauderdale. A Zimbabwean government official stated, "We feel we are being punished for our successful conservation efforts."[38]

The South African proposal was opposed by virtually all other African range states, including Zimbabwe.[39] The US delegation, while finding the proposal scientifically sound, said it could not support it in the face of range state opposition.[40] South Africa later withdrew its proposal when it became obvious that it could not garner sufficient votes for adoption.[41]

It is critical to understand why Zimbabwe did not support the South Africans in their effort. First, they believed that the South African proposal did not go far enough and therefore did not deserve their support.[42] The southern African states, and Botswana and Zimbabwe in particular, felt that since they had more elephants, South Africa did not have a legitimate right to move on an elephant proposal without them. "South Africa has only 7,000 elephants, all in Kruger [National Park]," a Zimbabwean official pointed out after the Fort Lauderdale conference.[43] Moreover, they feared that adoption of South Africa's proposal could cause the ivory trade to be banned permanently.[44] Finally, and perhaps most importantly, Zimbabwe was changing its strategies for dealing with CITES.

Zimbabwe began to combine its protests and denunciation of CITES with increasingly successful efforts to increase its power within CITES and change the way the organization worked. As one official put it:

> [We have discovered that it is] better to work on CITES from within. It doesn't end with elephants; once you are an outsider you have no input or involvement. We are interested in learning from other countries, especially on the breeding of endangered species … We realize we will benefit from staying in [CITES], and now we are hosting [the next COP].[45]

Zimbabwe's effect on CITES: changing the nature of the regime from within

Because of the high visibility and political volatility of the issue of elephant downlisting at the Kyoto COP in 1992, it appeared that the southern African elephant range states left that meeting very much as losers. In fact, however, on a number of less flashy issues, these countries, led by Zimbabwe, saw several of their resolutions passed. Some of these, including resolutions on listing criteria for species and the potential benefits of commercial trade for wildlife conservation, have the potential to influence the future of the ivory trade (as well as trade in many other wildlife species) in more permanent ways than would a conditional downlisting.

A SACIM proposal calling for CITES to recognize the benefits of trade in wildlife conservation resulted in CITES Conf. 8.3, which recognizes "that commercial trade may be beneficial to the conservation of species ... when carried out at levels that are not detrimental to the survival of the species in question."[46] The importance of this resolution was overshadowed by SACIM's defeat on the downlisting proposal, but it served as a precursor to bigger changes at Fort Lauderdale.

One of the most important documents to come out of the 1994 Fort Lauderdale COP was Conf. 9.24: Criteria for Amendment of Appendix I and II, which laid out new procedures for both listing and downlisting or removing species on CITES Appendices. The adoption of the new criteria can be traced to the previous COP, where Zimbabwe introduced a new set of listing criteria, which were referred to as the "Kyoto Criteria." Zimbabwe's proposal was rejected by the parties, but a resolution was adopted (Conf. 8.20) which directed the Standing Committee to draft a revision of the "Bern Criteria" for consideration in Fort Lauderdale two years later.[47]

The Bern Criteria were guidelines set forth at the first CITES COP in 1976 for amending the CITES appendices. These criteria rested primarily on the "precautionary principle," which says that when there is doubt about the danger of trade to conservation of a species, CITES should err in favor of protection in the form of listing the species. Among the new listing criteria Zimbabwe presented at Kyoto was the requirement that the party proposing the listing must consult with the range states prior to introducing the proposal to the parties. This was an important theme for Zimbabwe's charges – elaborated in the CITES II document – that the Convention was imperialist and dominated by wealthy wildlife consumer countries. The new criteria adopted at Fort Lauderdale refer explicitly on two separate occasions to the importance of consulting with range states, and require that details of range state management, monitoring, and conservation programs for the species in question be provided before listing is considered by the CITES parties.

Other new considerations which species must meet to be included in Appendix I now include thresholds, including such biological criteria as population status and trends, distribution, habitat, and threats. In addition, scientific data about utilization and trade in the species, as well as information about range state conservation and management plans, must be provided.[48] The net result of the new criteria, which are more scientific and objective than listings based on the Bern Criteria, should make it more difficult to list species in Appendix I, and easier to downlist from Appendix I to Appendix II. These results are clearly to the benefit of Zimbabwe and other pro-trade countries.[49]

Zimbabwe was also instrumental in changing the committee and power structure of the CITES regime itself to accord more weight to the input of developing countries and range states. Along with Malawi and Botswana, Zimbabwe demanded that developing nations have a larger role in the CITES Standing Committee, the most powerful constituent organ of the Convention. Prior to the Fort Lauderdale COP, the membership of the Standing Committee was composed of one party from each of six geographical regions: Africa, Asia, Europe, North America, Oceania, and South and Central America and the Caribbean. The host countries of the previous and upcoming COPs are also Standing Committee members. This formula gave disproportionately high representation to regions with fewer parties – such as North America, with three, and Oceania, with four – at the expense of the larger Asian and African regions. US State Department communications from the Fort Lauderdale COP stated: "This [Standing Committee debate] is one of several issues where a certain amount of South versus North tension can be felt."

Zimbabwe viewed the Standing Committee's composition as further evidence of the imperialist nature of CITES, and, according to US government officials, Malawi, Botswana, and Zimbabwe started the movement to change the composition of the committee in order "to dilute the influence of the US."[50] Malawi introduced the proposal at Fort Lauderdale to reapportion representation more fairly on the Standing Committee. This proposal met with great support from the majority of developing countries and was adopted by the parties. The new Standing Committee provides for approximately one representative for every fifteen parties, allowing Africa three, Asia two, Europe two, South and Central America two, and North America and Oceania one each.[51] The African representatives are Namibia, Senegal, and Sudan. Zimbabwe, as the next host country, is also on the committee.

In addition to composition changes, the Fort Lauderdale COP resulted in an unexpected change in the Standing Committee chairmanship. New Zealand, the chair at the time, tended to cooperate closely with the United States, and US government officials anticipated that the next chair would be the United Kingdom, which would tend to share US interests.[52] They were therefore taken by surprise when Namibia countered the nomination of the United Kingdom and successfully backed Japan for the next chairmanship.

Although Japan is a large industrialized country and a major consumer of many CITES-listed species and products, with regard to CITES, it tends to behave more like a range state than a consumer state.

Japan is firmly in the "pro-use" camp, and is in agreement with Zimbabwe and other southern African range states on the ivory trade issue, as well as on broader questions about the role of CITES. The Standing Committee changes that came out of Fort Lauderdale did much to bring CITES more in line with Zimbabwe's "pro-trade" and "anti-imperialist" visions.

Fort Lauderdale COP Doc. 9.18 provides evidence of the effective collaboration between Zimbabwe, Japan, and Canada in bringing CITES into a more pro-use (or sustainable-use) posture. The adoption of this document, entitled "How to Improve the Effectiveness of the Convention," may in the long run prove to be the most influential outcome of COP 9. The proposal, introduced by Canada, was a very general call for a study of the regime's overall effectiveness to be conducted by an independent consultant, with the findings to be reported to the next COP.[53] It was adopted in committee by a vote of 62 to 4, and no opposition was voiced in the plenary session.[54] Members of the US delegation are certain that the proposal is a direct descendant of the CITES II document circulated by Zimbabwe.[55] Zimbabwean officials readily acknowledge that the decision to contract the study is the result of four years of behind-the-scenes coalition-building on its part, and that CITES II was in fact "incorporated in the Canadian effectiveness proposal."[56] Most parties, which were previously consulted on the proposed content, were immediately supportive.[57] The United States was among the four opposing votes, arguing that the money could be better spent on improving CITES implementation.[58]

A US State Department report on the Fort Lauderdale COP expressed the following concerns regarding the effectiveness document:

> Although proposed by Canada, this is another issue which resonates with a division between those favoring greater sustainable use and those favoring greater emphasis on "pure" conservation ... Although the proposal states only that a consultant will evaluate the effectiveness of CITES, the enthusiasm expressed by Japan (which announced it will contribute $100,000, much of which it hopes will be used for this review) and Zimbabwe (which has said it can collect enough money from developing countries to pay for this review) make it clear what they expect from the project.[59]

The effectiveness proposal is not radical or critical in tone, as was the CITES II document, but several themes from CITES II nevertheless emerge in the effectiveness study motion. One is CITES' age. CITES II argued that the regime embodied outdated principles and goals which have since been discredited. The new proposal states, with a similar implication, that "during that period [since 1973] the number of conservation conventions has multiplied many times," thus supporting the need for review.[60] CITES II claimed that "there is only one measure [of the success of CITES] and that is the extent to which species populations have increased as a result of CITES."[61] Along these same lines, the effectiveness proposal directs the consultant to provide information about:

> the extent to which the conservation status of a representative selection of species listed in each of the three appendices of CITES has changed, and the extent to which the change can be attributed to the application of CITES.[62]

As researchers who have tried to assess the effectiveness of regimes know, it is extremely difficult – and sometimes misleading – to quantify such effects. "Effectiveness" may take the form of increasing public awareness, education, strengthening domestic conservation structures and procedures through economic assistance or technical support, decreasing demand in consumer countries, or deterring potential behavior that is prohibited by the regime.[63] In addition, because international trade usually represents only a tiny fraction of the pressure on threatened and endangered species, a narrow assessment, such as that outlined in the effectiveness proposal, is likely to conclude that CITES is doing little or nothing for its listed species. This could theoretically make it easier for Zimbabwe and others to steer CITES away from listing species, particularly on Appendix I, and toward a pro-use stance.

Finally, Zimbabwe will host the next CITES meeting, which is scheduled for the first half of 1997. Zimbabwe plans to take this opportunity to forge a common southern African position on the elephant that can be presented to CITES on its home turf, and to "educate delegations [to COP 10] about the real situation."[64] These changes will, if successful, prove favorable to Zimbabwe as a pro-use range state. In the process of changing the regime, Zimbabwe has also improved its leadership status within the organization, with possible spillover effects to regional and even multilateral arenas.

The domestic dimension

To understand Zimbabwe's shift from initial opposition to the Appendix I listing of the African elephant to its more recent efforts to promote a sustainable use paradigm within CITES, it is essential to understand the domestic politics of wildlife conservation. Zimbabwe's position within CITES has been shaped by economic, political, and cultural factors. Complex attitudes toward conservation create a tightrope which Zimbabwe's foreign environmental policy officials are continually challenged to walk. In order to earn the favor of the international community and the important development funding and trade benefits that come with it, Zimbabwe feels that it must be a part of CITES. However, there is a general lack of domestic support for CITES' approach to wildlife conservation.

Traditionally, the people of Zimbabwe have been animists who regard certain animals with reverence, and many wild animals are also prized for their economic utility. At the same time, there are wild animal species in Zimbabwe that are feared or avoided as dangerous and destructive. Jon Hutton, director of the NGO Africa Resources Trust, remarked: "The First World does not know what it means to have an entire maize field destroyed by animals, besides being terrorized."[65] President Mugabe told a regional conference on environmental management that "Green movements sometimes tend to overstretch themselves and put nature before the needs of human beings. ... Must human beings suffer to sustain other animal species?"[66] The relationship between humans and animals in Africa has become increasingly complicated due to rapid human population growth, especially in marginal agrarian areas, where humans and animals must compete against one another for land.

Government officials maintain that environmental protection is a high priority for the general population, and that a conservation ethic has been traditionally based on a symbiotic relationship between humans, plants, and wild animals.[67] This symbiotic relationship, they argue, was destroyed by white settlers who took the land from the indigenous people, converted it to large farms, and devastated much of the continent's wildlife.[68] Previously the British colony of Rhodesia, Zimbabwe has been ruled since its independence in 1980 by President Robert Mugabe and his Zimbabwe African National Union-Patriotic Front party. The Zimbabwe Constitution created a multi-party system with a bi-cameral parliament and provides for majority rule with protection of majority rights. Despite this constitutional structure, it has been President Mugabe's vision to create a socialist, one-party state, and he has ruled largely in accordance with this vision. A referendum for a *de-jure* one-party state was rejected by voters in 1990, but Mugabe retained the presidency.

Zimbabwe's economy is centralized, with large public ownership of industry. Nevertheless, a pragmatic relationship with the private sector has been pursued. In recent years, Zimbabwe has undertaken economic reform, including privatization, as a result of an IMF/World Bank-supported structural adjustment program. Zimbabwe is now considered a relative economic and political success in Africa.[69] Large farming operations and subsistence farming are both important elements of the economy. There are about 100,000 white Zimbabweans out of a total population of some 11 million people. While most of the whites have been in Zimbabwe for several generations, there nevertheless remain cultural and economic divides.

Before independence, environmental policy was under the purview of the Rhodesia Natural Resources Board. This Board continued to exist under the new government until 1985, when it merged with the Ministry of Tourism to form the Ministry of Environment and Tourism. The Parks and Wild Life Act, passed in 1975, granted private landowners rights to use wildlife on their land. Previously, such rights belonged to the colonial state. Most public wilderness and wildlife conservation programs in Zimbabwe are administered by DNPWM, which is within the Ministry of Environment and Tourism. In addition to DNPWM, government agencies with vested interests in communal lands and their development strategies include: the Ministry of Lands, Agriculture, and Rural Resettlement; the Ministry of Local Government, Rural and Urban Development; the Ministry of Community and Cooperative Development; and District Councils – the elected local level representation for rural populations.

CITES is implemented and enforced in Zimbabwe by the DNPWM. Zimbabwe's principal piece of legislation regulating the international trade of wildlife, passed for the specific purpose of implementing CITES, is "The Control of Goods – Import and Export of Wildlife Regulations of 1982."[70] Under this law, the DNPWM publishes a schedule of all species listed in the CITES appendices. These species must be accompanied by valid CITES Import Permits in order to enter the country. The law requires that all wildlife exports from Zimbabwe be subject to export permits issued from DNPWM, whether listed in CITES or not.[71]

While most conservation programs on public lands are administered by the DNPWM, private game ranching is competing with public management. Commercial farmers and ranchers, discouraged by falling beef and other commodity prices, are increasingly moving into wildlife production.[72] Particularly important in this regard is the Commercial Wildlife Producers Association (CWPA), which is part of the very powerful Commercial Farming Union (CFU). The CFU does not espouse environmental protection as a central tenet, but as increasing numbers of farmers are taking up game ranching as a means of supplementing their income, the organization is becoming more vocal in conservation policy. Because of the strong political power base of the agricultural sector, the CWPA has a high degree of access to policy- makers, and has thus heavily influenced the strength of Zimbabwe's sustainable use position.[73] The concept of game ranching for profit has been widely perceived as a white-dominated phenomenon because it is largely whites who own large enough parcels of land to engage in this industry.[74] The rights to use wildlife that were conferred on private land-owners in the 1970s did not extend to those blacks living on communal lands. These territories are rural, of marginal agricultural value, often share borders with the protected lands on the country's periphery, and still are home to the majority of Zimbabwe's black population. This fact reflects the continued dominance of white large land-owners, a legacy from the colonial land tenure system which has yet to be substantially reformed. According to outside analysts, this is because Mugabe continues to perform a "balancing act" around this issue, attempting to maintain both economic growth and civil peace through a cautious approach to land reform.[75]

Interestingly, while the DNPWM is in favor of more private involvement in wildlife management, support of a pro-use paradigm is not complete. Although the overall trend within the DNPWM and CWPA is consistent with the principle of giving value to wildlife, and thus alleviating animal population pressures in national parks, the department fears that the transfer of too much of its responsibility to the private sector will threaten its already precarious existence. Some senior DNPWM officials have reportedly "expressed concern" over the rate at which game transfers are occurring.[76]

Traditionally, the conservation movement in Zimbabwe has been perceived as dominated by white-controlled groups: the Wildlife Society, Zimbabwe Trust, Africa Resources Trust, Environment 2000, the University of Zimbabwe's Centre for Applied Social Sciences, IUCN, and the World Wildlife Fund.[77] Although Zimbabwe's environmental NGOs are indigenous in the sense that they are not merely chapters of international groups, they are suspect to political charges that they are not representative of the environmental concerns of all of Zimbabwe because they are dominantly white. Still, while US and European environmental NGOs often play the role of opposition to governmental power, in wildlife conservation policy in Zimbabwe, government officials and most NGOs tend to be in agreement. There is a small, close circle of association among scientists, policy-makers, the DNPWM, and NGO representatives. This conservation community agrees that the sustainable use approach to conservation and development is the correct approach, and that CITES' approach to wildlife conservation has thus far been inappropriate.[78]

Zimbabwe's conservationists overwhelmingly feel that the cooperation of the blacks on communal lands is essential for the success of any wildlife conservation policies. In order to secure this cooperation, DNPWM officials and NGOs agree that these groups must have a vested interest in the value of the wildlife on their lands.[79] With the creation in 1988 of an organization known as The Communal Areas Management Program For Indigenous Resources (CAMPFIRE), progress has been made in bringing more black Africans and "traditional cultural perspectives" into the field of wildlife conservation. CAMPFIRE was established in an effort to bring a greater degree of control and economic incentive to the marginalized black community. The theory behind CAMPFIRE is that individual communities can develop the most effective management plans for their own grasses (for livestock grazing), water, trees, and wild animals. Such management plans increase the availability of scarce resources, and provide hard evidence that wildlife conservation can provide revenue and jobs to communities, whether through tourism, selling select hunting rights, or selective exploitation for food and other products. The DNPWM claims that CAMPFIRE has been successful in those communities where it has been implemented. For example, the Nyaminyami district, which was the first to implement CAMPFIRE, raised $458,000 in 1992 by selling hunting permits, meat, and hides. This money has been put toward community health care, schools, water systems, and arming wildlife protection rangers.[80]

Government officials point to CAMPFIRE as an example of successful sustainable use in action, and Zimbabwe is urging CITES to adopt two of CAMPFIRE's guiding principles: ownership and empowerment of those who are most impacted by the species in question (in the case of CITES, this would be the range states), and imparting economic value to the resource (through its exploitation).[81]

Because CAMPFIRE's implementation coincided with the ivory trade ban, revenue from the international ivory trade has not benefited communities. DNPWM officials have argued that once legal ivory trade is resumed, communities' revenues will be enhanced. DNPWM officials have also argued for the need for further decentralization of the administration of CAMPFIRE to the district council level in order to improve CAMPFIRE's effectiveness. In addition, the same DNPWM officials would like to see their own department, which has experienced budget cuts in real terms of 88 percent between 1988 and 1993, benefit from revenues from a resumed ivory trade.[82] There is discussion of forming a "parastatal" organization whereby wildlife revenue could bypass the central treasury and be put directly into conservation and wildlife management.[83] The precedent of decentralization within CAMPFIRE would strengthen the case for enhancing DNPWM's budget in this way. At the same time, arguing that CAMPFIRE has been a success also supports DNPWM's arguments within CITES that the trade ban hurts elephant conservation efforts.

Zimbabwe as an advocate of sustainable use

Some international NGOs feel that Zimbabwe's claim to be an example of successful wildlife management and conservation has been weakened by a downturn in the national economy from about 1993 and the subsequent shortfalls in wildlife management funding.[84] Zimbabwe's claim to be an appropriate leading voice for advancing the concept of sustainable use within CITES has also been called into question by allegations of corruption within its armed forces, the DNPWM, and higher levels of government.[85] Suspicion has been raised that Zimbabwe has not been completely forthcoming regarding its ability to manage its own wildlife resources. Zimbabwean government officials acknowledge that the country has been largely unsuccessful at controlling rhinoceros poaching; only an estimated 300 rhinos remain in Zimbabwe.[86] Some Zimbabwean NGO officials claim that had a legal, managed rhino horn trade been introduced when rhinos were still plentiful, numbers would not have fallen so dramatically. Some outside observers feel the rhinoceros case does not bode well for Zimbabwe's elephants should the ivory trade be reopened.[87]

In addition to its problems controlling rhinoceros poaching, Zimbabwe's government has been accused of claiming that its elephant herds have increased at rates in excess of the natural rate of increase.[88] Such allegations, however, have not been proven and evidence to the contrary is also available.[89] These charges highlight the difficulties in determining the validity of various conservation strategies, including sustainable use, which are being debated within CITES.

Conclusion

The Zimbabwe case-study points to two conclusions. First, it supports the claims of Levy and Young (1994) and other international regime theorists that international regimes do make a difference in policy decisions taken by member states. By altering Zimbabwe's cost-benefit calculus in its decision whether or not to allow international trade in ivory, CITES exerted influence over Zimbabwe to adhere to the trade ban – at least temporarily. This decision stands in direct contrast to the state's previous conception of its national interest, and is clearly different from the decision that would have been taken in the absence of the regime.

Second, the case-study points to a somewhat paradoxical conclusion: Zimbabwe, as a member state, has learned to use the regime and has been instrumental in bringing about (and taking advantage of) profound changes in the intent, structure, and power relationships embodied in the CITES regime. In a twist on the "learning" behavioral pathway delineated by Levy and Young (1994), the member state's relationship to the regime has evolved from being the recipient of regime dictates to being the creator of some of those dictates – often in a form that serves the state's self-calculated rational interest.[90]

In some cases, these new directions represent a "spillover" effect for the regime, which has caused it to address other related issue areas. CITES, which was created to regulate international trade in threatened wildlife species, is now moving into larger habitat conservation and wildlife management principles. In part this is the result of learning; increased knowledge leads species protection regimes in this direction. However, it is also the result of member states learning to promote their individual economic interests through the regime.

In the case of Zimbabwe, learning how to influence the regime through participation has empowered the state, giving it more input into multilateral issues of import to itself than it would have had in the absence of the regime. Likewise, other range states within CITES have fundamentally improved their ability and willingness to speak out. The state–regime relationship is neither static nor limited to the regime dictating desired behavioral changes to the state. Rather, the relationship is dynamic and reciprocal; it develops over time as states learn to "play" the system. The regime is a political organization in which members use politics to jockey for changes in the regime itself, attempting to bring it into line with their own self-interested visions for the future.

Notes

1. CITES Update 32 (Washington, DC: US Department of the Interior, Fish and Wildlife Service, 1995.
2. Convention on International Trade in Endangered Species of Wild Fauna and Flora, Washington, DC, 3 March 1973, Article II.
3. Ronald Orenstein and Jeheskel Shoshani, "CITES at the Crossroads," *SWARA: Magazine of the East African Wildlife Society* (Nairobi, Kenya), 17:5 (1994), 12.
4. Interview with Claudius Nhema, counsellor, Embassy of Zimbabwe, Washington, DC, December 1994.
5. "Saving the Elephants: A Mammoth Task," *TRAFFIC USA*, 1987, p. 26.
6. Jorgen B. Thomsen, "Conserving the African Elephant: CITES Fails – US Acts," *TRAFFIC USA*, 9:1 (1989).
7. Ibid., p. 2.
8. EIA, "Living Proof: African Elephants: The Success of the CITES Appendix I Ban" (London: Environmental Investigation Agency, 1994), p. 3.
9. Raymond Bonner, "The War Over Elephants," *The New York Times Magazine*, 7 February 1993, pp. 17–30, 52–53.
10. See Ronald Orenstein and Jeheskel Shoshani, "CITES at the Crossroads."
11. H. T. Dublin, T. Milliken, and R. F. W. Barnes, "Four Years After the CITES Ban: Illegal Killing of Elephants, Ivory Trade and Stockpiles," a report of the IUCN/SSC African Elephant Specialist Group, 1995.
12. *Financial Gazette* (Harare), various issues, 1991.
13. For a discussion of cost-benefit analyses, see Marc A. Levy and Oran R. Young, "The Effectiveness of International Regimes," Annual Convention of the International Studies Association, Washington, DC, 21 March–1 April 1994.
14. General summary of the Lausanne meeting, *TRAFFIC USA*, January 1989, p. 3.
15. The Ivory Review Trade Group was composed of representatives from the World Wildlife Fund, the World Conservation Monitoring Unit, the European Economic Community, the CITES Secretariat, and the African Wildlife Foundation. Jeffrey Vail, "Halting the Elephant Ivory Trade: A True Test for International Law," *Wisconsin International Law Journal*, 9:1 (1990), note 15, 229.
16. Mozambique announced at Lausanne its intention to take a reservation, and Botswana, South Africa, and Burundi hinted in plenary that they were also considering reservations.
17. Ronald Orenstein (ed.), *Elephants: The Deciding Decade* (San Francisco: Sierra Club Books, 1991), p. 11.

18. Orenstein, *Elephants*, pp. 16 and 22.; EIA, "Living Proof," p. 4; Dublin, et al., "Four Years After the CITES Ban." The United Kingdom took a six-month reservation to the Appendix I listing on behalf of Hong Kong, to allow that former ivory-carving center to sell off its stockpiles of ivory. During the six months, however, Hong Kong was able to find buyers for only a small portion of those stocks.
19. Interview with Chief, Operations Branch, Office of Management Authority, US Fish and Wildlife Service, Department of Interior, December 1994.
20. "CITES 1989: The African Elephant and More," *TRAFFIC USA*, 9:4 (December 1980).
21. Edward R. Ricciuti, "The Elephant Wars," *Wildlife Conservation* (March/April 1993), 30.
22. Ronald Orenstein and Jeheskel Shoshani, "CITES at the Crossroads," *SWARA, Magazine of the East African Wild Life Society*, Nairobi, Kenya 17, 5(1994), 12.
23. The composition of SACIM had changed in the interim; Zambia withdrew because of a change in government, and Namibia joined CITES and SACIM upon becoming an independent nation. Besides Zimbabwe and Botswana, only South Africa also met the Somali Amendment conditions. These conditions were: 1. They had stable elephant populations; 2. They had "excellent management programs"; 3. They showed "effective control of poaching"; and 4. They had verification of the above from the Panel of Experts assigned at Lausanne. (US FWS report, 1992.)
24. CITES doc. 8:58: "Moratorium on the Ivory Trade, Draft Resolution Submitted to Kyoto COP by the Delegations of Botswana, Malawi, Namibia, and Zimbabwe."
25. In estimating the vote among African countries, Adrian Stefan, the US State Department representative to the US CITES COP delegation, predicted the African delegations would vote 35–5 against the downlisting proposals.
26. Botswana Minister of Environment, speech withdrawing SACIM elephant downlisting proposal at Kyoto COP. Kyoto, Japan, March 1992.
27. Rowan Martin, Assistant Director Terrestrial Research, Zimbabwe Department of National Parks and Wildlife Management, Written communication with author, October 1992.
28. Ginnette Hemley, "CITES 1992: Endangered Treaty?," *TRAFFIC USA*, 11:3 (1992), p. 18.
29. The issue of where CITES stood on promoting free trade versus inhibiting trade in the interest of species preservation, however, was not new. Richard Parsons, Chief of the US Fish and Wildlife Service Wildlife Permit Office during the first Reagan Administration, was quoted in 1983 as trying to strike a balance between these polar positions: "CITES is not a treaty to prohibit trade … It's not a treaty to be conducive to trade. It's a treaty to regulate trade." Cited in Norman Boucher, "The Wildlife Trade," *Atlantic Monthly*, 251 (March 1983), 12.
30. IUCN/UNEP/WWF, 1980.

31. An official of the US CITES Management Authority has said that "'sustainable use' can be a catch-phrase for anything and everything" (personal communication with author, December 1994).
32. Nigel Hunter, interview with author June 1992.
33. Ginnette Hemley, "CITES 1992: Endangered Treaty?," p. 1. Such arguments assume "science" to be objective and separate from the political process. This image of science, particularly regarding an evolving science such as ecology, is illusory, and sets up false expectations for an essentially political organization such as CITES.
34. "CITES II," 1992, p. 1.
35. Ibid., p. 5.
36. Michael Satchell, "Wildlife's Last Chance: Should Endangered Big Game be Killed in order to Save the Species," *US News and World Report* (November 15, 1993), p. 76.
37. CITES Update 31, "COP 9 Results" (Washington, DC: US Department of the Interior, Fish and Wildlife Service, December 1994).
38. Claudius Nhema, Embassy of Zimbabwe, Washington DC, interview with author, December 1994.
39. US African Elephant Statement, COP 9, 1994.
40. Ibid.
41. Ironically, a similar South African proposal to downlist its White Rhinoceros population was approved after amendment to allow trade only in live animals and sport-hunted trophies. Rhinoceros species are even more endangered than elephants, so this decision was a surprise to many participants and observers.
42. Andrea Gaski, Senior Program Officer, and Christopher Robbins, *TRAFFIC USA*, Interview with the author, December 1994.
43. Nhema, personal communication.
44. Radio South African Network, 1994.
45. Nhema, personal communication, 1994.
46. Ginnette Hemley, "CITES 1992: Endangered Treaty?," pp. 6–7.
47. US Department of State communications; CITES Com. 9.17 (Rev.), Ft. Lauderdale, FL, November 1994.
48. CITES Com. 9.17.
49. The new criteria were adopted at Fort Lauderdale after a Working Group produced a consensus resolution based on the Standing Committee draft resolution and an alternative resolution introduced by the United States. The United States opposed the original draft because it felt the criteria were too rigid and attempted to apply fixed population figures as thresholds to be used on all species. Japan argued in the Working Group for adoption of the "numbers threshold" approach. The final document is a compromise which does use numbers but allows flexibility across species. The United States, Japan, and Zimbabwe report satisfaction with the new criteria. (US State Department report on Fort Lauderdale COP, November 1994, and interviews with Lieberman, Tanaka, and Nhema.)

50. An official of the US CITES Management Authority, personal communication.
51. CITES Update 31; Wagner, personal communication.
52. An official of the US CITES Management Authority; Wagner, personal communication.
53. CITES Doc. 9.18: "Evolution of the Convention: How to Improve the Effectiveness of the Convention." Ft. Lauderdale (November 1994), Annex, p. 3.
54. Susan Lieberman of the US CITES Management Authority, personal communication, 1994; Edwards, personal communication, 1995.
55. Lieberman, Wagner, personal communication.
56. Nhema, personal communication.
57. Ibid.
58. Susan Lieberman of the US CITES Management Authority, personal communication, 1994.
59. US Department of State report on Fort Lauderdale COP. As chair of the new Standing Committee, Japan will play a leading role in selecting the independent consultant to conduct the study.
60. CITES Doc 9.18, p. 1.
61. CITES II, p. 1.
62. CITES Doc. 9.18, p. 3.
63. See Marc Charles Trexler, "The Convention on International Trade in Endangered Species of Wild Fauna and Flora: Political or Conservation Success?" Ph.D. Dissertation, University of California at Berkeley, 1990; Levy and Young, "The Effectiveness of International Regimes."
64. Nhema, personal communication.
65. *The Zimbabwe Herald*, 3 March 1995.
66. *Financial Gazette*, October 27, 1994.
67. Nhema, personal communication.
68. *Action: The Environmental Health Magazine* (Harare: Action Team, 1994), p. 5: "Then came a dark chapter in our history. White settlers came. They had guns and tricked us with their false promises. The land of our people was seized by force. Many brave warriors died. The settlers were greedy. They slaughtered wildlife and ploughed the trees under to make way for their large farms. The few animals that survived became their property. This was when most wildlife suffered." This argument is also echoed in a recent study of African wildlife that documents the history of the white presence in Africa and its disastrous effect on the environment. Raymond Bonner, "The War Over Elephants."
69. EIU Country Report for Zimbabwe, 1994.
70. CITES document 9.24, 9.24 Annex I, and 9.24 Annex II: National Laws for Implementation of the Convention, Provisional Ratings of the National Legislation for Implementation, Proposed Decisions of the COP, November 1994, p. 153.
71. Martin, written communication, 1992.

72. *Sunday Mail*, 27 November 1994.
73. Robert Jackson, Zimbabwe Desk Officer, interview with the author, December 1994. Although the CWPA's pro-use approach to conservation is consistent with the ethic being promoted by Zimbabwe's government agencies and NGOs, the economic benefits of wildlife ranching are largely concentrated among large land-holders.
74. Interview with Jackson.
75. Allen and Edwards, personal communication, 1995.
76. *Sunday Mail*, 27 November 1994.
77. Jackson, personal communication. See also Bonner, "The War Over Elephants" for more on the issue of race in conservation in Africa.
78. If there is a conflict within Zimbabwe, it exists not over whether to utilize wildlife resources, but over how much to decentralize control over that utilization.
79. Rowan B. Martin, "The Influence of Governance on Conservation and Wildlife Utilisation," plenary address at conference on "Conservation through Sustainable Use of Wildlife" (University of Queensland, Brisbane, 8–11 February 1994); Marshall W. Murphree, *Decentralizing the Proprietorship of Wildlife Resources in Zimbabwe's Communal Lands* (Harare: University of Zimbabwe, 1990).
80. Satchell, "Wildlife's Last Chance," p. 76.
81. District councils are directly involved in administering CAMPFIRE. There was opposition to the CAMPFIRE program from its inception. The 1975 Parks and Wild Life Act was amended in 1982 to allow the Minister of Environment and Tourism to grant authority to District Councils to manage their own wildlife. District Councils, however, were not successful in obtaining such authority until 1988, after "pressure on the Minister ... resulted in the granting of authority" (Rowan B. Martin, "Resolving the Conflict between People and Parks in Zimbabwe," unpublished paper, 1992, p. 3). Opposition persists among "those politicians and bureaucrats who do not really wish to see self-sufficient rural communities" (ibid., p. 4).

    There is a movement afoot to further decentralize the program by limiting the role of the district councils, which are seen in some communities as remote and corrupt. The councils themselves are understandably fighting this movement, but it is viewed among local communities and DNPWM officials as the next step to improving CAMPFIRE's effectiveness. See Martin, "Resolving the Conflict," p. 5, and Murphree, *Decentralizing the Proprietorship of Wildlife Resources*, 1990, p. 17. DNPWM now must prove the initial success of CAMPFIRE in order to back the case for further decentralization.
82. Dublin, et al., "Four Years After the CITES Ban," p. 14.
83. Allen, personal communication, 1995.
84. Gaski, personal communication.
85. EIU Country Report for Zimbabwe, 1994, pp. 9–10; Jackson, personal communication, 1994; EIA, "Under Fire: Elephants on the Front Line" (London: Environmental Investigation Agency, 1992); EIA, "Living Proof."

86. EIA, "Living Proof," p. 11.
87. Lieberman, personal communication, 1994.
88. EIA "Living proof," p. 11.
89. CITES Panel of Experts Report, 1992.
90. Levy and Young, "The Effectiveness of International Regimes." Levy and Young delineate various pathways through which regimes cause behavior changes in member states. One such pathway is "regimes as learning facilitators." In this model, regimes "initiate processes that give rise to individual and social learning ... changing information and values and, in the process, altering the incentives that shape the behavior of individuals and collective entities ..." This pathway implies that such learning causes regime members to move in increasingly convergent directions as their positions evolve. The findings in this paper suggest, however, that other types of learning can also be caused by regime membership – and that these may not move member states in the same direction. The model was developed from Joseph S. Nye, "Nuclear Learning and the US-Soviet Security Regimes," *International Organization* 41 (1987), 371–402; Ernest B. Haas, *When Knowledge is Power: Three Models of Change in International Organizations* (Berkeley: University of California Press, 1990); and Peter M. Haas, "Epistemic Communities and the Dynamics of International Environmental Co-operation," in Volker Rittberger (ed.), *Regime Theory and International Relations* (Oxford: Oxford University Press, 1993).

8 The European Union: bridging domestic and international environmental policy-making[1]

Angela Liberatore

Domestic and international linkages are increasingly being influenced by regional organizations such as the European Union (EU) and the Association of South-East Asian Nations (ASEAN), and arrangements such as the European Free Trade Agreement and the North American Free Trade Agreement. Although different in form and scope, these regional arrangements are important actors that challenge the adequacy of the terms "domestic" and "international." "Domestic" typically refers only to events and policies that develop within national borders, but increasingly we are confronted by the need to examine those that occur within regional settings. At the same time, not only nations, but also regional organizations, non-governmental and transnational interests, including environmental NGOs and multinational corporations, participate in the negotiation of "international" agreements. The Uruguay Round negotiations of the General Agreement on Tariffs and Trade (GATT) and the negotiations related to the United Nations Conference on Environment and Development (UNCED) clearly demonstrated how regional organizations and international interests have helped to shape "domestic/international" dynamics on economic and environmental matters.

The EU, which was formed by the Maastricht Treaty in November 1993 and does not substitute for, but includes the European Community (EC), has unique supranational responsibilities in economic and environmental matters.[2] It represents an important interface between the domestic and international dimensions of environmental policy-making. The EU has developed its own environmental policy and legislation, and it is party to several international environmental agreements. In developing EU policies or in participating in international negotiations, EU institutions do not act in isolation from EU member

188

states but rather represent a "bridge" between the EU members and the broader international community. This chapter analyzes the EU's "bridging" role between the domestic and international dimensions of international environmental policy formation by focusing on four of its main functions.

A primary function of the EU is to serve as an arena for intergovernmental bargaining among member states in the adoption of EU environmental measures. It provides forums for reaching compromise and managing distributive issues among member states. These include meetings of the Council of Ministers, the European Parliament, and expert committees. The EU also establishes the "rules of the game" for making decisions through treaty provisions and Community legislation.

The EU also plays the role of agenda-setter. EU environmental action programs and legislation have influenced the environmental policies of member states. The extent of the EU's supranational influence and impact on national environmental policies, however, varies depending on the degree to which the member states' existing environmental policies and practices are proactive or reactive and the resources available to the EU and its members. EU institutions can act as sources and distributors of expertise, information, and even legitimacy (despite the "democratic deficit" which is understandably a frequent criticism of the EU) through European research programs, information campaigns, training activities, eco-labelling schemes, patenting procedures, or decisions of the European Court of Justice.

Another important role involves tackling environmental problems on a broader European scale. On some occasions the EU has been the catalyst in bridging its interests and the interests of its member states with those of the broader region. Here too resources play a fundamental role. Through the use of technical, financial, and diplomatic resources, the EU has stimulated efforts to improve pan-European and Euro-Mediterranean environmental protection and cooperation.

Finally, the EU is also an actor within the global arena, mediating between its supranational and regional interests and the concerns of the international community. The EU is now a recognized, although still not uncontroversial, entity in international environmental negotiations. This controversy stems from the rather ambiguous international role of the EU, which tends to be a "minimum common denominator" representative of its member states at the same time as it tries to establish its own distinct identity. On various occasions, EU institutions (the

Council, Commission, and Parliament) have made it clear that they desire a greater leadership role in international environmental affairs for the EU.

These EU functions will be discussed below through a brief analysis of some representative environmental cases. The negotiation of the Large Combustion Plant Directive provides a good example of the inter-governmental bargaining that characterizes the adoption of specific environmental measures. The formulation of EU environmental action programs shows how "Brussels" influences – albeit differentially – the environmental agendas of its member states. The efforts to establish pan-European and Euro-Mediterranean cooperation through specific plans and resources illustrate the potential for, and obstacles to, the EU acting as the catalyst in a broader regional perspective. Finally, the EU's role in negotiating two international agreements – the Montreal Protocol and the Framework Convention on Climate Change – illustrates EU attempts not only to represent the interests of its members but also to assert leadership internationally.

These examples are not comprehensive, but serve to illustrate the complexity, multiplicity and, to some degree, the fragmentation of the issues, procedures, and actors involved in the four "bridging" functions discussed in this chapter. A brief background section first introduces some of the main aspects of EU policy-making processes and institutional structure; these are central to an understanding of the various roles the EU plays in regard to environmental problems on both the regional and global levels.

An EU vocabulary

Regionalization

The development of regional arrangements and institutions is both a cause and a response to growing economic, political, and societal inter-dependence. The establishment of the European Economic Community in 1957 spoke to the complexity of European interdependence. There was a need for mutual accountability and cooperation among neighboring countries if they were to promote industrialization and economic growth.[3] The process of economic integration within the EC began with six states and gradually expanded to the present membership of fifteen states in the EU.

Environmental protection was not included as one of the initial areas of responsibility attributed to the EC in 1957 by the Treaty of Rome. This is hardly surprising given the primacy of economic concerns on the newborn Community's agenda. Moreover environmental degradation was not yet an important policy issue within any of its member states. Environmental legislation was not enacted at the Community level until ten years later when the EC established the first in a series of chemical controls – a directive on the labeling and packaging of chemical substances in 1967. The first of five Environmental Action Programs was adopted in 1973 to define the main priorities, principles, and overall strategy of EC environmental policy. It was not until 1987, however, that the Single European Act officially added environmental protection to the EC responsibilities enumerated in the Treaty of Rome.[4] This expansion of EC authority to include the environmental field can be regarded as a form of "positive integration."[5]

Initially environmental regulation was introduced mainly for economic reasons. It was introduced with the intention of avoiding distortion of competition within the European Community and to maintain access to foreign (especially US and Japanese) markets which otherwise might use their own environmental legislation as a barrier to entry for EC products that did not meet their standards. A close relationship between the economic and environmental agendas continues to shape EU policy and discourse on sustainable development. Political and institutional factors, including pressure by environmental organizations and the desire of EU institutions to broaden the scope of their competence, also play an important role in the development of EU environmental policy.[6]

Supranationalism

The EU is a unique supranational organization by virtue of its doctrine of supremacy of EC law over national legislation, the direct national effects of its legislation, its exclusive competence in certain policy fields such as trade, and the regulatory authority of the European Commission, which has the power to initiate EU policies and laws and monitor their implementation. EU member states are subject to the rulings of the European Court of Justice, which arbitrates cases related to the interpretation and implementation of Community law. In addition, the European Parliament is the only "non-national" parliament in the world. The European Parliament does not enact legislation in the same way as national parliaments but, since the introduction of the co-decision procedure under the Maastricht Treaty, it participates in making decisions related to the establishment of EC law, a role previously limited to the Council of Ministers.

While possessing supranational features, the EU still shares similarities with other regional and international organizations in regard to the importance of intergovernmental negotiations. Especially before the Maastricht Treaty entered into force, Community decisions taken by the Council of Ministers were the result of bargaining and compromise among the representatives of the member states. Since Maastricht, the co-decision procedure gives binding, rather than merely advisory force, to the opinions of the European Parliament.[7] Given the early stage of the implementation of this new procedure, it remains to be seen whether and how it will reduce the scope of intergovernmental bargaining in favor of supranational decision-making in the EU.

The regulatory power of the Commission and the supremacy of EU law has led to the development of comprehensive environmental legislation at the EU and national levels. EU environmental legislation primarily takes the form of directives. Directives are legally binding instruments on member states although national authorities remain free to choose both the forms and means of implementation. Regulations, which are legally binding in their entirety upon member states, are much less widely used in the environmental field. They have been used principally to implement (and sometimes tighten) international environmental agreements such as the Montreal Protocol and other protocols to the Vienna Convention for the Protection of the Ozone Layer into EC legislation.

Subsidiarity

An important issue related to the formulation and implementation of EU policies is the question of the "appropriate level of action." The subsidiarity principle is intended to address this matter. According to Article 3b of the Maastricht Treaty:

> In areas which do not fall within its exclusive competence, the Community shall take action, in accordance with the principle of subsidiarity, only if and in so far as the objectives of the proposed action cannot be sufficiently achieved by the member states and therefore, by reason of the scale or effects of the proposed action, can be better achieved by the Community.

Interpretation of the subsidiarity principle is far from unequivocal. The principle can be used either to argue for the need to return areas of responsibility back to the member states or to support EU action on transboundary issues, including pollution, security, and migration.[8] Policy actions aimed at fostering the sustainability of the internal market and protecting the global environment are generally considered to be under the purview of the EU because of their scale and effects. However, this does not imply exclusive EU competence, but rather recognizes the need for cooperation among supranational, national, and local authorities.

Importantly for the future, the "double-edged sword" of subsidiarity is raising interest in the question of what is gained from EU actions versus national and international ones. Answers to this question need to be specified in action programs and proposed legislation. The actual and potential added value of EU functions are discussed in the following sections.

The EU as a negotiating arena

Decision-making in the EU

Intergovernmental approaches point to the crucial influence of domestic agendas and the relative power of member states on decision-making at the EU level.[9] The influence of national agendas on the EU's agenda can be seen in debates on basic principles, such as the subsidiarity principle, as well as in specific decisions, such as with the adoption of the Large Combustion Plant Directive (LCPD) discussed below.

The important role played by member states in EU decision-making, however, does not mean that there is a direct linear relationship between the domestic and the supranational levels. For example, rather than a "one state, one vote" formula, a qualified majority voting procedure was introduced in the EC Council. This procedure weights votes according to the size, population, and GNP of each member country. Under qualified majority voting, it is difficult for even a coalition of the largest and most influential member states to impose a decision on other member states since the agreement of at least two other smaller member states must also be obtained. On the other hand, unanimity voting, which is required in many cases, gives each member state the power to block decisions it opposes, even when they are supported by all other member states. Keeping the complexities of EU decision-making in mind, an examination of the influence of domestic systems upon the supranational arena must be considered in any discussion of the "bridging" role of the EU. The EU's function as an arena for reaching agreement on and managing distributive aspects of environmental issues can be effectively illustrated in a short account of the negotiation of the Large Combustion Plants Directive (LCPD).

The Large Combustion Plants Directive: reaching agreement by managing distribution

Evidence of acidification problems in Europe (especially in lakes) was first brought to international attention by Swedish scientists and authorities at the first UN Conference on the Human Environment in 1972. European negotiations regarding this issue culminated nine years later in the adoption of the Convention on Long Range Transboundary Air Pollution. The EC was a party to that Convention and began to develop specific instruments to combat acidification, among them the LCPD.

The first proposal for a directive on SO_2, NOx and particulates emissions from large combustion plants was submitted by the Commission to the EC Council in 1983.[10] The proposal referred to EC participation in the Long Range Transboundary Air Pollution Convention of 1979 and argued for the need to take specific action at the EC level in regard to emissions from large combustion plants.[11] This need was targeted not only for environmental reasons, but also because of the existence of national regulations (notably in Germany) that were likely to create unequal conditions of competition. The focus on trade and competition characterized previous EC measures related to the control of SO_2 and NOx emissions and was a crucial component, together with the transboundary dimensions of the acidification problem, in motivating and justifying an EC acid rain policy.

It was not by chance that the Commission's proposal, drafted in 1982, was submitted in 1983 during Germany's presidency of the Community.[12] Germany, initially skeptical that acidification was a real problem, became a champion of anti-acidification measures in part because of the scientific, political, and media attention to the *Waldsterben* (forest dieback) phenomenon in the country in the early 1980s.[13] This led to the adoption of the *Grossfeuerungsanlagen-Verordnung* (decree on large combustion plants) in 1983 and to attempts by German authorities to advance the acidification issue and related control measures in the EC policy agenda. An explanation of the emergence of acidification as an issue on the EC policy agenda and the adoption of the LCPD, however, requires more than just an understanding of the German position.

Because of opposition from various member states, it took five years before the LCPD could be adopted, and then in a version that was substantially different from the Commission's original proposal. During those five years, negotiations on the LCPD involved scientific and political debate on the causes and spread of acidification, limit values, technological progress, timing of emissions reductions, the size and location of plants, and especially issues of distribution. The Commission, which supported its own research on acidification, was in a position to reply on scientific grounds to the skepticism shown by some member states, and particularly the United Kingdom, on the nature, seriousness and scale of the phenomenon even if areas of uncertainty remained.[14] Distributive arguments were at the heart of requests made by some countries for exemptions. The Commission rejected the requests for delays or less stringent standards made by some countries (especially Italy and France) on the grounds of technical feasibility as well as requests for exemptions from other countries on the grounds of their negligible contribution to acidification and/or their lower level of economic growth. This argument was made by Greece, Ireland, and Luxembourg in the early stages of the negotiations and was later echoed strongly by Spain and Portugal upon their entrance into the EC in 1986. Distributive aspects were explicitly addressed in the debate on the "bubble approach" suggested by the Netherlands, and in the method which was finally adopted in 1988 (which allowed for different emission reduction targets by different countries).[15]

Only after lengthy negotiations at the EC level did member states reach agreement on the meaning of scientific evidence of environmental damage and its causes, and on how to deal with complex distributive issues. Of course, bilateral contacts between member state representatives were also important in formulating the LCPD. Still, it was the EC debate on the reasons for and features of a Community legislative proposal that set the context and the "rules of the game" for these contacts. The positions of the various member states were crucial in determining the outcome, but they were influenced by the features of the EC negotiating arena. Although far from "perfect", agreement was achieved because distributive issues concerning different levels of emissions and targets were handled at the regional level. It is also worth mentioning that while in the case of the LCPD, distributive issues primarily were resolved by differentiating emissions control targets, in other cases they were also addressed through the use of such financial instruments as the EC Structural and Cohesion Funds and LIFE (*L'Instrument Financiaire pour l'Environnement*/Financial Instrument for the Environment) which help to spread the burden of environmental protection measures between higher- and lower-income member states.

The EU as agenda setter

"Brussels": neither omnipotent nor powerless

EU competences have expanded in the environmental field and Community legislation and programs have contributed to, or directly caused, policy change in member states. While the effectiveness of EU actions is frequently undermined by problems ranging from delays in implementing directives into national legislation to outright non-compliance, national legislation in the member states has been substantially shaped by Community law.[16] EC strategic documents, such as the White Papers on the Common Market (1985) and on Growth, Competitiveness, and Employment (1993), or the environmental action programs, also influence policy decisions in the member states.

In this regard, the EU plays another important "bridging" role between the international and domestic levels, namely an agenda-setting role. While EU legislation and institutions provide the arenas and "rules of the game" for intergovernmental negotiations, the formulation of strategic policy documents and their "translation" in the form of laws also influence policy developments within the member states. The impact of the EU's agenda-setting role, however, is not uniform across member states. The influence of EU environmental policy on policy changes in the environmental area is greater in some member states than in others, as can be expected given the diversity of socio-economic and ecological conditions in Europe.

Agenda-setting through law-making and program formulation

EU institutions, and particularly the Commission, can play an agenda-setting role through initiating legislative proposals and formulating and diffusing principles and strategies for promoting environmental protection and sustainable development. Several different stages exist: consultation, the submission of legislative and policy proposals, the adoption of EU legislation and policy programmes, and the negotiation of accession to the EU by other countries.

Consultations within the Commission – and especially with member states' experts and representatives of interest groups at the formative stages of legislation and action programs – provide an initial channel for exchange of information. These consultations provide an early opportunity to exchange scientific information and to gauge the reaction of member states, interest groups, and/or certain services of the Commission, to a specific proposal or more general objectives and principles.

The submission of legislative proposals and action programs from the Commission to the Council typically involves intense discussions within and among member states and the formulation of opinions by the Socio-Economic Committee and the European Parliament, whose views in areas covered by the co-decision process became binding with the adoption of the Maastricht Treaty. These discussions encourage debate on the nature of the problems, the need for EU action vis-à-vis national and international action, the type of action to be taken, and the expected consequences.

The adoption of EU legislation and programs necessitates transposing Community law into national legislation. It also means incorporating EU priorities and principles into national environmental policies or plans, and should lead to the actual implementation of codified laws and plans.

Negotiations regarding the accession of new member states offer the EU a particularly valuable occasion for agenda setting. States wishing to join the EU are typically only able to influence the terms of their compliance with Community laws in terms of timing and form. While these states can introduce new issues onto the agenda for negotiation, they have first to determine whether or not they subscribe to the EU's main objectives as stated in the treaty.

Differences in the influence of "Brussels" on the environmental policies of member states can be found in each of the stages mentioned above. Generally, countries with less developed environmental infrastructures in terms of administrative, technical, and scientific capacities or in levels of public awareness and pressure are influenced more by EU environmental policy than countries with a strong endogenous policy and administrative capacity. The latter are influenced by a feedback rather than a linear process. This means that these states tend to play an active role in setting the EU's, and particularly the Commission's, agenda. As a consequence they are influenced by the outcomes of an EU decision process, but one over which they could wield substantial influence even if the results depart from their original goals or objectives. This, for instance, was the case of Germany in the LCPD negotiation and adoption process described above. The environmental agendas of pro-active countries are influenced by developments in Brussels – not directly set by them, unlike the environmental agendas of countries that tend simply to react to EC policy initiatives in the environmental field.

A north/south or, more accurately, a core/periphery divide seems to be at work.[17] Greece, Ireland, Italy, and Spain tend to react to environ-mental policy initiatives coming from Brussels.[18] Entire sectors of environmental legislation are introduced as a result of the need to implement EU law. National environmental plans are drafted directly from EU action program guidelines. For example, while Italy inde-pendently enacted legislation on some aspects of air pollution, such as its anti-smog law in the 1960s, it later imported most of its air quality, waste, and other environmental legislation from Brussels. Portugal and Spain, which joined the Community in the mid-1980s, likewise incorpo-rated entire sectors of EC environmental legislation which had not been previously covered at the national level.

EU influence, however, is not limited to countries with little or no history of indigenous environmental initiatives. The most recent EU members – Austria, Finland, and Sweden – each had extensive pre-existing environmental legislation. Nonetheless, these countries have supplemented their national laws in accordance with EU guidelines where discrepancies were found to exist.

In a slightly different vein, the EU has also compelled some of its members to take positions on particular environmental issues that they would have been unlikely to adopt on their own initiative. For example, it is unlikely that the United Kingdom or Belgium would have enacted legislation on emissions from large combustion plants or bathing-water quality in the absence of EU policy. Likewise, most member states did not have environmental impact assessment procedures prior to the adoption of the relevant EC directive.

Principles established at the EU level are also being circulated within the member states. It is now commonplace to find member states with plans such as those related to Agenda 21 or prepared in the wake of the Berlin Conference to the Framework Convention on Climate Change, which emphasize the importance of precautionary action (one of the guiding principles of EU environmental policy) or the need to integrate environmental concerns into all sectoral policies – the focus of the EU's Fifth Environmental Action Program "Towards Sustainability."[19]

With regard to global environmental problems such as ozone layer depletion and climate change, the EC quickly embraced these concerns and helped to establish them on the agenda of even reluctant member states at the earliest possible stage of the relevant international negotiations. This was due in large part to the process of EC institution-building and the related attempt by EC institutions to gain a broader scope of environmental competence. The first important EC policy document related to ozone layer depletion – a Council Recommendation on fluorocarbons in the environment – was presented in August 1977, soon after the United Nations Environment Program's policy meeting on the subject in March of the same year. The Commission developed a Community "ozone policy" and participated in the negotiation of the Vienna Convention and related Protocols. The policy placed emphasis on the control of CFC production capacity, making the issue especially important for major CFC producers located in France, Germany, Italy, and the United Kingdom, and later, via voluntary agreements at the EC level, for CFC users in all member states.[20]

Concerning the issue of climate change, the first Communication of the Commission to the Council on the Greenhouse Effect and the Community was presented in November 1988, again only a few months after the Toronto intergovernmental conference, "The Changing Atmosphere," which is generally acknowledged as the first important international policy event related to climate change. Developing more or less in parallel with the negotiation of the climate convention, the EC climate policy obliged even the most reluctant member states to agree on a target of stabilizing EC CO_2 emissions by 2000 at the levels of 1990 and to debate policy measures for meeting this target through, for example, energy-saving programs and the EC CO_2/energy tax, which after years of unsuccessful negotiation is still on the Commission's agenda.

A cautious conclusion with regard to the EU agenda-setting role is that while the EU has been successful as a sponsor of regional and global environmental issues – including the enactment and diffusion of related laws, principles, and programs – it has been much less successful with regard to their actual implementation. The gap between raising or sponsoring issues and acting upon them, or between policy formulation and policy implementation, is a crucial issue for the EU. As previously mentioned, implementation gaps are acknowledged by both scholars and policy-makers as one of the major weaknesses of EU environmental policy. On a more positive note, recognition of these implementation problems has led to a great deal of monitoring, periodic assessment, reporting, research on implementation, and other activities intended to identify the main sources of the problem. For example, annual reports monitoring the application of Community law (including environmental law) are submitted by the Commission to the European Parliament, and similar reports are issued and discussed within member states. In the environmental field, an "implementation network" established to review the Fifth Environmental Action Program published its first interim report in July 1994 and a second in 1995. Although these reports identified some progress, they also documented the many continuing difficulties in integrating environmental factors into all sectoral policies and in meeting EC commitments regarding the protection of the global environment.[21]

The EU as a regional catalyst

The EU shares a variety of transboundary environmental problems with neighboring European and non-European countries. Moving toward sustainability – as the Fifth Environmental Action program advocates – is thus not merely an internal EU affair. Environmental interdependence was first widely recognized in the mid-1970s with regard to the protection of the Mediterranean Sea and acidification problems and was dramatically reinforced by the Chernobyl fallout in 1986.

As a regional organization representing a cluster of industrialized countries moving toward economic integration, bounded by a treaty and supranational legislation, having common policies, and pooling together significant financial resources, the EU plays a catalytic role for other European and neighboring non-European countries. This role is exercised through the control over the direction and use of flows of funding, scientific information, technology, and other goods, as well as through the regulation and negotiation of access to EU markets and political institutions (for instance, by means of association and accession procedures).

As will be illustrated below, programs which target cooperation with Central and Eastern Europe (such as PHARE) and with New Independent States (such as TACIS) are major sources of international funding for these countries, and the EU is the main trading partner of North African countries. Far from being motivated by pure altruism, the EU's attempts to build and expand cooperation with its neighbors are necessitated by the complex socio-economic interdependence of the "old Continent" and the Mediterranean area. With regard to environmental protection and sustainable development, the EU's catalytic role is embedded in, and perhaps more often "diluted" by, the broader economic and strategic issues framing cooperation with non-EU countries. Environmental and sustainable development issues have not historically been a priority in the EU's pan-European and Euro-Mediterranean relations. Still, the EU has played and could play an even more important catalytic role in these areas in the future. Two examples are discussed below.

The Dobris process and Mediterranean cooperation

During a Conference of the Environment Ministers of all European countries held in Dobris, in the former Czechoslovakia in 1991, the formulation of an Environmental Action Program for Central and Eastern Europe (EAPCEE) was planned, and the call was made for a pan-European collaboration aimed at enabling its implementation.[22] The first step in the implementation of the EAPCEE was the drafting by the Task Force of the European Environmental Agency of a pan-European State of the Environment report,"The Dobris Assessment."[23] At the same time, follow-up ministerial conferences were scheduled every two years; the first was held in Lucerne, Switzerland in 1993, and the second in Sofia, Bulgaria in 1995. The "Dobris Process" (as these initiatives came to be called) suggests that there is significant potential for institutional and socio-economic innovation aimed at promoting sustainability on a continental scale. However, the development of such potential seems to be undermined by the lack of sufficient financial support for EAPCEE. During the Lucerne Conference of 1993, Central and Eastern European countries hoped for an "environmental Marshall Plan," similar to that proposed by Austria which would be funded by the West to the tune of US$24 million. Western countries, however, including Canada, the United States, and the EC, were only willing to commit themselves to increased investment based on concrete projects rather than devoting a specific amount of funding to the plan. Different evaluations emerged within the EU regarding the outcome of the Lucerne Conference. While Danish Minister Svend Auken, President-in-Office of the EC Council at the time of the conference, was alarmed by the extent to which Western countries underestimated the environmental dangers ahead, German Minister Klaus Topfer, who chaired the final stage of the preparatory work for the program, said that no finance minister could have accepted the massive expenditure demanded by an "environmental Marshall Plan," and he welcomed the practical realism of the conference.[24] The need to find a balance between these two different views and their practical implications represents a major hurdle which the EU will have to confront as it contemplates future contributions to regional and global sustainability.

This also applies to the utilization of funds available under the PHARE and TACIS programs. As noted above, these two programs form the core of the EU's broader initiatives for Central and Eastern Europe.[25] At the end of its first five years of operation, PHARE made available 4,283 million ECU to eleven partner countries; 9 percent of this funding was allocated to environmental protection and nuclear safety.[26] In the same period, TACIS provided 1,870 million ECU to launch more than 2,000 projects in the New Independent States (NIS), with 256.3 million ECU of this total allocated to top priority nuclear safety and environmental projects.[27] The joint focus on nuclear safety and the environment in the two programs, and especially the large percentage of funding allocated to these programs, are both reasonable and necessary given the increased concern for transboundary nuclear risk since the Chernobyl accident. On the other hand, other transboundary/global environmental problems tend to be overshadowed by this focus. Given the socio-economic instability still characterizing the "economies in transition," environmental issues run the risk of being marginalized in future attempts to redefine and optimize EU cooperation with Central and Eastern European countries and the NIS. The EU must still determine how it can best obtain and properly manage resources in order to continue to perform and strengthen its catalytic role in regional and global environment protection and sustainability.

This also applies to current and future relations in the Mediterranean area. The EU shares important socio-economic and environmental problems with countries of the Mediterranean Basin. South–north migration flows and security problems have traditionally been the focus of political attention in this important but unstable region. The EU is also the main trading partner of North African countries, and thus possesses economic leverage which can prove important in resolving environmental concerns.[28]

Mediterranean environmental problems are closely linked to economic issues. The protection of the Mediterranean Sea is the most prominent environmental concern in the Mediterranean region; and desertification has also gained attention in recent years. These are the areas in which the EU has been most active. The EC is a party to the

Barcelona Convention on the Protection of the Mediterranean Sea of 1976, and since 1990 the European Commission has collaborated with the World Bank, the European Investment Bank, and the United Nations Environment Program within the framework of the Mediterranean Environmental Technical Assistance Program (METAP). The EU is also active in the negotiation of a Desertification Convention.

In order to foster broader environmental cooperation in the area, the European Community has organized regular conferences of regional environmental ministers. At the 1990 Nicosia Conference, agreement was reached on the "Charter on Euro-Mediterranean Cooperation concerning the Environment in the Mediterranean Basin," which committed the signatories to the objective of achieving sustainable development in the Mediterranean Basin by 2025. The following were identified as priority areas: water and waste management, management of the Mediterranean landcover, nature conservation, energy efficiency, and exchange of experience with regard to technology transfer and institution building. In the 1992 follow-up meeting in Cairo, additional declarations and plans were adopted, but no specific financial commitment was achieved. In this case, as with the outcome of the Lucerne meeting mentioned earlier, the Community appears to have a strong preference for providing financial help for specific projects rather than for a "packaged" plan. While understandable in view of the greater financial risks involved in a plan, the project-by-project approach might be too piecemeal to tackle ecological interdependence and protect the regional and global environmental commons effectively.

The EU is in a unique position, in part because of its resources, to play a catalytic role in environmental agenda-setting in Central/Eastern European and non-EU Mediterranean countries. The specific programs and projects discussed above represent the "core" of such a role; further development and actual implementation of these core activities, coupled with an increased integration of environmental factors in EU trade policy with its neighbors, would help exploit the full potential of the EU's catalytic role. This also has relevance with regard to the EU's role in global international negotiations; by playing a stronger catalytic role at the pan-European and Euro-Mediterranean levels, the EU could in fact assist (by means of technology sharing, further scientific cooperation, and/or favorable trade provisions in certain areas) its European and non-European neighbors in the negotiation and implementation of global environmental accords.

The EU as representative and leader in international environmental negotiations

The EU is becoming an increasingly visible actor in international environmental negotiations. It contributes directly to the formulation of international agreements, is a party to all the main international environmental conventions, and provides binding means for the implementation by its member states of "soft" international law. The intergovernmental nature of EU decision-making may, however, clash with attempts by the EU to present itself as a truly supranational actor capable of taking on the leadership role it desires in the formulation and adoption of international environmental agreements.

The issue of EU leadership in international environmental negotiations is a recurrring theme in EU affairs. The Dublin Declaration of the European Council of 1990 states that the EC must use its position of moral, economic, and political authority more effectively in advancing international efforts to solve global problems and promote sustainable development and respect for the global commons. This theme was also prominently featured in the Fifth Environmental Action Program, and was especially apparent in spoken statements and documents prepared for UNCED and the negotiation of the Framework Convention on Climate Change.[29]

The examination of some particularly significant events related to the negotiation of the Framework Convention on Climate Change illustrates some of the problems faced by the EU during international environmental negotiations, where it tries to play two roles – that of a representative of its member states and that of a distinct actor with leadership ambitions. The example below focuses on the negotiations before and during UNCED, but also addresses some aspects related to the Berlin Conference of the Parties to the Framework Convention on Climate Change.

In the period preceding UNCED, many EC representatives began pushing for a "climate leadership" role for the organization. On several occasions, such as the White House Conference and the Bergen Conference in 1990 (these being forums which both addressed the climate change issue), the EC Commissioner for the Environment, Carlo Ripa di Meana, attacked the US Bush Administration's wait-and-see position on climate change and strongly advocated the need for an EC leadership role. Among the EC's credentials for such a role was the fact that the main goals of the upcoming UNCED conference – the stabilization target, measures aimed at increasing energy efficiency, and a proposal for a CO_2/energy tax – had already been incorporated into the EC global warming control strategies, culminating in the adoption in October 1990 of a plan to stabilize EC emissions of CO_2 at 1990 levels by 2000. Energy saving and efficiency measures (SAVE and THERMIE programs) had been developed, and the idea of the CO_2/energy tax, initially proposed by Ripa di Meana in May 1989, had already undergone extensive and controversial debate.[30] In addition, the EC, together with Austria and the Scandinavian countries, which are now, with the exception of Norway, EU members, had argued strongly in OECD forums that any future convention on climate change needed to include a CO_2 stabilization target despite opposition from the US administration. Their arguments stressed that as the main emitters of greenhouse gases, all OECD countries should commit themselves to stabilize and reduce CO_2 emissions in order to set an example to developing countries. The Bush Administration, however, refused to change its position.

On 9 May 1992, at the last meeting of the Intergovernmental Negotiating Committee for a Framework Convention on Climate Change, a draft treaty was approved which included guidelines for cutting CO_2 emissions, but set no specific targets. According to an EC official, this was a substantial compromise in the face of American intransigence; US President Bush would not attend the upcoming Rio Conference unless these minimal guidelines were in place. In the view of J. Ripert, chairman of the Intergovernmental Negotiating Committee, the lack of specific commitments in the text was an example of "constructive ambiguity."[31]

In the months preceding the Berlin Conference of April 1995, it became clear that the EU was not in an easy position. On the one hand, the Commission, Parliament, and several member states, including the host of the conference, were willing to play a leadership role and push for the negotiation of a protocol. On the other hand, some of the measures which had been proposed for reaching the EU stabilization target, such as the CO_2/energy tax, had not yet been adopted, and some studies and Commission documents questioned the very possibility that the EU could meet such a target with current measures.[32] The internal controversy on the tax and the doubts regarding the EU's ability to meet its own stabilization target undermined the EU's credibility as an international environmental leader. In preparation for the Berlin

Conference, the Commission prepared a working paper which enumerated some of the options available for stabilizing and reducing CO_2 emissions – including fiscal instruments, research, completion of the internal energy market, and change of transport modes – but failed to present any binding proposals, admitting that reaching the stabilization target would be a very difficult task. The weakened EU position influenced the outcome of the Berlin Conference, particularly the dilatory strategy resulting in the agreement to negotiate a protocol in two years.

Several points can be made about the role of the EU as a representative of its member states and as a distinct actor trying to play an environmental leadership role. When different views and interests of the member states are mediated and agreement is reached prior to international negotiations, the EU can speak with one voice and advocate positions and solutions that are not simply the "minimum common denominator" of diverging national positions. Unfortunately, the time necessary to reach such internal agreement over distributive and other issues rarely coincides with developments in international environmental negotiations. In addition, the EU has to deal with complex legal provisions regulating its external responsibilities.[33] Because it does not have exclusive authority in the environmental field, the EU can only be a party to international conventions in the form of "mixed agreements" where both the EU and its member states are parties; under such mixed agreements, the Commission can negotiate on behalf of the EU only if granted a unanimous mandate by the Council. However, even if such unanimity is reached, as was the case in the negotiation of the Framework Convention on Climate Change, problems may arise concerning the manner and timing in which instructions are given. The extent to which the Commission can play a visible and proactive role during international negotiations is proportional to the clarity of the mandate and the degree of flexibility it is accorded by the Council.

It can be concluded that although the EU, and particularly the Commission, was quick to sponsor the climate issue once it emerged on the international policy agenda, and although it continues to be energetic in drafting proposals to address this problem on the regional level, the EU continues to have serious problems in extending its role beyond that of a "minimum common denominator" representative of its member states. Thus the EU has yet to reach its potential as an international environmental leader.

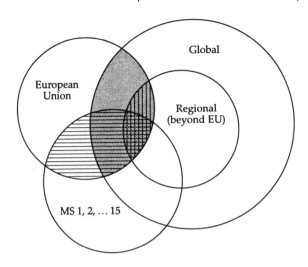

EU as arena for reaching agreement between member
states (MS) and as having agenda setting role

EU's catalytic role in a pan-European and
Euro-Mediterranean perspective

EU as representative of its member states in international settings
and as actor claiming international environmental leadership

Note:
The area "MS 1, 2, ... 15" represents each and all EU member states.
The area "Regional (beyond EU)" could also cover relations with other
regional organizations outside Europe and the Mediterranean Basin.

Conclusions and perspectives

The diagram above helps to summarize the EU's multiple roles as a
bridge between domestic and international environmental policy-
making. The EU provides a distinct policy arena which interacts with
those of its member states, the broader region, and the international
community. In some cases these policy-making areas overlap, as in the
cases where the EU and its members collaborate with non-EU countries
in the broader regional and global spheres. At the intra-EU, regional,
and international levels, the EU plays a distinct role in reaching consensus, agenda-setting, and acting as the catalyst for action by other actors

as both a representative of its members and as a fledgling international environmental leader.

The EU's expanding role in environmental politics demands that there be renewed attention given to the meaning of regional and supranational politics. The EU is playing an increasingly visible and important role in influencing environmental policy outcomes. Yet the EU's role is neither well established nor fixed in its present form. The debate on subsidiarity, together with the conflicting pressures to enlarge the EU or to create a "Fortress Europe," indicate that the EU is still evolving.

With regard to the EU's four main functions as identified in this chapter, one can expect changes. Advocates of the subsidiarity principle who interpret this principle as favoring "repatriation" of responsibilities from the EU to the national level, will challenge the EU's agenda-setting role. This is likely to promote further caution and prudence in advancing proposals for EU-level initiatives, especially with regard to legislative proposals. Certain interpretations of subsidiarity would also increase scrutiny of the EU's representative role in international environmental negotiations and its attempts to play a distinct leadership role. At the same time, the expansion of EU authority already granted by the Maastricht Treaty and the continued accumulation of policy experience by EU institutions will serve to counterbalance these trends, at least in part. Furthermore, the EU's catalytic role in pan-European and Euro-Mediterranean environmental politics seems likely to remain strong or even expand. Even professed "Euroskeptics" tend to prefer joint (EU) approaches to risk-taking in economically, socially, or politically unstable areas, at least when defense matters are not concerned (as has been the case in Bosnia). The role of the EU as an arena for reaching compromise and managing distributive issues among member states is also likely to expand since the system of pooling resources is already very advanced, and accepted rules of the game have been established. In conclusion, we may not witness the emergence of a stronger and more federalist Europe in the near future, but the EU will continue to be an important regional and supranational bridge between domestic and international environmental policy-making.

Notes

1. The views expressed are those of the author and do not necessarily represent those of the European Commission.
2. The EU was established by the Maastricht Treaty of 1993. The Maastricht

Treaty amends the Treaty of Rome of 1957 which established the European Economic Community. The EU includes the EC and has additional competences in the fields of justice and common security policy.

3. Robert O. Keohane and Joseph S. Nye, *Power and Interdependence: World Politics in Transition* (Boston: Little, Brown and Company, 1977).

4. This role was later explicitly acknowledged in the 1992 Maastricht Treaty on the European Union.

5. See Ernst B. Haas, *The Uniting of Europe: Political, Economic and Social Forces, 1950–1957* (London: Steven and Sons, 1958) and Leon N. Lindberg, *The Political Dynamics of European Economic Integration* (Stanford: Stanford University Press, 1963). For an overview, see J. Tranholm-Mikklesen, "Neofunctionalism: Obstinate or Obsolete? A Reappraisal in the Light of the New Dynamics of the EC," *Millenium* 20:1 (1991).

6. For detailed accounts and analyses of the development of EC environmental policy, see Nigel Haigh, "The European Community and International Environmental Policy," in Andrew Hurrell and Benedict Kingsbury (eds.), *The International Politics of the Environment* (Oxford: Clarendon Press, 1992), pp. 228–249; Ludwig Kraemer, *EEC Treaty and Environmental Protection* (London: Sweet and Maxwell, 1992); Angela Liberatore, "Problems of Transnational Policy Making: Environmental Policy in the European Community," *European Journal of Political Research* 19:2 (1991), 281–305; J. D. Liefferinck, P. D. Lowe and A. P. J. Mol, *European Integration and Environmental Policy* (London: Belhaven Press, 1993); and Eckhard Rehbinder and Richard Stewart, *Integration Through Law, Vol. 2: Environmental Protection Policy* (Berlin: de Gruyter, 1985).

7. The co-decision procedure is applied in relation to strategic matters such as the completion of the internal market, environmental action programs, research framework programs, guidelines for the TransEuropean Networks, and the mobility of workers within the EU. Procedures which leave the final decision to the Council (e.g., the cooperation procedure) are used in relation to the implementation or adoption of specific measures, such as environmental directives.

8. Useful discussions of the subsidiarity principle can be found in Renaud Dehousse, et al., "Europe After 1992: New Regulatory Strategies," European Union Institute Working Paper, Law N. 92/93, Florence, Italy; Stephan Kux, "Subsidiarity and the Environment: Implementing International Agreements", Basler Schriften zu europäischer Integration, Europa Institut, Basel University, Switzerland, 1994; and M. Wilke and H. Wallace, "Subsidiarity: Approaches to Power Sharing in the European Community," Royal Institute of International Affairs Discussion Paper, London 27 (1990).

9. See, for example, Andrew Moravcsik, "Negotiating the Single European Act: National Interest and Conventional Statecraft in the European Community," *International Organization* 45 (1991), 19–56.

10. For a more detailed account of the EC acidification policy, see Angela Liberatore, "The European Community's Acid Rain Policy," contribution to

the Project on Social Learning in the Management of Global Environmental Risks, 1993; on the LCPD, see Graham Bennet, "The EC Large Combustion Plants Directive," paper to the workshop, "Environmental Risk, Energy and Environment: The European Perspective on Risk," Como, Italy, 1988; and Nigel Haigh, *EEC Policy and Britain*, 2nd edition (Longman and Harlow, 1989).

11. COM (83) 704 final.

12. The presidency of the EC rotates among member states every six months.

13. On German acid rain policy, see Sonya Boehmer-Christiansen and Jim Skea, *Acid Politics: Environmental and Energy Policies in Britain and Germany* (London: Belhaven Press, 1991).

14. In 1983 a scientific symposium was convened by the Directorate General for Science, Research, and Development on "Acid Deposition: A Challenge for Europe" and a cost/benefit assessment of EC policy options to control acidification was published and sponsored by the Directorate General for Environment. See Environmental Resources Limited, *Acid Rain: A Review of the Phenomenon in the EEC and Europe* (London: Graham and Trotman, 1983).

15. The control of SO_2 emissions was to be modulated in three stages (1993, 1998, 2003). Belgium, Germany, France, Luxembourg, and the Netherlands were to reduce emissions by 40 percent. Spain was to stabilize emissions by 1993 and reduce them in the following years. Greece, Ireland, and especially Portugal were each allowed to increase emissions over these three stages (Directive 88/609).

16. On the implementation gaps and regulatory deficits that still characterize EU policy making see Dehousse et al., *Europe After 1992*; Giandomenico Majone, "Regulatory Federalism in the European Community," *Environment and Planning: Government and Policy* 10(1992); Rehbinder and Stewart, *Integration Through Law*; and A. Sbragia, "The European Community and Implementation: Environmental Policy in Comparative Perspective," paper presented at the Annual Meeting of the American Political Science Association, 1991.

17. See the special issue by Susan Baker, et al., "Protecting the Periphery: Environmental Policy in Peripheral Regions of the European Union," *Regional Politics and Policy*, 1994. The "core/periphery" distinction is more appropriate than a "north/south" one because the different ability of states to influence decision-making within the EU and their different levels and forms of economic development do not fully match their geographical locations.

18. On Italy see Marina Alberti and Jonathan Parker, "The Impact of EC Legislation on Environmental Policy in Italy," EIU, European Trends 2 (1991), and Antonella Capria, "Direttive ambientali CEE. Stato di attuazione in Italia," Quaderni della Rivista Giuridica dell'Ambiente, Giuffré, Milan, 1988.

19. "Towards Sustainability: A European Community Program of Policy and

Action in Relation to the Environment and Sustainable Development," adopted by the Resolution of the Council of 1 February 1993, published by the Office for Official Publications of the European Communities, Luxembourg, 1993.

20. On the EC ozone policy, see Michael Huber and Angela Liberatore, "The EC Ozone Policy, 1977 to 1992," contribution to the Project on Social Learning in the Management of Global Environmental Risks, 1993. On EC participation in the negotiation of the Vienna Convention see Markus Jachtenfuchs, "The European Community and the Protection of the Ozone Layer," *Journal of Common Market Studies* 28:1 (1990), 263–275.

21. See Interim Review of Implementation of the European Community Program of Policy and Action in Relation to Environment and Sustainable Development, "Towards Sustainability," July 1994, European Commission, DG XI, Brussels.

22. The Dobris Conference was largely shaped by the energetic role and long-term vision of Joseph Vavrousek, Minister of the Environment of Czechoslovakia at the time of the conference. His death is a sad loss to the continuation of the process initiated in Dobris.

23. D. Stanners and P. Bourdeau, *Europe's Environment: The Dobris Assessment* (Copenhagen: European Environmental Agency, 1995).

24. *Agence Europe*, 6.5.1993.

25. The importance of these EU initiatives is manifested in the proportion of aid provided to the states of Central and Eastern Europe by EU members: 61 percent of total aid in 1992; 71 percent of technical aid for economic restructuring; 76 percent of emergency aid; 69 percent of export credits; and 51 percent of macro-economic aid (*Agence Europe*, 6.5.1993).

26. See "What is PHARE? A European Union Initiative for Economic Integration with Central and Eastern European Countries," 1994, European Commission, PHARE Information Office, DG I, Brussels, Belgium.

27. See "What is TACIS? Partnerships and Cooperation with New Independent States," 1994, European Commission, TACIS Information Office, DG I, Brussels, Belgium.

28. According to B. Khader, *L'Europe et la Méditerranée: Géopolitique de la proximité* (Paris: l'Harmatan, 1994), the Maghreb countries are highly dependent on the EC, which is their main trading partner. These countries, in turn, account for about 10 percent of the EU imports from non-EU countries.

29. See "A Common Platform: Guidelines for the Community for UNCED 1992," European Commission, DG XI, Brussels.

30. On the CO_2/energy tax debate see Angela Liberatore, "Arguments, Assumptions and the Choice of Policy Instruments: The Case of the Debate on the CO_2/Energy Tax in the European Community," in Bruno Dente (ed.), *Environmental Policy in Search of New Instruments* (Kluwer Academic Publishers, 1995), pp. 55–71.

31. *International Environmental Reporter*, 20 May 1992.

32. See "Environment Watch: Western Europe," 17.2.1995 on the DRI's European Energy Forecasts. The doubts on the possibility of meeting the stabilization target are acknowledged in Commission documents such as the *Commission Working Paper on the EU Climate Change Strategy: A Set of Options* (SEC 95/288/final).
33. On this matter see Haigh, "The European Community," pp. 228–249, and Martin Hession and Richard Macrory, "The Legal Framework of European Community Participation in International Environmental Agreements," *New Europe Law Review* 1:2 (1994), 59–136.

Index

Index

Maastricht Treaty, 188, 191–92, 197, 208
Major, John, 64
Malawi, 166, 173
Malaysia, 48, 168, 169
Martin, Rowan, 167, 169–70
Mediterranean, 200–203
  desertification in, 202
  Dobris Assessment and, 201
  Dobris Process and, 201
  European Union cooperation with,
    200–3, 207–8
  environment–economy link in, 202
Mediterranean Environmental Technical
  Assistance Program (METAP), 203
Merck & Co., 46, 52
Milner, Helen, 5
Ministry of Agriculture, People's Republic
  of China, 28, 31
Ministry of Energy, People's Republic of
  China, 28, 31, 34, 36
Ministry of Foreign Affairs, People's
  Republic of China, 24, 30, 31, 32, 34,
  36, 38
Ministry of International Trade and
  Industry (MITI), Japan, 143, 147,
  150–52, 157
Ministry of Environment and Tourism,
  Zimbabwe, 177
Molina, Mario, 76–7, 83
Montreal Protocol on Substances that
  Deplete the Ozone Layer, 9, 88–93,
  134, 147, 150, 192
  amendments to, 142–43
  amendment procedure, 84
  comparison to Biodiversity Convention,
    54
  developing nations and, 75, 87
  European Community and, 84–87, 192
  implementation problems of, 88
  London Amendments to, 87
  Multilateral Fund and, 54, 88
  schedule of reduction for CFCs and
    halons, 75, 82
  United Kingdom and, 85
  United States and, 77, 82–84
  see also CFCs, halons, stratospheric
    ozone, Vienna Convention
Mozambique, 163, 165
Mugabe, Robert, 176
Müller, Edda, 140

Namibia, 173
National Climate Change Coordinating
  Group, People's Republic of China,
  30

National Environmental Protection
  Agency, People's Republic of China,
  11, 24, 26, 28, 31, 37
National People's Congress, People's
  Republic of China, 23
Natural Resources Defense Council, 77,
  83
Netherlands, 81, 144, 149, 150, 195
Newly Independent States (NIS), 114–15,
  200, 202
  EU cooperation on environment and,
    200, 202
New Zealand, 173
nitrogen oxides (NOx), 110, 194
non-governmental organizations
  (NGOs), 44–5, 49, 53, 57, 61, 77, 84–5,
  86–7, 89, 91, 115, 158, 163–64, 167,
  178–79
  informal, 111
Nordic Investment Bank, 118
North Africa
  EU cooperation with, 200
  EU trade with, 202
North–South relations, 33, 37
  Biodiversity Convention and, 45, 48
  climate change and, 31
  migration and, 202
  European Union and, 195, 198
  inequity in, 19, 23, 33
  Zimbabwe and, 162
Norway, 77, 119–20, 168, 205
nuclear power
  anti-nuclear activism in Soviet
    Union/Russia, 112, 122
  East-West interaction on, 107, 120–24
  Japan and, 14, 151–52

Our Common Future, 168
Office of Technology Assessment, report
  on IPR, 53–4
ozone layer *see* stratospheric ozone
Ozone Trends Panel, 84, 86

Parks and Wildlife Act, Zimbabwe, 177
particulates, 194
Pechenganikel smelting combine, 119–20,
  123
People's Republic of China (PRC), 13
  climate change and, 10, 12, 20–1, 33, 34,
    38
  climate change research in, 24–7, 37
  CITES and, 165
  CO_2 emissions in, 22, 148
  economic reforms in, 22
  energy debate in, 27–30, 37

218

CAMBRIDGE STUDIES IN INTERNATIONAL RELATIONS